BURT FRANKLIN RESEARCH AND SOURCE WORKS SERIES No. 26

THE ITALIAN RENAISSANCE
IN ENGLAND

Sir Thomas Wyatt by Holbein.

THE
ITALIAN RENAISSANCE
IN ENGLAND

STUDIES

BY

LEWIS EINSTEIN

BURT FRANKLIN RESEARCH AND SOURCE WORKS SERIES No. 26

BURT FRANKLIN
New York 25, N. Y.

Originally published New York, 1902.

Published by
BURT FRANKLIN
514 West 113th Street
New York 25, N. Y.

Printed in the U.S.A.

NOBLE OFFSET PRINTERS, INC.
NEW YORK 3, N. Y.

TO

My Father and My Mother

ERRATA

Page 23, line 8, for " Paul the First," read " Paul the Second."

Page 24, footnote, for "*verendam*," read "*venerendam*."

Page 50, line 5, for " Montepulciano," read " Montpellier."

Page 179, line 13, for " Vicario," read " Vacarius."

ADDENDA

Appendix B : Page 386, 1562 — La Guida Romana, by Peter (?) Shakerley.

Appendix C : Page 388, 1517 — Letters to Isabella d' Este, by Francesco Chiericati.

[NOTE. — On account of the brief time intervening between the first edition of this book and its re-impression, it is possible to mention only the most important corrections and additions.]

PREFACE

THE history of the Italian Renaissance in the countries of Europe outside of Italy still remains a subject half unexplored. No account has as yet been written of the successive steps by which Italian culture crossed the Alps, the different directions it took, and the extent of its influence. The purpose of these studies is, therefore, to supply a link in the chain, and trace the Italian influence in England from the beginning of the fifteenth century until the death of Elizabeth. Separate aspects of this have, it is true, been treated by others. Beginning with Warton and Nott, a number of scholars have searched especially for the Italian sources of English poetry. Although in recent years most work of this kind has been accomplished in Germany, Miss Scott's contribution to a similar subject ought not to pass unnoticed in the scholarly annals of our own country. No serious effort has, however, been made to discover a common impulse running through the Italian influences in England : to find at the university, at court, and among the people at large, in different and even opposite directions, the results of one and the same great movement.

In all, three stages can be discerned in the history of the Italian influence in England during the period of the Renaissance. The first, extending to the end of the fifteenth century, found a centre at the University of Oxford. It succeeded, after several attempts, in introducing the new classical and scientific learning of Italy into England, and thereby laid the foundation for all future English scholarship. The second and third epochs embrace respectively the two halves of the sixteenth century. The growth of Italian culture at court marked the former; it flourished there under royal protection, and assisted in creating the new types of accomplished courtier and learned traveller, often the same individual under different aspects. The third and last period witnessed a great extension of the Italian influence, as it spread gradually from the court to the people at large. At the same time, the moral and national reaction against Italy, which was further fostered by the growth of Puritanism, put an end to much of this influence.

These studies have been divided into two groups. The first is concerned mainly with the Englishman as affected by Italy in scholarship, court life and travel, and later with the movement against Italian influence. The second treats rather of the Italians in England, — merchants and artists, reformers and adventurers. Allusions of many kinds must necessarily creep into any work attempting to cover so wide a range. Such,

however, as refer to the historical and religious relations existing between Italy and England have so far
as possible been omitted.   Politics and religion in
the sixteenth century were everywhere very closely
connected, and the Anglo-Italian relations of this
nature belong more properly to a history of the
Reformation.   Only so far as they may have influenced English life and culture have they been
mentioned here.

It may seem idle to rehearse the Italian influence
in English literature, so much research has already
been expended on it.   The labors of scholars on this
subject, however, have never before been brought
together.   Several new ideas and suggestions will perhaps add some further novelty to what might otherwise seem of familiar interest to the specialist.

Most of the illustrations are from prints in the
British Museum, reproduced here for the first time.
The portraits of Wyatt and Surrey by Holbein are,
however, from the well-known Windsor Castle collection.   The tomb of Dr. John Yonge, by Torrigiano,
formerly in the Rolls Chapel, is now preserved in the
museum of the Record Office in London, and the
original of the manuscript letter in the Duke Humphrey correspondence is in the Royal Library at
Munich.

That these studies are not more incomplete is due
to the aid and advice of many friends.   Above all, the

writer wishes to express his gratitude to the unfailing courtesy and kindness of the officials of the libraries in which he worked, especially of the British Museum, the Record Office in London, the Bodleian at Oxford, and the Archives of Florence. Lastly he desires to thank Professor Donati of Siena, Professor Pasquale Villari of Florence, Monsignor Giles of the English College, Rome, Mr. Bliss of Rome, Mr. Horatio F. Brown of Venice, Mr. Sidney Colvin of the British Museum, Professor Charles Waldstein of King's College, Cambridge, Mrs. E. H. Blashfield, his sister, Miss Amy Einstein, Mr. Henry A. Uterhart of New York, and Dr. John G. Underhill of Brooklyn. In particular he wishes to thank Dr. J. E. Spingarn of Columbia University for aid, which has at all times proved valuable, and Professor G. E. Woodberry for his ever kindly criticism and advice extending over a period of years.

NEW YORK,
January 2, 1902.

CONTENTS

PART FIRST

CHAPTER I

THE SCHOLAR

CHAPTER II

THE COURTIER

CHAPTER III

THE TRAVELLER

CHAPTER IV

THE ITALIAN DANGER

PART SECOND

CHAPTER V

THE ITALIANS IN ENGLAND: CHURCHMEN, ARTISTS, AND TRAVELLERS

CHAPTER VI

THE ITALIAN MERCHANT IN ENGLAND

CHAPTER VII

ITALIAN POLITICAL AND HISTORICAL IDEAS IN ENGLAND

CHAPTER VIII

THE ITALIAN INFLUENCE IN ENGLISH POETRY

APPENDIX A

ENGLISH CATHOLICS IN ROME

APPENDIX B

ENGLISH ACCOUNTS OF ITALY IN THE SIXTEENTH CENTURY

APPENDIX C

ITALIAN ACCOUNTS OF ENGLAND IN THE SIXTEENTH CENTURY

BIBLIOGRAPHY

LIST OF ILLUSTRATIONS

LIST OF ILLUSTRATIONS

THE ITALIAN RENAISSANCE
IN ENGLAND

CHAPTER I

THE SCHOLAR

I

THE influence of Italy on English learning during the
Renaissance differed in several respects from that exercised by the other European nations. It was first in
the field, and for that reason long single in its power.
Its individual influence, moreover, proved the greatest
factor in modifying existing intellectual conditions,
while it supplemented the entire mediæval fabric of
learning by the new system it had itself originated.

Commencing, virtually, about 1425, a gradual development took place in English scholarship till by the
end of the fifteenth century, when Italian intellectual
life was beginning to enter on a decline, its lessons
had been mastered. Fifty years later, learning in Italy
had become a tradition rather than an actuality. Although scholars were plentiful, and foreign students
still attended its universities, the reasons which induced them to study there were no longer purely
scholarly. In the intellectual life of England at that
time, such foreign elements as existed owed their origin

to several nations, no one of which could claim exclusive supremacy. It is thus possible to limit to a definite period of time the Italian influence on English scholarship in the Renaissance. During this period its course can be traced without unnecessary subtleties. The field can be narrowed still further by remembering that during the fifteenth century in England, learning was almost entirely confined to the universities, and to churchmen who for the most part had received their education in colleges. Lastly, intellectual activity centred almost exclusively around Oxford. Although learned men lived elsewhere as well, they appear rather as isolated individuals than members of the great movement then preparing the way for the reception of the new learning in England. In studying, therefore, the history of the university and of its friends and patrons during that period, one might almost be said to witness the intellectual life of an entire nation condensed and focussed at one point. Oxford, in itself, thus affords an insight into the scholarly history of the English Renaissance from its beginnings in the decay of the Middle Ages, when the first desire arose to share in the benefits of the new learning rediscovered by Italians, until the time when humanism was no less firmly established in England than it had been in Italy.

II

The Middle Ages had looked upon learning primarily as the handmaid to theology. In the Renaissance, on the other hand, it was regarded as a guide to the conduct of life.   This difference in conception brought about the new idea in education which was to take the place of the encyclopædic teachings of the church.   The transition from one system to the other meant an entire revolution in methods of instruction. A decline came over the mediæval fabric of learning ; the old *trivium* and *quadrivium* were done away with, and studies which formerly had seemed of great importance were now either neglected or dropped entirely.

The questions which once agitated men now gave way to new ones.   More and more it was felt that the scholastic training, out of harmony with actual conditions, furnished no longer adequate preparation for life. In the early years of the fifteenth century, when the lowest depths of intellectual torpor had been reached in England, the efforts of a single man were to bring about a great change and introduce new rays of light. In Duke Humphrey of Gloucester, son of Henry the Fourth, and in the cultivated circle of his friends, the intellectual hopes of his country were centred.   His career is of interest to the literary student, not only as the first conspicuous English example of the Italian princely patron and lover of learning, but as the benefactor of a great university, the collector of classical manuscripts, and the correspondent and protector of learned Italians who dedicated their works to him, many of whom even visited him in England.

Duke Humphrey's first aim as a patron of letters was to surround himself with a circle of scholars.   Among

his English protégés were Pecock, Capgrave, and Lydgate, who translated from Boccaccio. His efforts were
also directed to bringing over from Italy some of the
younger humanists to instruct him in the ancient poets
and orators,[1] while at the same time he maintained a
correspondence with the greater men who could not be
tempted to cross the Alps. The scholars he induced
to come over translated the classics for his benefit.
Lapo da Castiglionchio brought with him as a fitting
recommendation a number of renderings from the
Greek. Antonio Beccaria of Verona, who had been
one of Vittorino da Feltre's pupils, was later regularly employed by the duke as a translator,[2] while Tito
Livio of Forli even styled himself the "Poet and Orator
of the Duke of Gloucester." Although the records of
this early period are scanty, there can be little doubt
that Duke Humphrey, in gratifying his own cultivated
tastes, was also trying to create in England a revival of
letters by employing the only means possible, since
Italy was then the intellectual centre of Europe — the
introduction into England of Italian scholars and
scholarly methods. At a time, moreover, when patrons
were a necessity to every literary man, the "good

---

[1] "Huic tanta litterarum est cura ut ex Italia magistros asciverit
Poetarum et oratorum interpretes." — Æneas Sylvius, *Epist.* 105.
Vide also *Epist.* 64, Dec. 5, 1443, Letter to Duke Sigismund of
Austria.

[2] "C'est livre est a moy Homfrey Duc de Glocestre, lequel
je fis translater de Grec en Latin par un de mes secretaires,
Antoyne de Beccaria de Verone." — Cited in Ellis, *Letters of
Eminent Literary Men*, Camden Society, 1843, p. 357.

Duke " acted the part of a Mæcenas to the humanists of Italy. Piero del Monte, sent to England as collector of the papal revenues, dedicated to him some philosophical dialogues. The Duke's attention was also called to the new translation of Aristotle's *Ethics* by Leonardo Bruno, the greatest scholar of his age, which pleased him so much that he urged Bruno to set to work on the *Politics*. After the first part of this had been completed it was sent to London with a dedication to the duke, but this was withdrawn when his acknowledgment was delayed, and it was dedicated afresh to Pope Eugene the Fourth.[1] More fortunate were his relations with another humanist, Pier Candido Decembrio, who offered him a translation of the first five books of Plato's *Republic*, first begun by Chrysoloras, which he, continuing his father's work, had at last completed. The documents referring to this affair have been preserved, and are of interest as illustrating similar negotiations between the scholar and his patron. The Archbishop of Milan first wrote to the duke, knowing his zeal in behalf of learning ; having heard that his relations with Leonardo Bruno had come to naught, he wished to inform the duke that an opportunity now presented itself in the translation of Plato's *Republic* by Pier Candido, a humanist versed in Greek no less than in Latin. If he cared for wisdom or true eloquence, it could be found in this book, which in former times had been a favorite with Ambrose, Jerome, and Augustine.[2] His

---

[1] Vespasiano da Bisticci, *Vite*, p. 437.
[2] Ms. Royal Library, Munich. Ms. Lat. 222, f. 113 *et seq.*

interest having been aroused by the bishop, a correspondence began between duke and scholar, which
brought out the interest of the former in the new learning of the Italian Renaissance. Pier Candido grace-
fully alluded to the fame the duke enjoyed in Italy, and
how much his efforts had accomplished in the revival
of letters. The duke was evidently very proud of his
patronage of scholars, and both styled himself and was
addressed as *litteratissimus*.[1] He received at first but
a portion of the work, and in acknowledging this, he
urged the humanist to finish the remainder as speedily
as possible, at the same time warmly praising the
scholarship displayed in the translation. To this encouragement came a reply, written in the true style of
the humanists. Just as the shade of a tree was pleasing
to the weary traveller, as the gentle breeze was welcome
to the sailor, and the crystal spring to the thirsty man,
so were his letters welcome even as those of a great
poet. As soon as he [Pier Candido] heard that the
learned Aretine [Bruno] had changed his dedication
of Aristotle from Humphrey to the Pope, he at once
determined to celebrate the duke in no inferior manner, and for that reason had selected the *Republic* as
in itself a great work and one of benefit to rulers. He
compared Humphrey to Julius Cæsar, to Octavius and
other cultivated princes of former times whose names
had been the brighter for their devotion to learning.
For this reason he begged him to accept this offering
of good will and preserve it as a comfort in his own

[1] Ms. cit., f. 246 *et seq.*

dirigat ipse bonoꝝ omniũ equissimus retributor

P. candidi decembris ad illustrissimũ et littatissi=
mũ principem dñm humfredum ducem clouces-
trensem fratrem serenissimi et muictissimi domini henrici regis anglie et super nona traditor
totius poliue platonis feliciter incipit Epistola

Clarissima apud italos omnis uirtutis
tue fama prebuit princeps illustriss-
ime ita ut ignota sane tuam excellenti-
am omnes litterati apud nos uiri fama nouer-
int inter quos precipuus tue dignitatis laudator
fuit et auctor reuerendissimus pater bauorensis
episcopus uir non solum doctrina harum sed
humanitate caritate et obsequio mitissimus itaqꝫ
nonnis precipuus amator Is tu multa de uir-
tute de humanitate de prudentia tua nobis re-
tulisset tum mirũmodum extulit diligentia
et amorem tue claritatis erga studia harum q̃-
dere profecto gaudent hi qui bonarũ artiũ studiis
solent oblectari quod etate nra non omnino extincta
sint simulata principum optimorũ Quippe cũ talis
cesar fuerit talis augustus tales multi predari uiri quoqꝫ fama est immortalis Itaqꝫ cum multi ex
hac gloria amore tuum certatim appetant ipse-
m primis tuam gram non uerbis tantu sed ope-
ribus assequi confido et quidem optimis et dignita-
te tua dignis Cum igitur intelligam leonardum
arretinum uiriũ grece latineqꝫ lingue satis eru-
ditum aristotelis politicam quã tuo nomine uerte-
dam susceperat non tue excellentie sed dñi nostri
pape sanctitati diuisse statim nomen tuũ per se
satis illustre non meliori munere exornare et ex-
imiam laudem tuam penitus extollere felicis-
sime igiturꝫ exgrens litteris traducere inchoa-
ui politicam platonis philosophi omniũ clariss-
imi et excellentissimi quam tue dignitati dedi-
caui quo quidem ope nil excellentius nil utilius

*Letter of Pier Candido Decembrio
to Duke Humphrey of Gloucester*

studies. In his reply the duke expressed delight at the beauty of his translation, saying he knew not whether to be more grateful to the author or the scholar whose efforts had once more brought it to light after it had for so long been buried from view; through Candido he was at last able to admire Plato; in the immortal fame which awaited this labor he wished him happiness.[1] A considerable amount of miscellaneous information was scattered through these letters; the duke, for instance, was told of Manuel Chrysoloras, whose work had made possible that of an Aretine [Bruno] and a Veronese [Guarino], as well as of many others who now were laboring when but a short time before there had been none. In the last letter of the series, the scholar bade the duke farewell, addressing him (perhaps by reason of his dedication) as *Immortalis Princeps.*[2]

Duke Humphrey had studied in his youth at Balliol, and in after years the devotion he showed his university was to be his noblest trait. Oxford about that time had sunk to her lowest level. Scholasticism was dominant, but her reputation even in these studies was behind that of Paris. The long wars with France and civil strife at home had greatly affected all scholarly pursuits. For a time the university was reduced to the greatest misery, and the ruin of education seemed imminent.[3] Scarcely a thousand students remained in her ruined halls, and those who studied were said to

---

[1] Ms. cit., f. 113. [2] *Ibid.,* f. 248.
[3] *Epistolæ Academicæ Oxonienses,* I, 128.

find no reward awaiting them amid the poverty and distress of the nation.[1] In their plight appeals were made at different times to Thomas Arundel, Archbishop of Canterbury,[2] the Duke of Bedford,[3] and others, informing them of the condition they were in. The one truly generous patron they found proved to be Duke Humphrey of Gloucester. Not only were his gifts of books of great assistance to them, but his active support in the defence of their privileges as the special protector of the university was to help them through a period of virtual anarchy. There can be no doubt that he also advocated reforms in their education. At one time, indeed, his relations with them appear to have been somewhat strained, probably on account of their refusing to adopt certain innovations he had pressed.[4]

In first advocating the new Italian humanism in England, Duke Humphrey proved himself far in advance of his age. The time was not yet ripe, however, although general dissatisfaction existed with the old scholastic training as a valueless preparation for life. The credit for whatever was then accomplished in England belongs rightly to the Duke of Gloucester and his circle. What this was, as well as the practical purpose of the new humanism he introduced from Italy, can perhaps best be judged from a letter written in 1444 by Æneas Sylvius Piccolomini, who later

[1] *Epist. Acad.*, I, 154.
[2] Beckynton, *Correspondence*, I, 277.
[3] *Epist. Acad.*, I, 94.   [4] *Ibid.*, I, 64.

became Pius the Second, to Adam Mulin, Bishop of Chichester and Keeper of the Privy Seal : —

" I read your letter with eagerness, and wondered that Latin style had penetrated even into Britain. It is true that there have been amongst the English some who have cultivated the eloquence of Cicero, amongst whom common consent would place the Venerable Bede. Peter of Blois was far inferior, and I prefer your letter to any of his. For this advance all gratitude is due to the illustrious Duke of Gloucester, who zealously received polite learning into your kingdom. I hear that he cultivates poets and venerates orators ; hence many Englishmen now turn out really eloquent. For as are the princes, so are the people ; and servants progress through imitating their masters. Persevere, therefore, friend Adam. Hold fast and increase the eloquence you possess ; consider it the most honorable thing possible to excel your fellows in that in which men excel other living creatures. Great is eloquence ; nothing so much rules the world. Political action is the result of persuasion ; his opinion prevails with the people who best knows how to persuade them." [1]

Numerous letters passed between the duke and the university during the many years in which he defended its privileges. His first benefactions had begun in the early years of the fifteenth century. His last were to be almost forty years afterward. During

[1] *Opera, Epist.* LXIV; cited by Creighton, *Early Renaissance*, p. 19.

this time it was his wisdom alone, the authorities wrote him, which had revived learning and enabled scholars to devote themselves to it with fresh energy. It was almost a divine inspiration, they added, which led him to revive the studies of philosophy and the liberal arts ; they only trusted he would provide for the continued maintenance of this learning ; there was urgent need for books and money to carry on the lectures in science and philosophy which they knew enjoyed his favor, and they furthermore requested his aid in providing a permanent foundation for these.

From time to time, he gave them the books they wanted, and assisted them in other ways as well. Many letters of gratitude were written him ; if refinement of life, munificence and liberality, it was said, could confer immortal fame, that fame would be his. It was in vain they had searched the records of antiquity : there was no one to surpass him in learning and literary culture ; nor was his fame confined to England, but had crossed the sea and the Alps, so that among all the Christian princes none was more renowned for his knowledge of the Greek and Italian writers. Night and day they now were able to devote to their scholarly tasks ; not only they themselves, but even eloquent and learned Italians toiled over the work. It was a pleasant sight to see the number of volumes received from Greece and Italy. Under his patronage, Greek literature, buried for so many centuries, had again come to life, and once more the philosophers could be studied in their original tongue. The very foundation of eloquence, which he had carried over to England from Italy and Greece, would be exhausted in the effort to render him due thanks. If the Latin races owed him this, how much greater gratitude ought the English to feel. Previously there had been, it is true, a university at Oxford, but study there was none, for there were no books; now, however, through his gifts, they too could discern the secrets of learning. Oxford must, therefore, always be the home of his glory: if, then, the Trojans vaunted their Hector, the Macedonians their Alexander, the Romans their Cæsar, it was for Oxonians to extol Humphrey; and while distant rays might reach the students of every clime, it was they who enjoyed, so to speak, the very beams of the sun itself.[1] However great the exaggeration and flattery of these letters, they yet show a decided zeal for learning, and the beginnings of the Renaissance feeling for antiquity. On Duke Humphrey's part, the taste was encouraged by presenting Oxford at various times with from three to four hundred books, purchased, for the most part, in France and Italy. Among these were the writings of Petrarch and Boccaccio, the text and commentaries of Dante, and the great writers of antiquity, whose works had been rediscovered by Italian humanists.[2] By these gifts, it was said, from having been almost without books, the university had grown rich. Once more in their long-forgotten majesty the ancient tongues had been re-

[1] *Epist. Acad.*, I, 203, 240.
[2] Vide *Munimenta Academica*, Indentures of 1439, 1444, etc.

vived, and everything which had been written was now accessible to students.[1]

Around Duke Humphrey were grouped the other scholars of the age in England. His protégé was Thomas Beckynton, Bishop of Wells and a doctor of laws of Oxford, who corresponded also with many learned Italians, among whom were Flavio Biondo of Forli, Angelo Gattola and Piero del Monte. His letters reveal quite a little group of English humanists, — such men as Adam Mulin, Thomas Chandler and William Grey. Nicholas Bildstone, the Archdeacon of Winchester, and Richard Pettworth, the secretary to Cardinal Beaufort, were also among the few English scholars then familiar with the new Italian studies. Certain other foreigners resident in England should be mentioned as well. Simon de Taramo, the papal collector, wrote a letter to Duke Humphrey in 1427, full of the new Renaissance spirit of humanism, realizing the duke's weakness in that direction.[2] The most important, however, was Vincent Clement, who, although perhaps a Spaniard by birth, had yet been educated in Italy. He was at different times the papal collector in England and Duke Humphrey's orator at Rome, where he may well have purchased books for Oxford.[3] He was certainly known as " the star of the university," and in all probability had studied there. Later, King Henry the Sixth requested that the degree of doctor of divinity be conferred on him, since it was

---

[1] *Epist. Acad.*, I, 244.
[2] *Beckynton*, I, 283.   [3] *Ibid.*

intended to add to his prestige as papal proctor at the English court.[1]   Various indications point him out as a man of great cultivation.   His correspondence with Thomas Beckynton was full of classical and humanistic allusions, as for example when the latter thanked him for a volume of poems by the Italian, Pontanus.[2]   In this early group of Clement and Beckynton, Chandler and Mulin, the first indications of the new spirit brought in by the Italian Renaissance can be found in England.   The scholars centred around Duke Humphrey, who acted as their patron.   With his death, however, in 1447, the first period of English humanism may be said to have ended.   It was not a great age ; its scholars were for the most part obscure men, whose names, with scarce an exception, have been forgotten. Its very knowledge of Greek, even if not confined to the Italian humanists in England, probably died out. Nevertheless, in marking the first stage of a new movement, in providing the foundation on which succeeding generations might build, in evincing a zeal for letters, the age deserves a place in the annals of English scholarship; and Duke Humphrey's name, perpetuated by his library, should live for the encouragement he gave the new learning.

[1] *Beckynton*, I, 223.   [2] *Ibid.*, I, 178.

III

Neither the scholarly zeal shown by certain of the great English churchmen, nor the travels of such Italian humanists in England as Poggio and Æneas Sylvius, strictly enter the new scholarly tradition which from the first had centred around Oxford and Duke Humphrey. In the succeeding age, beginning about the middle of the fifteenth century, the chief progress in English humanism came through the journeys of university students to Italy. In all likelihood they were unaware of the significance of the movement they had started afresh. It probably seemed to them only a continuation of the mediæval migrations which in former days united the learned world, before the feeling of the intellectual kinship of Europe had disappeared amid the struggles of rival nations. During the Middle Ages, English scholars were by no means unknown in Italy. At the University of Bologna there was an English "nation," and both Vicenza and Vercelli had English rectors,[1] while on the registers of Padua, British names appear frequently.[2]

The Italian humanists assumed at first a somewhat patronizing attitude toward Englishmen, which was not without a certain justification. Thus, although Richard

[1] Rashdall, *Universities of Europe*, I, 157; II, 14. Vide Dallari, *Rotuli di Bologna*.

[2] Andrich, *De Natione Anglica . . . Universitatis Patavinæ*, p. 129.

de Bury, the most learned man of his day in all England, had met Petrarch, he was unable to grasp his new point of view toward the classics, which revolutionized the scholarly world. Much later, Leonardo Bruno said of Thomas of England, an Augustinian monk who went to Florence to purchase manuscripts, and lectured there in 1395,[1] that he keenly loved the new Italian humanism, as much as one of his nation was able to understand it.[2] Such early instances of Englishmen in Italy formed part, however, of the great mediæval fabric of learning, and bore no direct relation to the new age soon to dawn. In spite of examples like Osbern Bowkenham, the poet, who lived five years in Venice, or even of Oxford men who crossed the Alps, like Master Norton in 1425 or Master Bulkeley in 1429,[3] not till later can one feel assured that English students went to Italy in search of the new learning.

About the middle of the fifteenth century several Englishmen were studying in Italy. One of these, well known for his love of the classics, and in whose veins flowed the royal blood of England, was Reynold Chicheley, who later became rector of the University of Ferrara, where he had studied.[4] Andrew Ols[5]

[1] Gherardi, *Statuti della Università e Studio Fiorentino*, p. 364.

[2] "Studiorum nostrorum, quantum illa natio capit, ardentissimus affectator." — Leon. Bruni, II, 18. Cited by Voigt, *Wiederbelebung*, II, 258. [3] *Epist. Acad.*, II, 564.

[4] *Calendar of State Papers, Venetian*, Vol. VI, Pt. III, 1581.

[5] Could his name have been Ellis? All that is known of him comes through Italian sources, and English names became

was among the first English humanists of whom anything at all is really known. Like most scholars of that age, he occupied a minor church preferment, although he never sought ecclesiastical advancement. Most of his life was devoted entirely to the cultivation of letters. His appointment, however, as royal envoy to the Pope gave him an opportunity to pass some time in Florence, where he associated with the learned set which had gathered around Lorenzo da Medici. Among the friends he entertained there, were Matteo Palmieri, Giannozzo Manetti and many other celebrities of the day. It was noted particularly that he had abandoned the English fashion of remaining several hours at table for the more sober Italian manner of living.[1] The main purpose of his Florentine residence was to have certain books copied there, to take back with him. Like all lovers of learning whose means permitted, he was a great collector of manuscripts. His were said to be so numerous that, as it was impossible to send them overland, he was obliged to wait until a ship left for England. A supply of manuscripts was, however, a necessity at a time when printing was barely known, and public libraries still in their infancy. On his return, he retired to a living in the country, and there in the seclusion of his study passed the rest of his life, leaving at his death the manuscripts he had collected to the library of his

curiously twisted when pronounced by Italians: thus Hawkwood became *l' Acuto*, Southampton, *Antona*.

[1] Vespasiano, p. 238.

church. His gentler nature, with its grain of selfishness and perhaps of scholarly reserve, felt out of touch with the world of the unlearned. He remained content amid his bookish surroundings, feeling unequal or unwilling to preach the gospel of the new learning. For this reason he was not so well known in England as in Italy, where he was celebrated alike for his scholarly attainments and the purity of his life. His Florentine biographer, Vespasiano da Bisticci, who knew him personally, thought that few foreigners were his equals in character and cultivation.

The small band of scholars, Grey, Free, Flemming, Gunthorpe and Tiptoft, who now crossed the Alps were to be the pioneers of the new movement. It certainly seems more than a mere coincidence that they were all Oxonians, while at the same time whatever means then existed in England to acquire the rudiments of humanism were only to be found at Oxford. It is almost natural to suppose that the mediæval traditions of the university had in part been superseded by others of more recent growth, and that the desire for learning encouraged by the facilities offered by Duke Humphrey's library brought about these new conditions.

The reasons which drew English scholars to Italy are not hard to find. The new spirit of the Renaissance, in passing over the Middle Ages and going straight back to antiquity, had effected a revolution in the intellectual world. Italy was conscious of this discovery long before the rest of Europe had awak-

ened to it. Italian scholars had been the first to see
the ancient world in its true light, and to study the
classics, not as allegorical explanations of Christianity,
but from the literary point of view. The Italian
universities, moreover, were then eminent above all
others ; philosophy, natural science, medicine, civil
law and Greek, elsewhere almost unknown, flourished
at Padua and Bologna. The brighter minds at Oxford, seeing beyond their own limited horizon and
conscious of the progress in Italy, were anxious also
to take part in this advance.

Beyond the fact that they were all Oxonians, the
early group of Englishmen who went to Italy in
search of the new humanism possessed other traits
in common. Excepting Robert Flemming, all were
Balliol men, which was also Duke Humphrey's college.
Excepting Tiptoft, Earl of Worcester, they were
churchmen. It seems likely, too, that all were friends.
One last point of resemblance was that all either
studied or else were connected with the famous
Guarino Veronese, who after long years of wandering
had at length settled down at Ferrara, and was conducting there, under the protection of the house of
Este, the most celebrated school of his age. His fame
was then on the lips of every English scholar ; his
name, it was said, was dear to all Englishmen. It led
John Free (better known as Phreas), almost from
another world, to cross strange lands and unknown
seas to seek him in Italy.[1] John Tiptoft likewise, on

[1] Ms. 587 Bodleian, f. 165 *et seq.*

his return from Palestine, went especially to Ferrara to visit the aged scholar. Ludovico Carbo, in his funeral oration on the dead humanist, also bore witness to the number of scholars who, regardless of all difficulties, came from England itself to hear and acquire from him a polished elegance ;[1] and Battista Guarino, who later continued his father's work, wrote proudly that students were thronging to him from Britain itself,[2] which was situated in the furthest confines of the earth.

William Grey, a connection of the English royal family, was his first scholar of note. His name had already appeared in Beckynton's correspondence, which connects him with Duke Humphrey. Carbo, in the funeral oration delivered on Guarino, alluded to Grey as one well able to bear witness to the greatness of the dead humanist. Grey had begun by studying logic and theology at Cologne, but had realized that it was only in Italy that the new learning could properly be pursued. After crossing the Alps, his first care when in Florence had been to order as many books as were there to be purchased. He then went to Padua, where he heard of Guarino's fame, and this took him to Ferrara, where he studied under the master, living at the same time in princely style, and maintaining Nicolo Perotto, then a young man, as a scholar in his own household. Henry the Sixth appointed

---

[1] Cited by Leland, *De Scriptoribus Britannicis*, p. 462. Vide Mattaire, *Annales Typographici*, I, 91.

[2] " Ex Britanniæ ipsa, quæ extra orbem terrarum posita est." — Vide Voigt, II, 261, note.

him his proctor at the Curia, and later Pope Nicholas the Fifth selected Grey to fill the vacant bishopric of Ely.   After remaining in the Royal Council until the king's death, he retired from public life and passed his remaining years in retirement, leaving his collection of manuscripts to Balliol.[1]   William Grey was among the first great English churchmen of the Renaissance whose interest in humanism was more than a passing fancy.   He was not only a keen student himself, but his great wealth permitted him to follow Italian examples and be a patron to others less fortunate in that respect.   He represented a type common enough in Italy, where learning formed so large a part of the churchman's life, where no prelate considered his household complete without scholars in his retinue, and where a humanist like Æneas Sylvius had been raised to the papacy.   But all this was almost unknown in England, and William Grey was among the very first to carry back to his native land the love of the new learning and the desire to assist its growth.

John Free's career was typical in a different way of the life of the English scholar in Italy.   William Grey had gone there as a great lord, who established a princely household wherever he went.   John Free, on the other hand, represented the poor wandering student, who later raised his station in life by sheer force

---

[1] Among these were the works of Poggio, Guarino, Bruno, Petrarch and other humanists.   Vide Coxe, *Catalogus Codicum Collegiis Oxoniensibus*, I, Balliol College.

of ambition and personal ability. It has been stated
by Leland the antiquary, that some Italian merchants
whom Free met in his native town of Bristol induced
him to cross the Alps. It seems more likely to suppose however that his patron William Grey advised
Free as a promising student to go to Italy, offering, as
stated by him, to aid him in his travels. Free's letters
to his patron tell the story.[1] He left England with
only ten pounds in his possession, which he carried in
bills of exchange; barely six remained by the time he
had reached Ferrara, and after purchasing the necessary food and clothes, a very small sum was left over.
This he had spent, and poverty stared him in the face;
he swore to his patron he had not received a penny
since leaving England. All he asked for was sufficient
money to enable him to continue his work; for whoever wished to perfect himself in the humanities, he
wrote, must first be freed from all mental worries, especially such as related to the necessities of life. He
was particularly anxious to be able to study, in order to
help swell the scanty number of Englishmen then proficient in Greek and Latin; this, he wrote, would contribute to his patron's glory. The bishop of Ely sent the
needed remittance, and for a time everything went well.
Free however, who wished to translate something from
the Greek, begged for an addition to his usual allow-
ance in order to purchase the necessary texts.[2] His
complaints were frequent not only of his poverty, but

[1] Ms. 587 Bodleian.
[2] *Ibid.*, f. 162.

of homesickness, as well, and the thought of having left friends and country.

The new humanism also had its influence over him. Grey's nephew, who had been sent by his uncle to study in Italy, had died there. In attempting to console his patron, Free made use of arguments taken from Petrarch; he bade him remember that although nothing could prevent death, yet beyond its threshold were glory and everlasting fame. His letters plainly betrayed the Renaissance spirit, and were full of the expressions and feelings of Italian humanism. He spoke of men " of ancient faith and virtue "; he called " Immortal God " to witness, and not the Blessed Virgin; he paid a fitting tribute to the scholarly attainments of Valla. In every way he tried to show that he had left far behind him the scholastic traditions of the Middle Ages, and looked forward to the new ideals of the Renaissance. He was not only the most learned Englishman of his age, but the first who even attempted to reach the goal of universality Italy had created. In his love of learning he took up not only the classics and philosophy, but medicine and civil law.[1] In the classics he achieved considerable success, and his funeral ora-

---

[1] On the margin of f. 1, Ms. CXXIV Ball. Coll. (a universal cosmography in the writing of John Free) is a note by a more recent hand. "This book on cosmography was written at Padua in Italy, by John Free of Bristol, who studied at Padua and at Rome and was a professed doctor in medicine, civil law and Greek." Free also wrote and compiled the first six books of Diodorus Siculus, perhaps from Poggio's translation. — Coxe, I, 35.

tion on Guarino was highly praised for its Latinity by Carbo of Ferrara. His principal study, however, was probably medicine, which he taught for some years in different Italian cities. About 1465 he went to Rome, where he found a patron in John Tiptoft, Earl of Worcester, to whom he dedicated his Latin poetry and several translations from the Greek. For his scholarly attainments, Pope Paul the First granted him the bishopric of Bath and Wells, but he died, not without suspicion of poison, before his consecration.

John Gunthorpe and Robert Flemming were among the other scholars who belong to this early generation. The former had been Free's companion in Italy. He too had collected there many books, most of which were later distributed among the colleges at Oxford.[1] On his return to England he became royal chaplain and Dean of Wells where the deanery house built by him showed the Italian influence in its architecture.[2] His remaining literary work was confined to a rhetoric,[3] remarkable for its occasional use of Greek words and letters, and the minute analysis of the Latin parts of speech. Leland however mentions certain Latin epistles and poems also by his pen.

Robert Flemming had perhaps been induced to visit Italy by his kinsman, Richard, who at the Council of Constance, where Italian humanism first crossed the

[1] Leland, *Script. Brit.*, p. 463, also Leland, *Collectanea*, III, 16.
[2] Creighton, *Early Renaissance*, p. 29.
[3] Ms. 587 Bod.

Alps, had distinguished himself by the violence of his attacks on Wyclif.[1]   Flemming's desire for learning was strong enough to make him leave the cathedral of which he was the dean, to undertake the Italian journey.   After visiting the famous universities and studying at Ferrara under Battista Guarino, he settled down for some years in Rome.   There he formed a friendship with Platina, the papal historian and librarian of the Vatican, while from Sixtus the Fourth he obtained a preferment.   He dedicated to the Pope his *Lucubrationes Tiburtinæ*, written at Tivoli, where he passed the warm summer months.   This poem in heroic metre was probably the first important humanist verse written by any Englishman.[2]   In addition he compiled a Greek and Latin dictionary, no longer extant.   The remaining years of his life were uneventful.   After his return to England he settled at Lincoln, and on his death the manuscripts collected by him were left to the Oxford college which bore his cathedral's name.

One more English scholar who belonged to this early group will be mentioned.   John Tiptoft, Earl of Worcester, proved himself a quite different type of man from the others, whom he resembled only in his love of letters.   He was revered in Italy as a second

[1] Voigt, II, 260.

[2] A few lines are cited by Leland, *Script. Brit.*, p. 461.

> " Sane quisquis in hunc oculos defixerit acreis
> In vultu facieque viri cœleste videbit
> Elucere aliquid majestatem verendam."

Mæcenas, known alike for his scholarship and the zeal
with which he collected manuscripts. Like the Italian
despots of that age, he united a fondness for learning
and patronage of the arts with tyranny and oppression.
He has often been considered the first example of an
"Italianate Englishman," a type so common a hundred
years later. This is untrue in so far as the name stands
for the affected dandyism of Elizabethan courtiers. On
the other hand, he represented the blood and iron of
fifteenth century Italy, with its energy impatient of
restraint, eager only to accomplish its end, heedless
of difficulty. He represented, too, its zeal for learning,
perhaps the one love in which it was sincere.

Tiptoft had gone to Padua to continue his Latin
studies; afterwards he visited the aged Guarino at
Ferrara, and then went to Florence to have manuscripts
copied. Everything interested him, and arm in arm
with the bookseller, Vespasiano, he saw the sights of
the city, and even heard John Argyropulos lecture.[1]
In Rome Tiptoft is said to have caused Pius the Second
to weep with joy at hearing such eloquence flow from
English lips.[2] He met scholars as well, in Italy, while
humanists like Francesco d'Arezzo dedicated their
works to him.

No mean scholar himself, he is supposed to have
translated into English, Cicero's essay on friendship,
and Cæsar's commentaries. His great wealth, moreover, allowed him to take back with him such a
number of books that he was said to have despoiled the

---

[1] Vespasiano, p. 403.   [2] Voigt, II, 258.

libraries of Italy to enrich those of England. Oxford
shared in his benefactions and gratefully acknowledged
them.   Through him the authorities wrote[1], the university approached nearer to his Padua since the
fame of his attainments, and with it of their own, had
become known to the Italians, the masters of eloquence.   Just as no reward could have been too
great for the late Duke Humphrey who had favored
their cause, there now was no one worthier than himself to succeed to his place in their affections.   They
felt it time for others than Italians to enjoy his fame.
Such lavish praise did not fail to obtain its reward.
A letter of some years later mentioned the fact that
the earl had left Oxford a large number of books.[2]

Caxton also eulogized Tiptoft's love of letters,[3]
and praised his learning and cultivation of the arts;
like praise can be found as well in the Canterbury
Necrology.[4]   Unfortunately the less pleasant side to
his life earned for him the title of the "butcher of
England."   He was especially hated for introducing
the so-called *Paduan* law, which attempted to
substitute the Roman law, revived at Bologna and
Padua, for the common law.   This change, while
of advantage to trained jurists, seemed like an
infringement on the rights of the poorer people

---

[1] *Epist. Acad.*, II, 354.   [2] *Ibid.*, II, 390.

[3] Leland, *Script. Brit.*, p. 480.

[4] "Vir undecumque doctissimus, omnium liberalium artium
divinarumque simul ac secularium litterarum scientia peri-
tissimus." — Cited by Gasquet, *Eve of the Reformation*, p. 23,
note 3.

who had been accustomed to plead for themselves. Tiptoft was hated in consequence, for having introduced what was considered a foreign and tyrannous system in opposition to the liberties of England. The important judicial positions he occupied permitted, moreover, a free rein to his cruelty, and when, during the civil wars, he fell a prisoner in his enemies' hands, all alike demanded his execution, on account of his having oppressed the people and curtailed their just rights. To the Italian priest, who accompanied him to the place of execution, he apologized for his cruelties, on the ground of their having been necessary for the safety of the state,— an explanation which satisfied neither priest nor people. The examples for his life's work were both Italian. On the one hand, he had found in Italy models of tyrannous government and the absolute rule of the prince. To carry this into effect he introduced an alien system into England, the purpose of which was to elevate the sovereign's power. On the other hand, as a cultivated scholar, an eloquent orator, a collector of manuscripts and a patron of learning, he also found examples in Italy where once he had gratified his tastes.

What may be called the second period in English humanism came to an end with Tiptoft's death, even though Flemming and Gunthorpe lived many years longer. Although those who had been its principal actors accomplished but little, they forged a link in the development of the English Renaissance, and showed that the new learning at Oxford, far from being a sudden outburst, was silently prepared by a small group of scholars. Disturbances at home and wars abroad proved obstacles, however, to the student's life, while, furthermore, no commanding names lent lustre to the period. Excepting as they distinguished themselves in other fields, the scholars of this time have all disappeared from memory.

England was still unripe for the new learning. The only chance for its success lay in concentration of effort. But the young and ambitious band of Balliol scholars who set out for Italy, full of hope, did not return to Oxford, where alone in England their work might have borne fruit. United in their early zeal, they separated when the immediate goal had been reached, and in consequence failed in their work. John Free, the most learned and gifted of all, died before returning home. Tiptoft, who shared their love for letters, was led away from scholarly pursuits to perish miserably on the scaffold, while the others passed the remainder of their lives apart from each other in retirement. Their labor, however, was not in vain. The task they accomplished was to provide books for later students to use; to bring back with them, even though sterile, the learning of the Renaissance, and show that Greek and natural science, philosophy and medicine, were all within their reach. John Free, at least, proved the type of humanist to be possible for Englishmen. But most important of all, they pointed out that guidance for the new learning must be sought for in Italy itself.

IV

The fifteenth century was already nearing the end, with the new learning in England still in its infancy. Its growth, although slow, had nevertheless been constant during the fifty years before Oxford began to emerge from mediævalism. In the face of many difficulties, there had been a steady movement in the direction of progress. A second generation of Oxonians now found the task before them of laying the foundations of English scholarship, and beginning in their own country the study of the humanities as it had flourished for a century in Italy.

William Selling of All Souls, a Benedictine monk, may almost be called the dean of this younger generation. With another monk, William Hadley, he had first gone to Italy in 1464. The two studied together at Padua and Bologna, and met, among other scholars, Politian and Chalcondylas. Selling on his return gave particular attention to Greek, which was still unknown in England. He took back with him many ancient manuscripts,[1] and tried to make a centre of learning out of the monastery at Canterbury, of which he became the prior. The first real facilities in England to learn Greek were to be found there. He himself translated into Latin a work of St. John Chrysostom's, probably the first Greek book translated in that century on English soil. The wandering friar of the Middle

[1] Leland, *Script. Brit.*, p. 482.

Ages, the teacher of humanism and the scholar diplomat of the Renaissance were the elements in Selling's nature. As a diplomat he accompanied the embassy sent to the Pope by Henry the Seventh to announce his succession to the throne, and delivered a Latin oration before him and the College of Cardinals. As master moreover of the Christ Church School, he first taught Thomas Linacre the classics. He was thus one of the earliest English examples of the all-round man of broad culture, so frequent in Italy in the Renaissance. Prominent alike in scholarship and diplomacy, as a churchman and a teacher, he yet failed to excel in any capacity.

With the work of three Oxford friends, Thomas Linacre, William Grocyn and Thomas Latimer, modern English scholarship really began. Unlike their predecessors, who after studying in Italy, had accomplished little, both because the time was not ripe and their efforts were too scattered to produce any effect, they centred their work at Oxford and taught what they had themselves learned across the Alps. After the new learning had once rested on a firm foundation at the university, it was an easy task for its usefulness to be acknowledged by the rest of England.

William Grocyn, the eldest of the three friends, had been a fellow of New College, and afterwards prebendary of Lincoln Cathedral, where Robert Flemming was dean. From him came probably Grocyn's desire to visit Italy. Most of the Italian humanists of Flemming's generation were dead, but new ones continued worthily the old traditions, although the favorite city for study was no longer Ferrara, but Florence. That William Grocyn, already a man of forty and a scholar of some reputation, should have considered it necessary to cross the Alps in search of learning, shows how much Italy had then to offer and Englishmen wished to learn.

Linacre set out in 1488 to study under Politian,[1] then the acknowledged master among Italian scholars. There had been many learned humanists before him, but all had lacked the taste and perfect style, which he united to his great erudition. The new method taught only by him attracted to his lectures students from all Europe,[2] among whom were Grocyn, Latimer and Linacre. Linacre, after his first schooling at Canterbury, went to Oxford and then accompanied his former master, William Selling, on his embassy to the Pope. He was left, however, at Bologna in the care of Politian, whom he later followed to Florence. From him Linacre acquired his living knowledge of the classics, and the purity of style for which he was celebrated; for Politian boasted of his students, that they knew Greek as if the ancient Athenians had settled in Florence. Lorenzo de' Medici, the patron of the school, allowed him moreover (perhaps on account of having been with Selling's embassy) to attend Politian's private instruction to the young princes, Piero and Giovanni, who afterward

---

[1] Erasmus, *Epist.*, CCCI.
[2] Prezziner, *Studio di Firenze*, I, 162 *et seq*.

became Leo the Tenth. Many years later, the English scholar dedicated his edition of Galen to Leo, to recall, as he said, the common studies of their youth.

After a year in Florence, Linacre visited the other Italian centres of learning. In Rome he met Aldus, who held him ever afterwards in high regard and was later to publish his books. While studying Plato in the Vatican Library, he also became acquainted with the great Hellenist, Hermolaus Barbarus, who urged on him and his two English companions the task of translating Aristotle into Latin; Linacre alone is said to have completed his share of this work.[1] The study of Aristotle probably led him to devote himself to natural science and especially to the medical writers of antiquity; later he graduated a doctor of medicine at Padua. To perfect himself further in these pursuits, he studied at Vicenza, under the celebrated scholar and physician, Leonicenus, who had been the restorer of the medical treatment of Hippocrates through observation, which then was practised only by Italians; for the great development of medicine in the Renaissance came from the rediscovery in Italy of the methods of the ancients. Six years were spent by Linacre in his efforts to acquire there the new sciences. When finally he was ready to depart, he built an altar of stones dedicated to Italy, bearing on it the words, *Sancta Mater Studiorum.*

Cornelio Vitelli, a wandering Italian scholar, was called by Polydore Vergil the first teacher of

[1] *Collectanea Oxford.,* II, 346.

humanities (*bonas litteras*) at Oxford, and it has even been suggested that Grocyn and Linacre may have studied under him. Both Erasmus and George Lily wrote that Grocyn taught Greek before his Italian journey,[1] but no evidence to this effect can be found. It was certainly not until 1490, the date of Grocyn's return from Italy, that his teaching of Greek at Oxford began to exert its influence, and all indications point to its having been taught then for the first time. The materials for the study of the new learning had for some time been accumulating at Oxford, until everything was ready. In the university library were the books which Duke Humphrey and the Earl of Worcester donated, while Grey and Free had been similar benefactors to Balliol, and Flemming to Lincoln College. In this way, the discoveries of Italian scholarship had become known at Oxford, while the methods of the humanists were likewise brought back by English students on their return from Italy.[2]

The close friendship which existed between Grocyn and Linacre induced them to work together, once they were back at Oxford. Humanism, though affecting them equally in their love for the classics, had influenced each one in a different manner. It led the former to scriptural criticism ; William Grocyn had not taken up the new studies until comparatively late

[1] Erasmus, *Epist.*, CCCLXIII.

[2] Among other books in Grocyn's own library were the works of Ficino, Valla, Filelfo, Perotti, Petrarch and Boccaccio, *Collectanea*, II, 317 *et seq.*

in life. In spite of having been the introducer of Greek at Oxford, he always remained half a schoolman; even Erasmus had to admire the wide extent of his scholastic training.[1] He did not, however, allow this to blind him to the merits of the new learning. With a rare devotion to the cause of scholarship, he gathered in Italy the fruits of its best instruction to expound them later to those still immersed in mediæval traditions. In the face of many obstacles cast in his way, he succeeded in establishing at Oxford the study of Greek.

The fame of Grocyn, besides resting on his reputation as a teacher, resulted also from his lectures on the works of the so-called Dionysius the Areopagite, which marked the beginnings of biblical criticism in England, and showed the effect of his own humanistic studies. He began by vigorously attacking Lorenzo Valla, who had disputed the authenticity of the work; but realizing his error, with characteristic frankness he openly acknowledged it and retracted.

Little is now left to confirm the extraordinary reputation Grocyn enjoyed as a humanist. He shared the distaste of the other scholars of his age for appearing in print; excepting an epigram, nothing has been preserved of his writings save a letter written in 1499 to his friend Aldus, the Venetian printer,[2] in which he thanked him for the " singular kindness " shown his best friend Linacre, who had just returned to England, and congratulated him on completing the first publication

[1] *Epist.*, XIV.　　　　[2] Cited in *Collectanea*, II. 351.

of the Greek text of Aristotle by "that extremely ingenious artifice which you have invented for spreading
Greek literature by means of the press. . . . Go on
then, my Aldus, with this work and prosper."

There were two sides to William Grocyn; in his
nature the spirit of the Middle Ages blended with that
of the Renaissance. On the one hand was the schoolman and the quiet recluse, who, after satisfying his
thirst for knowledge in Italy, returned to settle down
in almost monastic seclusion at Oxford. On the other,
was the humanist, the theological critic, the introducer
of Greek. It was this which has entitled him to a
place in the foremost ranks of English scholarship,
and almost justified the verdict which makes him
share with his friend Linacre the glory of beginning
the English Renaissance of learning. Unlike the
latter, however, he lived within a small circle, caring
little for the applause of the world, but known to
his friends as "the most upright and best of all the
Britons." [1]

Thomas Linacre, the first great English humanist
and the foremost physician of the time, was a different
type of man. What John Free attempted in the previous generation, Linacre had accomplished. For the
first time England found a universal scholar who, like
the great Italians of the fifteenth century, was learned
in all branches of knowledge. He was a humanist in
every sense of the word ; although his learning was
essentially secular, he was skilled in ancient dialectic

---

[1] Erasmus, *Epist.*, CII.

and rhetoric, no less than in the classics and sciences. It was even questioned of him "whether he was a better Latinist or Grecian, a better grammarian or physician."

On his return from Italy, Linacre had lectured at Oxford, and with Grocyn taught such students as More, Colet and Erasmus. He wrote as well as taught, and his book on grammatical distinctions in Latin — a line of work already accomplished by Valla and Perotti — produced a considerable effect in England, where nothing of its kind had previously been attempted.[1] His reputation increased, and about the year 1500 he was called to court to be tutor to Prince Arthur, who died, however, shortly afterward. Neither his fame nor Grocyn's was confined to England, but spread to the other countries of Europe. The two were brought into especial prominence by the death of the great fifteenth century humanists, who left no Italian scholars to take their places. The new learning had, however, crossed the Alps, and now, firmly rooted in the different countries of Europe, united once more the learned world, insuring for its leaders an international celebrity. Vives the Spaniard, Lascaris the Greek, and the Frenchman Budaeus, to say nothing of his own pupil Erasmus, all joined in praising Linacre. Aldus, in publishing his edition of the *Sphere* of Proclus, regretted that Linacre had not sent him more books to print. He paid a striking tribute to the new English scholars who were now surpassing their masters. Admiring their

[1] Hallam, *Literature of Europe*, I, 344.

eloquence and style, he expressed the hope that their example might shame the Italian philosophers out of their uncultured mode of writing, so that from Britain itself, whence formerly there had issued a barbarous and rude literature, which threatened the Italian sanctuary of knowledge, true aid to learning might now come.[1]

Linacre had been able to cultivate, even if he had not acquired in Italy, his taste for medicine and the natural sciences. There had been other classical scholars, but he was the first English scientist and physician of distinction. On his return to Oxford he is supposed to have lectured on medicine as well as on other subjects ; Erasmus considered him the introducer of medical science in England.[2] His translation of Galen began its classical study there ; this was also the first work of a Greek author printed in that country. Aldus desired to publish other scientific books by him ; but Linacre shared the dislike to appear in print. He later became prominent in London through his medical practice, and succeeded the Italian Battista de Boeria as court-physician, attending the king with the other doctors, Fernando de Vittoria and John Chamber, who had also studied medicine at Padua.[3]

Linacre had felt the need of adequate facilities in England for scientific studies, which could then only

[1] Cited in *Collectanea*, II, 347. Vide E. Legrand, *Bibliographie Hellénique*, II, 396.

[2] *Epist.*, CCVII.

[3] J. N. Johnson, *Linacre*, pp. 170, 279; *Marini Transcripts*, Brit. Mus., XXXVII, 826.

be properly pursued in Italy. Before him, the practice of medicine in England had been chiefly in the hands of charlatans. To remedy this, he left the fortune he had accumulated, for the foundation of medical chairs at both universities ; and to dignify further the profession,[1] he established the College of Physicians, which was modelled on similar Italian institutions. The lectureships he endowed were only realized in a modified form, without embracing the wide scope he had mapped out for them. His public spirit and foresight in regard to the future of science made him, however, a benefactor of the nation. He was regarded generally as the first English type of universal humanist. He corresponded with foreign scholars in other lands; his real work lay in teaching to his countrymen the lessons he had learned in Italy. With him, the example of the scholar whose knowledge should rest on a broad secular foundation, and embrace the wide range of the arts and sciences, was brought over to England from across the Alps. Erasmus, writing to Latimer, said that had he only Linacre or Tunstall as his teacher, he would not seek Italy.[2] It was no longer necessary for scholars to go there ; the new learning had been definitely established in England ; the new type of scholar now flourished there as well.

William Latimer was the last of the three Oxford friends who had studied together in Florence. He is known chiefly by his friends, whose dislike for appear-

[1] Caius, *De Antiquitate Cantabrigiensis Academiæ*, II, 126.
[2] *Epist.* CCCLXIII.

ing in print he felt even more strongly; Erasmus
compared him on account of this to a miser hoard-
ing his gold.[1] His scholarship, however, was greatly
appreciated, especially by Erasmus. Bishop Fisher,
eager in spite of his advanced years to learn Greek,
wished him to be his teacher; but he advised instead
that one be sent for from Italy.[2]

It will scarcely be necessary to go through the increasing list of English scholars who had either studied
in Italy, or else betrayed the influence of Italian scholarship. The humanist movement in England was
well under way, and each year saw eager students has-
tening to Padua and Bologna. Even at the provincial
university of Siena, out of some three hundred students
in the school of philosophy, one-half were foreigners,
among whom were English, Germans, Portuguese, and
even Swedes.[3] The greater number who returned to
their homes helped in silence to build up the new
humanism and spread the learning they had acquired
in Italy. A few remained, however, in their adopted
country. Before the close of the fifteenth century one
Thomas Penketh " for his admired learning and eloquence " had even been called from Oxford, it was
said, to teach at Padua.[4]

Several differences, as well as resemblances, appear
between the two groups of Oxford scholars who went

---

[1] *Epist.* CCCLXIII.

[2] Mullinger, *History of Cambridge*, I, 519, note.

[3] Zdekauer, *Studio di Siena*, p. 96.

[4] S. Lewkenor, *Discourse of Foreign Cities*, 1600.

to Italy in search of the new learning. The first
devoted themselves only to individual study. Their
scholarship, however, was neither so profound nor so
broad as that of their successors, who were teachers as
well as students. The first had failed when they tried
to encourage the new learning by offering only their own
individual example. The others succeeded because
they built on a surer foundation. In both instances
nearly all concerned in the movement were churchmen ; but the secular tendency was gradually growing,
and when Linacre took orders in his old age, it was
rather to enable him to obtain preferment than for
any other reason. Both groups were composed entirely of Oxonians, but while the first (excepting John
Tiptoft) kept up their connection with the university
only through gifts and bequests of books, the latter
showed in their life work a far greater academic devotion. Their task was not only to bring back but
actually to teach their countrymen the studies of
Greek and science, medicine and Biblical criticism,
which Italian humanism had opened to the world.
By their instruction, as well as by their personal example, they created the new type of English scholar, who
was to equal his Italian model in learning, while he
surpassed him in purity of life. The efforts of this
small band of scholars succeeded at last in firmly establishing the new learning at Oxford. Before them,
it had been almost impossible to place it on the secure
foundation necessary. Englishmen lacked interest in
humanism so long as civil anarchy, desolation and

lawlessness conspired to forbid the necessary repose for scholarly labors. All that could be hoped for, and had in fact been accomplished, was to preserve what little learning was left from earlier generations. The day came, however, when the strong arm of the Tudor monarchy made itself felt through the land, and people realized that the age of civil strife was over, and the arts could now be practised in peace. Amid the novel feeling of quiet and repose, the new learning developed and prospered. Just as in Italy scholars had lived under the patronage of princes, who granted them adequate rewards for their labors, so humanism, newly introduced into England, was fostered and encouraged by Henry the Seventh, first of a new race of English monarchs.

V

Already in the early days of English humanism, a definite growth can be traced, marked by separate stages of development. This growth coincided for a time with the extension of Italian influence, and was in part its result. To the very end of the fifteenth century, and even later, Italy remained the fountain-head of the new learning. Yet England, as a whole, was still strangely insensible to Italian scholarship, which flourished only at Oxford. During the sixteenth century however, a great transformation took place. On the one hand, the silent preparatory work of previous years was to spread beyond the narrow limits of the university. On the other, the single dominant influence of Italy, which had been till then the living breath of the new learning, was greatly to diminish, while other countries in part took its place. This change was neither so sudden nor so unexpected as might appear. The diffusion of the new learning beyond the college halls, was largely the work of Oxford men trained in the methods of Italian scholarship. The decay of learning in Italy at the same time, caused Grocyn and Linacre to be regarded by the Italians themselves as the successors to their own great humanists. The foreign scholars who had been trained in Florence, Bologna and Padua were now to take up the work where it had left off in Italy, and spread the Renaissance learning in their own countries.

The desire to move in a broader sphere than the narrow world of Oxford can be observed in Linacre. The great connecting link, however, between court and university was to be Sir Thomas More. His task was to foster the desire for learning in circles where hitherto it had been unknown. His training and nature had fitted him for this work. As a young boy he had been sent to Oxford by Archbishop Morton, and had there learned Greek from Grocyn and Linacre,[1] with both of whom he formed enduring friendships. "Grocyn is in your absence the master of my life ; Linacre, the director of my studies," he wrote Colet.[2] Still other links than the affection he

---

[1] Erasmus, *Epist.*, DXI.
[2] T. Stapleton, *Tres Thomæ*, p. 23.

bore his masters bound him to Italy. Not only had Colet and Lily, with both of whom he was intimate, studied there, but he himself conceived a hero-worship for Pico della Mirandola, whose life he translated into English. Among his best friends, moreover, was the Luccan merchant, Antonio Bonvisi, to whom before being led off to execution he wrote in most affectionate terms, saying he had been a son rather than a guest in his house.

The opportunity soon arose for More to prove himself a friend of the new learning. Its very success had stirred up a violent opposition in Oxford itself. The contest came over Greek, as being the most important of the new studies brought from Italy. To know Greek was the next thing to heresy in the minds of many who regarded its literature as unorthodox.[1] Others, skilled in dialectics, were hostile, because unwilling to take up a new study in which their former work would prove of no use. Some, too, regarded all innovations as dangerous. The opponents of the " Grecians " united, therefore, under the name of "Trojans," and ridiculed in the streets those who pursued the new learning.[2] A priest who should have delivered a Lenten sermon preached in its place an invective against Greek and other polite literature.[3] William Tyndale, writing only a few years later, recalled the fact that the disciples of Duns Scotus " raged

[1] Jebb, *Erasmus*, p. 41.
[2] Maxwell-Lyte, *History of Oxford*, p. 435 *et seq*.
[3] Jortin, *Erasmus*, III, 359.

in every pulpit against Greek, Latin and Hebrew,"[1] and proclaimed openly that if there existed only a single copy in the world of Terence or Virgil, they would burn it, though it cost them their lives.

At this point, More wrote a letter to the university authorities, directed against mediæval scholasticism, which severely censured those who desired it once more. After presenting strong arguments in favor of the new learning, he warned them that further opposition would alienate the favor of their chancellor Archbishop Warham, their patron Cardinal Wolsey, and even the king, who was much interested in the progress of letters.[2] For More, besides awakening the court to the new learning, was also high in the royal favor, the king often sending for him to converse on learned subjects. It was through the influence, too, of More and Pace that the king took up the matter and finally silenced the Trojans.

Erasmus and Colet were among the other famous pupils of Grocyn and Linacre. The former went to Oxford because he thought it no longer necessary to proceed to Italy for classical learning, which could then better be obtained in England than anywhere else. There were fewer good scholars in Italy, he wrote, than in the days of Latimer's youth.   In his own judgment whoever was really learned was an Italian, even though born among savages.[3]   It was not till later

---

[1] Tyndale, Works, III, 75.   [2] Erasmus, *Epist.*, CCCCXIII.

[3] " Mihi Italus est quisque probe doctus est etiamsi fit apud Juvernos natus." *Ibid.*

that Erasmus went to Italy, accompanying the sons of Battista de Boeria, the king's chief physician. His life however, is too European to belong distinctively to English scholarship. It was otherwise with John Colet, whom Erasmus regarded as a leader among learned men.[1] After studying at Oxford, wishing to follow in the footsteps of his masters, he too visited Italy, attracted rather by a general love of culture than any great desire to learn Greek. Nothing really is known of the details of the three years he spent there, although it has been suggested that he may have met Savonarola. The puritan in his nature seems, however, to have been brought out by Italy. He was greatly impressed by the contrast presented between the corruption of the church and the lives of " certain monks of true wisdom and piety." [2] What chiefly influenced his later life was the Neo-Platonism and scriptural criticism of the Italian scholars. Returning to Oxford he lectured on Paul's *Epistles*, abandoning the allegorical interpretation of the Middle Ages for a free exposition of the whole. He compared the references of St. Paul to the state of Roman society, and rejected in consequence much of the doctrine of verbal inspiration, thus adopting the new historical method introduced in Italy. In these lectures, as in his work on Dionysius the Areopagite, he cited no schoolmen, but referred frequently to Ficino and Pico della Mirandola, quoting freely from the Platonic theology of the former, while often borrowing the latter's theological

[1] *Epist.*, XLI.   [2] *Ibid.*, CCCCXXXV.

doctrines.[1]   Colet was one of the first, with Grocyn, to
criticise in England the subject-matter of the Scriptures, as Valla had done in Italy.   In a different
direction, his work in beginning the study of the new
learning at the public schools was analogous to what
More accomplished at the court.   The wealth he inherited from his father was made use of by him to
found a school in St. Paul's churchyard.   William Lily,
the grammarian, who had studied in Italy under
Sulpitius and Pomponius Lætus, was its first head-
master.   There Colet and Lily put into practice the
new principles of education, and gave an example soon
followed by other schools.

The direct influence of Italy on English scholarship may be said to have ended with the generation
succeeding Grocyn and Linacre.   At the same time,
amid the blending of continental influences then
apparent in English culture, it would be unfair not to
assign proper importance to the strong leavening of
Italian thought and scholarly training.   The system
which Italy had built up, at a time when the rest of
Europe was still in the darkness of the Middle Ages,
was not to be shattered in a day.   Its intellectual influence could not so quickly be shaken off.   The
brilliant scholars in the other countries of Western
Europe who then began to make their appearance,
had all imbibed the Italian humanistic training, either
directly themselves or else through nameless masters,

[1] Vide Seebohm, *Oxford Reformers*, pp. 39, 151 *et seq.*
Lupton, *Life of Colet*, p. 51 *et seq.*

who transplanted it to their own land. The Italian Renaissance had moreover, given a vast impetus to learning, which in the Middle Ages was only to be found at the universities and in the higher ranks of the clergy. The courts of Europe now welcomed it with open arms, and everywhere men sought to gather its best fruits, whose ancestors had either scorned it as worthy only of poor clerks or else ignored it entirely. Largely owing to such changes as these, as well as to progress in other directions, scholars who had in former years been either of the academic or ecclesiastical types, were now divided into many classes. A few of the main paths along which scholars found their way will very briefly be outlined.

The wandering scholar was among the commonest of mediæval types. He had often been a man without a country, who found refuge at the universities, or else with patrons of learning. In the Renaissance, Erasmus, whom four nations claim, was the greatest example of the wanderer. An Englishman, by the name of Florence Volusenus, was of this type, although on an inferior scale. At the same time that he sent political information to Thomas Cromwell, he was in the patronage of the Cardinal of Lorraine, and then of Cardinal du Bellay. His real interest in life was supplied however by scholarship. He tried to go to Italy to gain his livelihood at a university;[1] failing in this, he was appointed, by Sadolet's influence, to a professorship of humanities at Carpentras,

[1] *Letters and Papers of Henry VIII*, IX, 573.

where, save for occasional visits to Italy, he passed the remaining years of his life. A similar exile was Peter Bisset, a graduate of St. Andrew's, who at the time of his death was professor of canon law at Bologna. Both men exemplified certain ideals of the age, which often placed learning above everything else, and made the scholar find a home in the land where his intellectual tastes could best be gratified.

Antiquarianism was a new direction the Renaissance gave to learning, and John Leland, if not so early as William Worcester, was yet the first great English antiquary. Conforming to the fashion then beginning, he had been on the grand tour; and after studying abroad, where he met some of the distinguished humanists, he returned with a good knowledge of Italian. Emulating Bembo and his school, he showed his scholarly tastes in his works on the writers of his own country no less than in his Latin verse. He was also a tutor to the Duke of Norfolk's son, for many well-known scholars taught then in the households of the nobility. The influence of such masters contributed as much as anything else to fostering the zeal for learning among the upper classes. On the other hand the new interest in learning found its way to court and royal patronage through the efforts of a few like Sir Thomas More. Of greater importance than Leland was Sir John Cheke, Secretary of State and tutor to Edward the Sixth. He was perhaps the finest example of a scholar selected to teach men of great position. He had also been long in Italy, especially at Padua, where he lectured and seems, moreover, to have exercised a kind of general supervision over all Englishmen in residence there.[1] When he returned, he became known as one of the chief promoters of Greek learning in England. What his real influence was with Edward is difficult to say, as that monarch's short reign offered few opportunities for his personal advancement of culture. The king's library, however, contained many Italian books,[2] urged on him, perhaps, by his tutor.

The study of Greek, once established at Oxford by Grocyn and Linacre, had not been long in spreading to Cambridge, where, owing to Bishop Fisher's influence, it was allowed to develop in peace. Erasmus, then professor of divinity, taught it unofficially,[3] but the first real teacher of Greek was Richard Croke, who, like many Italians, united learning with diplomacy. In this double capacity he had been sent to Italy at the suggestion of Cranmer, to collect opinions regarding the king's divorce, and had there visited the chief centres of learning.

The early work done in science by Free and Linacre was continued by Thomas Starkey, a Magdalen man, who, after studying at Padua, became a lecturer at Oxford. The famous Dr. Caius had also been at Padua; later in life he founded at Cambridge the

---

[1] T. Wilson, *The Three Orations of Demosthenes*, Preface.
[2] Nichols, *Literary Remains of Edward VI*, I, cccxxxv.
[3] Jebb, p. 27 *et seq.*

medical college, designed on an Italian model, which still bears his name ; among its provisions was one which stipulated that holders of travelling medical scholarships should be required to study at Padua, Bologna, Montepulciano, or Paris.[1]

The Italian Renaissance was first known in England in the scholarly world. Its progress in the arts, in social life, in a hundred ways, did not come until after it had penetrated the intellectual classes. What may therefore be called the first period of Italian influence in England, beginning in the second quarter of the fifteenth century and lasting for a hundred years, was essentially a scholarly influence which found its home at the universities. The initial impulse toward the new learning was thus given by Italy to England. By holding up its own example as a model, Italy formed the English secular type of scholar and directed his intellectual interests. Its influence, however, in the scholarly world was one of foundation rather than of development. It was paramount in assisting the one ; it diminished with the growth of the other. It was practically over with the generation which followed after Grocyn and Linacre, when English scholarship was developing along its own lines, barely affected by foreign influence. Its purpose had already been accomplished in the very beginning of the sixteenth century. The new learning of the Italian Renaissance had been transplanted to England, the new type of humanist established there. The influence of Italy

[1] Mullinger, II, 163.

first felt by Oxford men had spread thence to Cambridge, to the court, the homes of the nobility, the public schools, and by degrees through all England.

VI

The patronage of learning which has always been one of the proudest boasts of the Catholic Church existed especially in the Renaissance, when a genuine love for it on the part of churchmen atoned for many other shortcomings. The higher clergy, moreover, were mostly university men, whose scholarly interests had been awakened early in life, and who later were placed in a position to show their gratitude. An account of Italian influence on the new learning in England therefore requires some brief mention at least of the great churchmen who aided in fostering the movement.

The many ecclesiastical ties which bound all Europe to Rome had long familiarized the English clergy with Italy. Already in early mediæval times an Englishman named Nicholas Breakspere, had ascended the papal throne as Adrian the Fourth. During the long period of the Crusades, and the centuries when religious enthusiasm still stirred mankind, English pilgrims passed as a rule through Italy on their way to Palestine. So long as scholastic theology and canon law were studied as much at Bologna as at Oxford, there was little for Englishmen to bring back with them. A new era dawned, however, when the wave of the Renaissance swept over one country while the other was still un-affected by it.

The Church Councils, especially, brought the prel-ates of different nations, and their numerous retinues, in close contact with one another.   Henry Chichely, Archbishop of Canterbury, after returning from that of Siena, gave valuable gifts to Oxford, and founded All Souls College.   At the Council of Constance, where gleams of the new humanism for the first time crossed the Alps, Henry Beaufort, Bishop of Winchester, and an uncle of Henry the Fifth, met Poggio Bracciolini and invited him to England.

During Poggio's residence there, from 1420 to 1422[1], while he himself accomplished little, the great Florentine scholar found in John Stafford, Archbishop of Canterbury, Nicholas Bildstone, the Archdeacon of Winchester, and especially Richard Pettworth, Beau-fort's secretary, men of considerable cultivation.[2]   Still another learned prelate of this early period was Thomas Arundel, also Archbishop of Canterbury, who corre-sponded with the scholarly chancellor of Florence, Coluccio de' Salutati.

English learning, however, was to make its progress at Oxford and not in the ecclesiastical centres.   Even such churchmen as Grey, Flemming and Gunthorpe were to assist by their gifts of books rather than their personal example.   In developing the new learning, there was thus at the outset an essential difference be-

[1] Vide p. 180.

[2] Poggio, *Epistolæ*, II, 12, 18, 20, 22, 35; V, 22, etc.

tween the scholars and the dignitaries of the church. Both were university men, and the former were also for the most part in orders; but their preferments as a rule were only minor ones. The work in which they achieved real success was in their teaching at Oxford; while the assistance lent the cause by the great churchmen came rather through protecting the interests of scholars, as well as in gifts and donations of manuscripts.

Many prelates, however, set a personal example of learning, among whom were Bishop Waynflete, and Peter Courtenay, the Bishop of Exeter, who had studied at Padua. Thomas Langton, too, the Bishop of Winchester, had in his youth been in Italy, and was later sent by Richard the Third on an embassy to Rome. Returning to England, he founded a school for boys in his own house at Winchester, desiring perhaps to emulate Vittorino da Feltre. He showed further interest in the new learning by his connection with Oxford, and in sending Richard Pace to study in Italy. The many churchmen who displayed a similar interest, or were in some way connected with Italy, are far too numerous to mention here. A few examples only of the learned ecclesiastics — a type so prominent in the Renaissance — can be given. Of these William Warham, Archbishop of Canterbury, was among the most prominent. After having been at Oxford, he visited Italy, where he perhaps developed his interest in letters. The examples of the great Italian cardinals may also have urged him to follow them in his patronage of learning.   His wit, his genial temper and courtesy, no less than his own culture, made him the friend and protector of the scholars who were preaching the new learning in England.   To Erasmus he was " my special Mæcenas " : [1] Warham's kindness alone kept him from seeking the rich libraries and cultivated circles of Rome.[2]

A zeal for learning and the patronage of scholars became almost an affectation on the part of the higher clergy.   Some like Pace and Tunstall had studied at Padua, while the former even published in Venice a portion of the works of Plutarch, which he dedicated to Cardinal Campeggio, who was also interested in the success of humanism at the court.[3] Stephen Gardiner, too, the friend of Erasmus, and Richard Foxe, the founder of Corpus Christi, had both been on embassies to Rome.   Edward Bonner was also eager to learn Italian.   In all ranks of the church an interest in the new learning was shown, even by those who were to leave the Roman faith, but who in their zeal for letters continued former traditions.   The great patrons of learning were most beneficial in establishing scholarly foundations.   This was especially true of Cambridge, where the new learning came far later than at Oxford. During the entire fifteenth century the traces of Italian learning were barely noticeable there.   A copy of Petrarch's poems had, it is true, found its way to the library of Peterhouse so early as 1426.[4] A few similar books were gradually acquired, and John Gunthorpe

---

[1] *Epist.*, CXLIV.
[2] *Ibid.*, CLXVIII.
[3] *Ibid.*, CCCCXXXVII.
[4] Mullinger, I, 433.

left some of his manuscripts to Jesus College. Very few indications of the new learning can, however, be found, although an Italian named Caius Auberinus acted as Latin scribe toward the end of the century, and gave in addition occasional lectures on Terence.[1]

The impulse, when it came, was chiefly from Bishop Fisher, who, encouraged in his efforts by Lady Margaret, was determined to raise Cambridge to the level of her sister university. In 1511, he summoned Erasmus, who for a time gave unofficial instruction in Greek. The intellectual condition of things may be judged from his complaint that the masters at Cambridge were trying to bring back dialectics.[2] He said himself he did his best to deliver the rising generation from ignorance, and to inspire them with a taste for better studies. Ten years later, however, he was able to write differently, and declare that Cambridge could then compete with the chief universities of the age. Bishop Fisher was largely instrumental in bringing about this improvement; not only did he assist in establishing St. John's College, but he founded lectureships as well in Greek and Hebrew. His generosity, moreover, enabled Richard Croke to go as the first professor of Greek to Cambridge, instead of to Oxford where his friendship with Linacre and More would naturally have led him.

Similar foundations were also established at Oxford, the first by Richard Foxe, Bishop of Winchester, who

---

[1] Cooper, *Athenæ*, I, 9.
[2] *Cal. St. Pap.*, *Henry VIII*, I, No. 1404.

endowed Corpus Christi in 1516. This was a college founded in the interests of humanism, and attracted for that reason considerable attention; for, up to that time, the new plant had been grafted on the old, usually without success. In the statutes of Corpus Christi, however, all former hindrances were swept aside. A public lecturer in Greek was to be among its principal officers, and Greeks and Italians were declared especially eligible for the position. A complete humanistic education was required of its graduates; for the long vacation, the works of Valla and Politian were especially recommended as subjects of study; candidates for scholarships, in addition to knowing the ancient writers thoroughly, must themselves be able to compose Latin verses, although in ordinary conversation within the college Greek was thought acceptable as a substitute for Latin. By such means as these it was intended that " all barbarism " should be suppressed.[1]

The torrent of opposition greeting Foxe's daring innovations was ended by More's influence at the court, and Cardinal Wolsey's similar foundation of Christ Church, which he endowed from the revenues of the suppressed monasteries. Consent for this was obtained at Rome by Wolsey's agent, Ghinucci, who was also instructed to search for books, and order copies to be made of the Greek manuscripts in Italian libraries.[2] Wolsey made a similar request of the Venetian envoy, Orio, requesting him, as a great favor,

---

[1] Maxwell-Lyte, p. 412.
[2] Creighton, p. 25.

to ask the signory for transcripts, for the college library, of the Greek manuscripts which had belonged to Cardinals Grimani and Bessarion.[1] The college itself was filled with the spirit of the new learning; the great writers of antiquity were to be expounded daily, and all conversation conducted in either Latin or Greek. The foundation of similar institutions thus marked the final overthrow of scholasticism by the new learning of the Renaissance. Its further development at both Oxford and Cambridge was to be more especially along purely English lines.

In the early stages of the new learning the English scholar's dependence and example came almost entirely from Italy. Even much later, although great foreign scholars like Vives and Erasmus, both of whom aided so largely the growth of English learning, were not themselves Italians, yet the one had studied long in Italy, while the other, before crossing the Alps, had sought instruction at Oxford from those who had themselves studied there. So far-reaching was the influence of Italy in the sixteenth century, that much which may seem French or Spanish at first glance was, in reality, Italian, but once removed.

In Italy, therefore, English scholars had first been taught the new humanism, while English churchmen found there an example for their patronage of letters. It was the joint effort of both that brought about the Renaissance of learning in England, to which patron and scholar alike contributed.

[1] *Cal. St. Pap., Ven.,* III, 515.

CHAPTER II

THE COURTIER

I

In the last quarter of the fifteenth century the nations of Western Europe began to pass through similar phases in their transition from the Middle Ages to the Renaissance. The dominant political feature of the age was the concentration of the supreme power of the state in the person of one sovereign prince. This had begun already in Italy, where petty despots gathered into their hands the power of the nobility and burghers, whom they reconciled to the loss of political liberty by the attractions and splendor of their courts. Similarly, beyond the Alps the centralization of the sovereign power in the king brought with it, on the one hand, a diminution in the influence of the great nobles, while on the other, it fostered the growth of the court. Thus it came about that the political characteristic of the age was likewise to mark its social development, and the descendants of feudal lords were gradually transformed into courtiers.

Court life in the Renaissance assumed of a sudden far greater importance than ever before. More and more the activities of the nation centred around and emanated from it. While during the Middle Ages

Thomas Linacre professeur en medecine a son feld. Angloif
homme cortel docte aus deux langues grecq' q' latine
ayant coposé plusieurs doctf liures, mourut à Londres l'an a.

Thomas Linacre

every castle was a miniature court, complete in itself, the life of the nation was now focussed, so to speak, around one sovereign, about whom there gathered the best in the land. The court became almost the only means of entering the service of the state, which at that time depended so largely on royal favor. It led as a stepping-stone to the great careers of arms, diplomacy and administrative employment. Whoever found favor in his prince's eyes might well hope to be intrusted with the command of an army, the charge of an embassy, or the government of a province.

Toward the end of the fifteenth century, Italian influences began to appear at the English court. Through the scholars, the new humanism had spread from Oxford to this larger sphere, where it could more readily be felt; a noticeable growth, moreover, had taken place in direct intercourse with Italy. The Dukes of Ferrara and Urbino were on the friendliest footing with Henry the Seventh,[1] and he himself employed numerous Italians in his personal service: among others there may be mentioned Silvestro Gigli, his master of ceremonies, Polydore Vergil, his friend, historian and adviser, and his poet, Peter Carmeliano. In its hearty welcome to Italians, the English court in the sixteenth century was only following the example of France and Spain. Monarchs could, indeed, find their most servile adherents in these foreigners, who

[1] *Cal. St. Pap. Ven.*, VI, Pt. III, 1603 *et seq.* Dennistoun, *Memoirs of the Dukes of Urbino*, II, 443 *et seq.*

without ties binding them to their adopted land were courtiers and diplomats by nature. Another reason, moreover, added to their success. A new type of courtier had grown up in Italy. At the courts of Urbino, Mantua and Ferrara, a higher conception had been formed of what the companion of the prince ought to be ; his manners and accomplishments became an outward reflection of the new life of the Renaissance, infusing its spirit in the court. By degrees these were formed into a system ready to be taught as a part of the courtier's education. A definite and distinct type having thus gradually been created in Italy, the courtier who had received this training became superior to any other. During the sixteenth century, England in common with the other nations of Western Europe acquired considerable familiarity with this new type, through the observation of Italians at home and abroad, and partly, too, through the translation of Italian books, especially of such as related to manners ; from these could be obtained the new theory of the courtier as it presented itself to the Italians of the Renaissance.

It was especially in Italy that the inquiring spirit of the race endeavored to analyze the principles of conduct determining all matters of social intercourse ; hence great numbers of manuals of courtesy, and guides to conversation, were written there. Conversation and courtesy were then treated almost as fine arts, which could both be taught and practised. Books professing to give such instruction endeavored to direct the entire social existence of man, advising him even in regard to the most intimate details of life. Two kinds of such courtesy books can be distinguished in the literature of the age : the one intended for men in general, gave sound advice in the direction of refinement of manners ; the other, on the contrary, confined its attention to the courtier class, quite unconcerned with the ordinary individual. Della Casa's *Galateo* and Castiglione's *Cortegiano* severally were the representatives of each type. Although written in Italian their influence was in fact European, and they were well known in translations throughout Western Europe. Any account of court life in England in the sixteenth century, would, indeed, be incomplete without attention to such books, which both gave a definite expression to the underlying principles of the courtier's art, and advocated likewise a new ideal of social conduct. Scores of allusions can be found to these books in the English literature of the age, and especially to the *Cortegiano*, which in itself may almost be said to have given voice to the undefined mass of Italian influences at the Tudor court, and assisted in forming in England the new type of courtier.

II

In the sixteenth century, even more than now, the question as to what constituted a gentleman was discussed among the living problems of the age. This great subject centred around the respective merits of nobility by birth and nobility by virtue.[1]   Different, often contrary, views were expressed on the subject, but opinions tended to group themselves in two separate camps.   On the one side was the so-called popular idea which considered nobility to be by birth alone, and seemed to think it showed itself in a tone of luxury and sport, an overbearing manner and a quick temper.[2] On the other was the opinion of alleged "philosophers," who maintained that since all men owed equally their origin to God, in whom the highest nobility found its centre, every one, irrespective of birth, was noble so long as he lived a virtuous life ; if, however, he inclined toward vice, he was base, no matter from whom he traced his descent.[3]   Between these two extremes most opinions varied.   Especially debatable were the qualifications necessary to the eligibility of the courtier —a question of the greatest importance, since gentle- men then found an active career open at court.   It was thought by some that the courtier should be a gentle- man born and of good family ; his nobility, however, was not to excuse in him any lack of virtue, since such deficiency would be far less reprehensible in one of low birth than in a gentleman.   Others argued in favor of wit and beauty taking the place of noble descent. Still a third eminently practical view was held by some. Although high virtues, it was acknowledged, were often present in one of base extraction, yet the courtier

---

[1] Vide *Nennio, or a Treatise of Nobility*.

[2] Humphrey, *The Nobles or of Nobility*.

[3] Romei, *Courtier's Academy*, p. 187 *et seq.*

should be of noble birth, since prejudice played so large a role in all human affairs, and people respected noblemen far more, although their qualities were no greater.[1] The first view prevailed for the most part, especially in the first half of the sixteenth century. Liberal opinion complained bitterly that "the world commonly reputeth gentry by birth as legitimate, and gentry by virtue as bastardly and far inferior to the other . . . [Men had] rather be born gentlemen and have nothing in the world but their rapier and cloak, than to be descended of base parentage and to be senators or presidents."[2] Virtue, however, was thought by all to be the first cause of nobility, and its truest expression was said to consist in its union with famous ancestry.[3] He who was noble without virtue, or virtuous without nobility, could never properly be termed a gentleman.[4] Even such of the later writers as were imbued with a more democratic spirit recognized the advantages of noble descent. A sentiment frequently expressed was that one ought not to boast of ancient lineage but prove one's self worthy of it. It was said that the great advantage of noble blood was in making men ashamed to degenerate from the virtue and valor of their ancestors.[5] Laurence Humphrey only echoed Castiglione in his saying that faults were far more excusable in one of base

---

[1] Castiglione, *The Courtier*, p. 44 *et seq.*
[2] Guazzo, *Civil Conversations*, f. 83 *et seq.*
[3] Humphrey, *op. cit.*   [4] Romei, p. 225 *et seq.*
[5] Guazzo, f. 86.

extraction than in a nobleman of famous lineage. Italian views on this and kindred subjects were frequently repeated in England, with a certain moral element usually added to them. English writers on this topic, from Sir Thomas Elyot, Humphrey, the anonymous author of *The Institution of a Gentleman* and still later, William Segar, were all familiar with the works of Italians, from whom they frequently quoted, often without acknowledging their indebtedness. The theory of the gentleman was, however, a far more popular subject of discussion in Italy than in England, where its echoes were mostly of Italian origin, and but few original views were set forth.

A question often discussed was the compatibility of commerce with nobility. It was urged by some that the Venetians and Genoese, who thought themselves the first gentlemen in the world, considered it no disgrace to be merchants as well.[1] The great argument advanced in favor of trade was the practical one that nobility could neither be brought to perfection without wealth nor be preserved without money. Even in the sixteenth century, riches played a far greater part in the consideration of the gentleman than is commonly supposed. Money, however, of itself was not sufficient to ennoble a man, although three generations of wealth might suffice to do so.[2] On the other hand, poverty would often force a man to marry a woman of low birth, and thus debase his blood.[3] If any conclusion

[1] Segar, *Honor, Military and Civil*, ch. 18.
[2] Romei, p. 187.   [3] Guazzo, f. 89.

was reached at all in regard to the part played by riches, it was, perhaps, that though they could add in no degree to gentry, yet they permitted certain virtues pertaining to it to be practised, which poverty did not allow. A mere vulgar exhibition of wealth was, however, frowned on severely, while those who called themselves gentlemen, simply because they could afford to live idly, were sharply censured.[1]

Underneath the surface, especially during the latter half of the sixteenth century, a strong democratic tendency can be observed, which revealed itself chiefly in the growing importance assigned to such qualities in the individual as were independent of birth. Humble parentage had never been a bar to success in England where real ability forced its way to the front at all times, and especially in the sixteenth century, when many commoners were ennobled. It was usually accepted that children of men of distinction were gentlemen, regardless of their parents' birth.[2] The new Italian idea of gentlemanliness, which was penetrating England, was to include, moreover, such men as had formerly been debarred in theory. Whoever had studied the laws of the realm, had been at the university, or professed the liberal sciences, whoever could live without manual labor, and bear the port, charge, and countenance of a gentleman should be taken for one.[3] A reaction naturally followed; men complained that the old ideal of gentlemanliness had been suffered

[1] Romei, p. 226 *et seq.*   [2] *Institution of a Gentleman.*
[3] Sir Thomas Smith, *Commonwealth of England,* p. 37.

to decay, that many who were no better than handi-craftsmen had assumed the title and bore the arms which rightly belonged to the old gentry. "As for gentlemen, they be made good cheap in England," wrote Sir Thomas Smith,[1] with ill-concealed dislike for this new democratic movement.

More and more, however, new tests of learning, civility and virtue were applied to the judgment of the gentleman. It was even maintained that only such as excelled in an art or science acquired thereby a true nobility, far superior to one of birth or descent.[2] This nobility should spring from inward virtue, and not consist merely of outward form.[3] Men were to be respected not by reason of their ancestors, but for such virtues as were within them. The self-made gentleman possessed a twofold advantage over the gentleman only by birth : the first was virtue, the other courtesy, "the right ornament of a gentleman ; for of courtesy and gentleness, he is termed a gentleman."[4] Some even argued that it was an impossibility for men to be gentlemen who had no other qualification than their birth. "If they be uncivil how are they gentle-men? and if they be gentlemen how are they un-civil? . . . Gentry and renown is not got by our birth but by our life, yea, and sometimes by our death."[5]

---

[1] *Commonwealth of England*, p. 37.
[2] *V. Saviolo, his Practise*, Preface.
[3] Humphrey, *op. cit.*
[4] Guazzo, ff. 85 *b*, 88.   [5] *Ibid.*, ff. 85 *b*, 92.

A loftier and more democratic ideal of what the perfect gentleman ought to be had arisen in Italy, and found its way to England. It was no longer sufficient to follow in the footsteps of worthy predecessors: "Whoso vaunteth of his ancestors seemeth without any good thing of his own."[1] The new conception of gentlemanliness by personal effort, which sprang up, looked rather to individual *virtù* than to outward factors. This feeling was well expressed by a contemporary writer: "If it be a great delight for a man to know that from time to time out of his house (as out of the Trojan horse) there have issued captains, colonels, and knights, . . . how much more shall it be to him, who may say that he hath, according to the proverb, wings broader than the nest, and by the excellence of his deeds, and sufficiency in learning and feats of arms, hath surpassed the deserts, dignities, and degrees of his predecessors, and alone, as it were, carried away the prize."[2]

The influence of this new democratic doctrine of the Renaissance extended beyond the Alps. Even though in practice it was not to be realized till centuries later, it yet found frequent expression in literature and life. At the very court of Elizabeth it was echoed by William Segar, almost as a promise of the future liberty and freedom of the individual to rise by his own merits. The doctrine upheld by the Italians of the Renaissance was later to be realized among English-speaking people. "I say that the true no-

[1] Segar, *Book of Honor*, p. 34. [2] Guazzo, f. 87.

bility of man is virtue, and that he is truly noble that is virtuous, be he born of high or low parents; and the more highly he be born, the worse reputation he meriteth, if he cannot continue the honor left him by his ancestors."[1]

III

The Renaissance, more than any period in the modern world, endeavored to develop, as far as possible, the different faculties of man. The ideal of universality, once aimed at, was consciously pursued and attained by the best spirits of the age. This was especially true in Italy, where the perfect man of the Renaissance strove for excellence in every branch of human activity, both intellectual and physical, trying at the same time to be statesman and athlete, poet and scientist, philosopher and courtier. The excellence of the courtier, however, was by no means limited to the qualities of his mind. He was to possess every grace and accomplishment, but never to push into undue prominence what he did well; nor even appear to have given much time or study to it, since that would have spoiled the artistic effect produced on the spectator.[2] Everything was therefore to be done with grace, as though presenting no difficulty. He was to be nimble, quick and light, continually showing pluck and spirit; good at all games and excelling at the tourney, in hunting, swimming, leaping, running and casting the stone; even tennis and vaulting

[1] Segar, p. 34.   [2] Castiglione, p. 115.

were recommended. On the other hand, tumbling, climbing a rope and jugglers' tricks should never be practised by the courtier, who ought to preserve his dignity in all his actions. Above everything else, the superiority of his station in life was to be real, not merely a matter of convention; thus, if he wrestled or ran with countrymen, he should appear to do so for courtesy only, and not to win; but first he must be sure of himself; "for it is too ill a sight . . . to see a gentleman overcome by a carter, and especially in wrestling."[1] This scorn of social inferiority, it may be remarked, was by no means universal. In later years, especially, a kindlier and more democratic view was often taken of the relations which ought to exist between the different classes. Gentlemen were urged not to despise the society of their social inferiors, who would love and honor them in consequence. "There is no more difference between the gentleman and the yeoman than there is between two bricks made of selfsame earth, whereof the one is set in the top of a tower, the other in the bottom of a well."[2]

It is curious to think that England, which to-day claims superiority in sport, should have submitted in the sixteenth century to Italian methods and instruction. The accomplishments and pleasures of the courtly life had, however, first been systematized in Italy, and in sport, as well, its guidance was supreme. Even in horsemanship, Edward the Sixth had his Italian riding-master at the court; another Italian, known as Alex-

[1] Castiglione, p. 115. [2] Guazzo, f. 90 b.

ander, who had studied under the celebrated Grisone, also taught in England, and to him was ascribed, in part, the improvement in English teachers of riding. Elsewhere it was the same; Sidney spoke of Pietro Pugliano at the Emperor's court instructing his pupils both in the practice and theory of horsemanship, and even later Robert Dallington advised his traveller to learn riding under *Il Signor Rustico* at Florence.[1] The first English book on horsemanship was Blundevile's translation of Grisone, which appeared about 1560. What Alexander had failed to accomplish was left for this book to effect; after its publication, says Bedingfield, riding-masters who before " were not of much knowledge " improved considerably. The popularity of similar books was very great. Bedingfield was only one among their numerous translators.[2] Even Florio gave as a reason for his Italian dictionary, that without it English gentlemen would be unable to understand Grifonio's work on riding.

In falconry, and hunting as well, George Turbervile, in one of the most elaborately prepared books of the age, openly acknowledged his debt to the many Italian writers on the subject.[3] It was in fencing, however, then so essential a part of the gentleman's education, that the skill of the Italian showed itself to the greatest advantage. Even the Italian terms of the art were employed in England. English travellers were advised

---

[1] *Method for Travel.*

[2] *Art of Riding*, translated by Thomas Bedingfield.

[3] *The Book of Falconry or Hawking.*

when abroad, to study fencing either at Padua under *Il Sordo* or else at Rome.[1] This was scarcely necessary, however, since numerous Italian masters of the art gave instruction in England. George Silver mentioned three such schools in London.[2] A Signor Rocco had one in Warwick Lane, which he called a college, where " he taught none commonly under twenty, forty, fifty or an hundred pounds." On the walls of his school, according to Silver's contemporary description, hung the coats-of-arms of the noblemen and gentlemen who were his pupils, and beneath these were their rapiers, daggers and gauntlets. He even had a room he called "his privy school, with many weapons therein, where he did teach his scholars his secret fight, after he had perfectly taught them their rules."[3] In addition to its ordinary use, the school was also a sort of club for the young gallants of the court who found there "ink, pin-dust and sealing wax, and quires of very excellent fine paper gilded, ready for the noblemen and gentlemen upon occasion to write their letters."[4]

The most celebrated, however, of the Italian fencing-masters in England was Vincenzo Saviolo, who had as patron the Earl of Essex. Saviolo has been described as the perfect fencer by Florio, in words which Shakespeare almost certainly knew — "He will hit any man, be it with a thrust or *stoccata*, with an *imbroccada* or a charging blow, with a right or reverse blow, be it

---

[1] Dallington, *Method for Travel.*
[2] *Paradoxes of Defence.*
[3] *Ibid.*, p. 65.　　[4] *Ibid.*, p. 64.

with the edge, with the back, or with the flat, even as it liketh him."[1]

The Italian schools of fencing enjoyed a great success in London. Their methods of instruction, like their weapons, were both new to Englishmen, but proved none the less popular in an age when novelty was appreciated for its own sake. Their pupils were even taught to wear leaden soles in their shoes, to be the more nimble-footed in a fight. An English fencing-master of the time complained bitterly that his art, like fashions of dress, changed every day; that Englishmen had forsaken their fathers' virtues with their weapons, and lusted after the strange devices of Italian fencers and their imitators : " O you Italian teachers of defence, where are your *stoccatas*, *imbroccatas, mandritas, puntas*, and *punta reversas, stramisons, passatas, carricadas, amazzas*, and *incartatas*. . . . apish devices with all the rest of your squint-eyed tricks."[2]

The influence of this new Italian school made itself felt, however, in different ways. Among its other effects was the improvement of manners. Even George Silver, who hated the Italians as dangerous rivals, felt obliged to concede this : " It hath been commonly held that since the Italians have taught the rapier fight, by reason of the dangerous use thereof, it hath bred great civility amongst our English nation, they will not give the lie, nor with such foul speeches abuse

[1] *Second Fruites*, p. 119.
[2] Silver, p. 55.   Vide Marston, *Works*, III, 373.

themselves ; therefore there are fewer frays in these times than were wont to be. It cannot be denied that this is so, that we are more circumspect in our words than heretofore we have been." [1]

Italian treatises on fencing also enjoyed great popularity in England ; Giacomo de Grassi's *True Art of Defence* treated in detail the theory of the art, with illustrations and diagrams describing the various kinds of weapons used, rapier and halberd, partesan and javelin, and also of the falsing of blows and thrusts. Saviolo's *Practise*, dedicated to " the English Achilles," Robert, Earl of Essex, obtained, however, a far greater celebrity, and still remains of interest as the great source from which the Elizabethan dramatists acquired their knowledge of duelling.

Saviolo's work in combining practice with theory illustrated one of the causes of Italian success in such matters. Not only was the practical side of his art treated at length, but selections from well-known historians were also given. A large part of the book was further taken up by discussion ; thus, the point of honor, and the relations to be observed between men under strained circumstances, were treated. From his warnings, some idea can be had of the frequency of treachery in such matters ; for instance, it was thought unwise to ask to see another man's rapier, since it gave an opportunity to kill an unsuspecting enemy. He alluded also to the cowardly practice of hiring *bravos* to aid in murdering an

[1] *Op. cit.*, p. 56.

adversary, by no means an uncommon thing at that time. Even the Earl of Oxford, returning from his travels abroad, had with great difficulty been dissuaded from employing this Italian custom to revenge himself on Sidney. Other dangers were to be guarded against as well; thus, friends coming up suddenly in the midst of an encounter, as though to separate the combatants, might treacherously slay their favorite's opponent. He spoke also of quarrels, beginning between two or three men, and then spreading until whole families were engaged in them, and often not ending without great bloodshed.[1] Saviolo, like Castiglione, advised gentlemen to keep close guard over their tongues, neither to bear slander nor tell tales, and always to behave rightly to men of inferior station. To illustrate his point, he related the story of a wrestling match, which later Shakespeare made use of in *As You Like It*. Saviolo's tale was of an overbearing Moor vanquished by Rodomont, the Duke of Mantua's brother, who though himself a wild sort of fellow, would yet not "suffer so beastly a creature to stain the honor of Italian gentlemen." Touchstone's description of the different kinds of lies[2] was likewise taken almost certainly from Saviolo, who discussed conditional and foolish lies, lies in particular and lies in general.[3]

[1] It was perhaps some similar sentence which first suggested the dramatic possibilities of *Romeo and Juliet*, and gave Elizabethan playwrights an insight into the feuds of Italian cities.

[2] *As You Like It*, V, iv, 70 *et seq.*

[3] A similar account may be found in Segar's *Book of Honor and Arms*, 1590.

According to Saviolo, giving the lie was at the bottom of most duels, and he therefore cited the Italian code of duelling to be used on such occasions.

Even in that age the ethics of the duel were in debate. Men argued on the wickedness of private combat,[1] and Bryskett in his rendering of Giraldi Cinthio, condemned duels as " contrary to all virtue, odious to all laws, to all good magistrates, and to God himself,[2] " saying that the way to shake off an injury was to despise it.[3] Saviolo, without discussing the moral side of the duel, described the proper etiquette to be observed, the forms of cartels and letters of defiance, and the manner in which they were to be sent; he entered also into conduct on the duelling ground, the treatment of the vanquished and the inequality of adversaries; his advice was, that excommunicated persons, usurers, and all who did not live as gentlemen or soldiers, should be refused satisfaction in honorable combat.

Saviolo's book was probably the first in the English language ever written by an Italian. It stated openly the Italian ideal of arms and letters, weapons and books, as the two sources of greatness. By the one, the small man could overcome the larger, the weak the stronger; by the other, man could raise himself to any height by his own unaided merits. The entire Renaissance conception of the dignity of the individual lay in these words, the spirit of which gave conscious

[1] Romei, p. 129.
[2] *Discourse of Civil Life*, p. 70.   [3] *Ibid.*, p. 77.

assurance to the Italians in their careers beyond the Alps, making a Rizzio prime minister of Scotland, and the descendants of Florentine bankers queens of France.

The revival of the tourney was still another courtly practice which England copied largely from Italy. Jousting as a court amusement became fashionable once more in Elizabeth's time. Sir Christopher Hatton, well known as a patron of letters, and himself a student of Italian, was especially prominent among those who revived it. William Segar, garter king-at-arms, in his *Honor, Military and Civil*, alluded frequently to Italian practices, describing their method of conducting tournaments.[1] At Urbino and Ferrara, jousting had long been regarded as an amusement of the court; even Castiglione had advised his courtier how to conduct himself at the tourney; never, for instance, to be last in the lists, since women, especially, paid far greater attention to the first than to the last.[2]

In many other courtly practices, as well, the influence of Italy was felt. Hall, in his *Chronicle*, described the first mask held at court in 1512-13, as being in the Italian fashion. "On the Day of Epiphany, at night, the King with eleven others were disguised after the manner of Italy, called a Mask, a thing not seen before in England." The very names of *Maskelyn* and *Masculers*, occurring in the *Records of the Revels*, point to the Italian equivalents of *Maschera* and *Mascherati*.[3]

---

[1] Ch. 50.   [2] Castiglione, p. 114.
[3] Symonds, *Shakespeare's Predecessors*, p. 320.

The best artists of the period lent their assistance to contribute to the success of these masks; the records still exist of two Italians, Vincent Vulpe and Ellis Carmyan, who had been engaged in their decoration in the reign of Henry the Eighth.[1] Even Holbein was similarly employed, while considerably later Inigo Jones did not consider it beneath his dignity to devise and introduce new stage mechanisms which he had learned in Italy.

The Venetian Spinelli left an account of one of the earlier masks, which was presented at court in 1527, and may be given as an example of the early scenic development of similar spectacles in England. To describe it very briefly : admission to the hall in which it took place was through a lofty triumphal arch, fashioned after the antique, with vaulted entrances beneath, and Greek words written over the archway. The Renaissance spirit in which it was conceived showed itself even in the neo-classicism of the decorations, reminiscent of Mantegna's allegories or the paintings of the Ferrarese school. The actors of the mask first appeared on the scene and then withdrew, leaving behind a youth in the guise of Mercury, who, pretending to be Jupiter's envoy to the king, delivered a learned Latin oration in praise of his Majesty. When he had departed, eight boys led by Cupid and Plutus entered, clad in cloth of gold. Afterwards a like number of maidens appeared, supposed to be goddesses, also draped in gold cloth, and with richly jewelled garlands

[1] Brewer, *Henry VIII*, II, 150.

in their hair. First they danced, and then came the turn of the young men, each of whom took one of the nymphs by the hand.[1]

The popularity of these spectacles was very great, and they continued for long to be the favorite amusement of the court; Marlowe, for instance, made Gaveston, the royal favorite, say : —

> I'll have Italian masques by night,
> Sweet speeches, comedies, and pleasing shows.

Italian players, both men and women, later came over to England to play in masks, performing both at Windsor and Reading in 1574. At court, moreover, the masks were usually presented by Italians, often aided by English players. In the one presented before the queen and the French ambassador, the Lord Chamberlain gave instructions for the speeches written in English to be translated into Italian.[2]

The later development of masks under Jonson, Campion and Heywood, belongs to the history of English poetry. The musicians, however, were chiefly Italians, and Alfonso Ferrabosco composed much of the music for the later court masks. Inigo Jones, moreover, who designed the mechanism and stage scenery, brought back the new mechanical devices from Italy, where he learned his art. Among the articles most in use for spectacles and state occasions, was the cloth of gold, which was imported largely from Italy. King Henry the Seventh sent at various times to Florence to pur-

---

[1] Brewer, II, 152 *et seq.*
[2] F. G. Fleay, *History of the Stage*, pp. 22, 26.

chase gold cloth, as well as silks.[1] Many other Italian articles were also in great demand in England, for the Renaissance brought with it a perfect passion for novelty, which welcomed the introduction of foreign fashions. This was especially true of the luxuries Italy had to offer. Its embroidered gloves, sweet bags, perfumed leather jerkins, and costly washes, were all said to have been introduced into England by the Earl of Oxford, returning home from his travels. Even earlier, in 1559, already a parliamentary consideration alluded to the perfumed gloves of the Italians with which they endeavored to curry favor,[2] while Stowe mentioned the fact that women's masks, busks, muffs, fans, periwigs and bodkins, first used by courtesans in Italy, were all imported into England.[3]

In the matter of costume, especially, the influence of foreign fashions was felt. Italian, French, and Spanish articles of dress became fashionable at different times. The poor Englishman, bewildered, knew no longer which way to turn. Andrew Borde, a contemporary physician, drew his likeness standing naked, unable to decide what to put on : —

> I am an Englishman and naked I stand here,
> Musing in my mind what raiment I shall wear ;
>
> For now I will wear this, and now I will wear that ;
> Now I will wear I cannot tell what.[4]

[1] Archives, Florence, *Atti Publici*, 1502, July 6.
[2] Historical Manuscript Commission, Hatfield House, I, 163.
[3] Harrison's *England*, II, 34.
[4] *Early English Text Society, Extra Ser.*, 1870.

Among the foreign fashions introduced, the Italian long dominated. At the " Field of the Cloth of Gold " the Mantuan ambassador spoke of King Henry and his courtiers " dressed in long gowns in the Milanese fashion, checkered with hoods of gold tissue and gold brocade." [1] Later, the Venetian ambassador, Jacopo Soranzo, mentioned the fact that the costume of Englishmen was largely copied from the Italian. The long-breasted doublets and the so-called Venetian breeches were popular at one time.[2] Italian terms of dress, *bragetto* and *capuccio*,[3] were then in ordinary English use. The dandyism of the Elizabethan courtiers was sharply commented on and satirized by many writers of that age.[4] It was even said that men changed daily the fashions of their clothes, no longer thinking a hundred pounds a great sum to spend on the wearing apparel of a gentleman. How different from the old days, when an English squire wore the same dress for " twenty years " ; the days when there was simplicity in the land, and Englishmen were con-querors, and not " scholars " trying to imitate every new trifle in costume ! [5]

[1] *Cal. St. Pap., Ven.*, III, 72.

[2] Fairholt, *Costume in England*, I, 213, 252.

[3] *Faerie Queene*, Bk. III, Canto XII, 10.

[4] G. Harvey, *Letter-Book*, p. 97 *et seq.;* G. Puttenham, *Art of English Poesie*, p. 305; R. Greene, *Quips for an Upstart Courtier*, etc.

[5] *Institution of a Gentleman.*

IV

If a 'single book were to be chosen, typical of the Italian influence in the Renaissance in refining European manners, it would in all likelihood be Della Casa's *Galateo*. Castiglione's great work, though admirable in so many ways, yet narrowed its scope by appealing to only a limited court circle. The *Galateo* was intended, however, for more general use. Like the *Courtier* it had also been translated into French and Spanish, before appearing in England in 1596. In this form it was to make its appeal to the English people at large, to such as were entirely ignorant of Italian and had never been abroad. The effect of the book was to assist in spreading the new reform of manners first brought about in Italy. This task was a far more necessary one than may seem at first glance. Social intercourse had been rough and uncouth in Europe in the Middle Ages. Nowhere better than in the *Galateo* can this be appreciated after noticing the things condemned by writers on manners, like Della Casa. Much of his advice may appear ludicrous at the present day : he bade the reader neither yawn in company, nor grind his teeth, nor sneeze too loud ; not to eat like a glutton, nor wipe his brow with his napkin. In like manner, the ordinary relations of life and rules of social conduct were prescribed at great length. But in addition to what to-day seem platitudes, much sound and good advice was given : anything unpleasant to the imagination ought to be avoided, "for we must not only refrain from such things as be foul, filthy, loathsome, and nasty, but we must not so much as name them; and it is not only a fault to do such things, but against good manner by any act or sign to put a man in mind of them." Similarly, one ought not to "wash in the presence of others, since that suggests filthy matter." Many more personal details of this nature were mentioned, not necessary to dwell on here. It was from Italy that there came the first protest against the uncouthness which had been handed down almost as a tradition of social life from the Dark Ages, not only in England but in France, where later the Florentine Marquise de Rambouillet was to set a personal example of Italian refinement. This new Italian influence in matters of social intercourse can perhaps best be appreciated by examining contemporary books on conversation and letter-writing. In both, Italian models and examples were frequently employed. Robert Hitchcock's *Quintessence of Wit* was indeed little else than a collection of maxims and aphorisms, collected for English readers from Italian writers; while Fulwood's well-known *Enemy of Idleness* gave as illustrations the letters of Italian humanists. Politian, Ficino, Lorenzo de' Medici, and Pico della Mirandola were alike quoted for the benefit of such Englishmen as were anxious to acquire the art of letter-writing. Even the lover, languishing for his mistress, could find in this book the proper Petrarchan type of love-letter for him to send.

The Italian influence in conversation was largely felt in Platonism, for the Platonic ideas of the Renaissance came from Italy to England, not only through Petrarch's poetry but by a hundred different ways of which but little was from Plato himself. Those unable to read Italian could find it expressed in Castiglione's *Courtier*, and Romei's *Courtier's Academy*. Lodowick Bryskett, the friend of Sidney and Spenser, in his *Discourse of Civil Life* was translating Giraldi Cinthio's Platonic doctrines. In this literary expression of Platonism, so common during the Renaissance, the dialogue form was especially employed. In Italy, Bembo's *Asolani* had given it a stamp which impressed itself on the culture of the age, even more perhaps than the influence of the original example. Following Bembo, the other writers likewise selected for their scene a garden, or some other suitable place, for the knights and ladies of the court to meet. Castiglione wrote of Urbino, Romei of Ferrara. The usual proceeding was for a queen to be elected from among the ladies present. She then assigned to the different members of the company a topic of discussion. In this manner the important subjects of conversation were treated in turn, and the ideas and opinions of the age, on love and honor, beauty and riches, and so forth, were all expressed. Love especially was always a favorite subject, and innumerable treatises were written about it, many of which were familiar to English readers. Thus Leon Battista Alberti's *Art of Love* was translated into Eng-

lish.   Castiglione also had much to say on the subject.
He treated his courtier as a lover and gave him practical advice as such.   In his great discourse on love,
placed in Bembo's mouth, he expounded the noblest
ideas of Renaissance Platonism, and regarded love,
freed from all ideas of sensuality, as the desire to
enjoy beauty, which was most perfect when severed
from every earthly tie.[1]   Similar elevated discourses
were held in the less well-known *Courtier's Academy*,
translated into English by John Kepers.   In this the
Countess of Scandiano, chosen by lot to be the leader,
had been crowned with a garland of laurels.   She commanded " Signor Francesco Patritio," who was " very
learned, but especially in Platonical philosophy," to
discuss the subject of beauty, inquiring into its true
nature, whether it had actual existence or was merely
a creation of the imagination.   His discourse is typical
of others on the same subject.   Heaven only, he declared, could be termed really beautiful ; the beauty of
the human body came from contemplating that divine
light which was reflected in the soul's beauty ;[2] it was
virtue which made the soul approach this divine beauty ;
next in order came the beauty of the world-soul known
as nature.   Colors were but divine ideas infused into this
soul ; the pattern of form imprinted on it by the seal
of divinity, giving beauty to the deformed, was propor-
tion.   The soul shone in contemplating the divine ;
its beauty was only obscured when debased by sensual

---

[1] Castiglione, p. 342 *et seq.*

[2] Romei, p. 11 *et seq.*

delights. God, he went on to say, was the "creator and giver of all beauty because He alone was absolute perfection, perfect wisdom and incomprehensible beauty." Angelic understandings could contemplate His beauty face to face; the human intellect, however, so far as it formed part of the material body, was blind to it. Beauty proceeded from form, deformity from matter, since matter resisted ideal reason. To sum up his ideas in a sentence, "The beauty of this worldly frame, and all the parts thereof, dependeth on ideal form in mind divine comprehended."

Just as human beauty was the image of divinity, so beauty was also the mother of love. Love had been defined in various ways. Thus, Plato had called it, in the *Phædrus*, a desire to unite with the beautiful; in the *Banquet*, to bring forth what was beautiful. The first definition, although true, seemed too restrained; the second was only suitable to one kind of human affection and was by no means a general definition. To the Italian Platonist, love was rather a violent commotion of soul and mind stirred by some known beauty. It was of several kinds; one was divine love, defined by Plato as a kind of sacred fury; another consisted in discoursing and conversing with the beloved. "Kissing unto this love is permitted for a reward, in that a kiss is rather a conjunction of soul than body." [1] Divine love, however, was said to be a union with the beautiful which was the true image of divinity, raising the mind toward beauty and inflaming it with love for the creator.

[1] Romei, p. 40.

In all matters of human affection Petrarch was regarded as "the Grand Master in love."[1] The numerous questions arising from his writings, the use of the eyes in love, the conduct of the lover and the lady, the great problem of whether man's love for woman or woman's for man was the greater, were all discussed; but the authority of Petrarch was regarded as final by most writers.

These manuals of polite conversation presented to an English public the Italian Neo-Platonism of the Renaissance. They possessed, in addition, other elements of interest. "Conversation," it was said, "is the beginning and end of all knowledge."[2] It should be treated as a fine art, worthy to be practised for its own sake; George Whetstone for this reason in the *Heptameron of Civil Discourses* repeated some of the "conversational entertainments" he had listened to in Italy, "that Englishmen might profit by the example of Italians." Similar books, many of which were translated into English, signified a more important result than discussing problems of thought. The mixed assemblages meeting on a footing of equality proved that the position of women had been raised. Woman no longer occupied the fictitious position she had held during the Middle Ages, when, lifted by convention to a false height, she was in reality too often degraded. During the Renaissance woman was to become the equal of man. Even then the avowed object of conversation was to promote friendly intercourse between

---

[1] Guazzo, f. 210.   [2] *Ibid.*, f. 14.

the sexes. Advice was given how best to conduct it; questions too deep or subtle were not to be discussed, nor things spoken of out of place. Men were warned to refrain from rehearsing "friar's sermons to young gentlewomen when they are disposed to sport themselves;"[1] the learned were likewise to beware of all affectation and of patronizing attitudes.

The woman of the Renaissance was in no sense of the word an inferior creature. Although in former times she had known only how to knit and sew, yet now, "I am sure, I have seen the rôle of more than a thousand [women] who have been excellently seen in divinity, in philosophy, in physic, in music, in painting, and in all sciences."[2] Among the arguments advanced for the education of women it was urged, that they would thus be able to keep their household accounts, and write to their husbands without employing a secretary. Some maintained, however, that a woman able to read and write "will turn over Boccaccio only and write lascivious letters."[3] Even in the sixteenth century the "new woman," with her love of manly sports, was by no means unknown. "In my time I have seen woman play at tennis, practise feats of arms, ride, hunt, and do (in a manner) all the exercises besides that a gentleman can do."[4] But condemnation greeted her if she went too far. There were many opposed to her practising manly exercises, wishing her to preserve womanly grace and beauty.[5]

---

[1] Della Casa, p. 30.   [2] Guazzo, f. 158.   [3] *Ibid.*, f. 158 *b.*
[4] Castiglione, p. 220.   [5] *Ibid.*

Some even called it "a monstrous and naughty
thing to see a young girl use such liberty and
boldness in her gesture, looks, and talk, as is proper
to men." [1]

A description of the perfect woman has come down
to us from the pen of more than one writer of the
Renaissance. As a conversationalist she should have
sweetness of voice, gravity of expression, and purity
of meaning ; and although knowing a subject perfectly,
should only speak of it with modesty.[2]   She must possess, however, numerous other accomplishments, for
even in the sixteenth century men were hard to please.
"I will that this woman have a sight in letters, in
music, in drawing or painting, and skilful in dancing and in devising sports and pastimes, accompanying with that . . . the other principles also that have
been taught the courtier.   And thus in conversation,
in laughing, in sporting, in jesting, finally in everything, she shall be had in great price . . . and albeit
staidness, nobleness of courage, temperance, strength
of the mind, wisdom, and the other virtues a man
would think belonged not to entertain, yet will I have
her endowed with them all." [3]

V

The courtier has been considered hitherto more in
the spirit of the modern meaning of the word than in
its Renaissance significance.   Thus far his sports and

[1] Guazzo, f. 158.   [2] *Ibid.*, f. 115 *b*.   [3] Castiglione, p. 221.

pastimes and the lighter side of his life have alone been noticed. His more serious aspect remains still to be regarded. The underlying shadow of slur which to-day unconsciously attaches itself, especially in a democratic community, to the idea of courtier, is of quite recent growth. In the sixteenth century there was no more honorable career open to a gentleman. Before the courtier there lay the paths of distinction and glory; it was his task to fit himself to merit the success which lay ready before him.

During the Middle Ages, when the clergy had almost exclusive charge of the intellectual requirements of the nation, skill at arms had alone been thought necessary for the gentleman. A great secular growth accompanied, however, the new centralizing tendency of the Renaissance. The court became, as it were, the nucleus of the nation; from its centre stretched out in each direction countless threads which not only connected it with every activity in the land, but bound it in diplomatic relations with other countries. To fit the courtier for this development in the national life, a different education was necessary, which the new humanism in part provided. Its general nature, however, reacted on men in different ways; some were to find their careers in diplomacy and statecraft, others in letters, still others in war, since that too had become a science. The courtier, properly speaking, was therefore to be found under all these aspects, as a diplomat and adviser to his prince, a literary man and scholar, and lastly as a soldier.

A striking difference can be found in comparing the English embassies sent to Rome in the sixteenth century with what they had been in former years. During the earlier ages, diplomatic relations with the Vatican had been transacted almost exclusively by churchmen. Adrian de Castello, Ghinucci, Giovanni and Silvestro Gigli, were among the better known Italian prelates in the king's service, most of them holding English benefices. A change, however, was gradually effected, largely owing to the royal divorce and its consequences. Although churchmen were employed until the first quarter of the new century was over, courtiers were by degrees filling their places. Men like the Earls of Bedford and Wiltshire, Sir Francis Bryan, Sir Thomas Wyatt, and Sir Philip Hoby were beginning to conduct for England the new diplomacy of the Renaissance. Italians often accompanied them on their missions ; Sir Thomas Spinelli, Sir Gregory and John da Casale, Peter Vannes, and others, were all in the English service, but they were for the most part laymen, as were also the numerous Italian agents employed by Cromwell, and later by Cecil.

The progress of the Reformation in England had naturally for its effect the withdrawal of all diplomatic charges from the Roman clergy, while at the same time it ended in breaking off direct intercourse with Rome. Courtiers were therefore more and more intrusted with the conduct of diplomatic affairs. This had been the case for some time already in Italy, although there the true reason lay rather in the Papacy being considered

an Italian principality, so that those owing it allegiance
could not well be in the service of other states.

In advance of the rest of Europe, the career of the
courtier as a diplomat had long been foreseen in Italy.
In addition, however, his main function was thought to
be as the adviser of his prince, informing him of the
truth on every matter, and warning him when about to
do wrong.[1] Just as music, sports, and pastimes were
held to be the flower of courtliness, so its fruit was in the
proper advice to a prince, and in guarding him from
evil.[2] It was the courtier's place to see to it that his
prince should not be deceived by liars or flatterers ; to
this end he ought to advise him, and spur him on to
win further greatness. Regarding his personal relations
to his lord, the courtier ought neither to flatter him,
nor repeat scandal nor idle talk ; never to be forward
and pushing, nor ask favors ; nor do such service as
would put him to shame, nor even obey his master in
" dishonest matters." If his prince was wicked, he
should leave his service.[3]

For the courtier to be able to properly advise his
prince, he ought to possess "readiness of wit, pleasant-
ness of wisdom, and knowledge in letters."[4] This last
was the great change effected by the Renaissance, which
made the courtier wish to excel in branches which
he had formerly despised. In Italy, men like Castiglione and Navagero, who were courtiers, diplomatists,
and poets at the same time, had set a personal ex-

[1] Castiglione, p. 297. [3] *Ibid.*, pp. 130, 339.
[2] *Ibid.*, p. 298. [4] *Ibid.*, p. 297.

ample. The former not only bid his courtier speak
well, having great care in the selection of words, but
also cultivating and polishing his own language, to write
" both rhyme and prose." [1]   In addition, he should be
able to play on several instruments, and know also
how to draw and paint. [2]   Most of all he ought to
cultivate learning ; a knowledge of history would teach
him many things of value.

In studying the lives of great men, he would himself
desire greatness, for who could read the mighty deeds of
Cæsar or Alexander, of Scipio and Hannibal, and not
desire to be as they were, preferring the everlasting
fame, which is attained even by death, to ordinary life ;
" but he that savoreth not the sweetness of letters cannot know how much is the greatness of glory." [3]   The
courtier should also be learned in the humanities, reading the poets no less than the orators and historians.

This new conception of learning as a necessary part
of a gentleman's education had first obtained root in
Italy.   It was otherwise in France, where letters were
long disparaged, and men thought it " a great villany
when any one of them is called a clerk." [4]   Castiglione
looked forward to an improvement with the accession of
Francis to the throne, but even later it was said that
" learning is so little accounted of that a gentleman
though he be scarce able to maintain himself, thinketh
scorn to apply his mind to the study either of the laws
or of physic." [5]   In the Middle Ages, skill at arms was

[1] Castiglione, pp. 69 *et seq.*, 85.   [2] *Ibid.*, p. 89 *et seq.*
[3] *Ibid.*, p. 84.   [4] *Ibid.*, p. 82.   [5] Guazzo, f. 84.

indeed the only necessary part of the gentleman's education, nor did this old ideal disappear altogether in the Renaissance. The courtier might still be a soldier, but he must be learned as well. The Italian courtly ideas can be seen reflected in England in the books of William Segar, who expressed himself forcibly on this subject. "Very rarely doth any man excel in arms that is utterly ignorant of good letters. . . . This only I say that the endeavor of gentlemen ought to be either in arms or learning, or in them both. And in my poor conceit, hardly deserveth he any title of honor that doth not take pleasure in the one or the other."[1]

It was hardly to be expected that those brought up in the old system would look with favor on the importance now assigned to learning. One of the favorite questions of the age, around which stormed a controversy, regarded the two rival professions of arms and letters. Since books, however, were mainly written by scholars, the arguments ended generally in their favor. Learning was said, first of all, to increase gentry. Letters being no less esteemed than martial feats, it followed that the gentry of the one was no less than of the other.[2] But learning was superior to arms, since it might of itself achieve immortality, which arms could not do without its aid. Hence it followed that "the deeds of famous captains and worthy soldiers died with them, if they have not some to set them forth in writing;" unless they happened to join to their prowess in

[1] *Honor, Military and Civil*, p. 200 *et seq.* Cf. Spenser, *Faerie Queene*, II, iii, 40.   [2] Guazzo, f. 86 *b.*

arms a knowledge of polite letters.[1]   A fierce discussion
raged in Italy on this subject ; such writers as Muzio
who concluded in favor of the scholars were attacked
by others who held the profession of arms to be the
nobler because the older, and also because in many
countries letters were unknown.[2]   Saviolo, who gave
an English echo to the controversy, yielded prece-
dence to arms, since princes obtained their titles and
dominions merely by virtue of them, and only afterwards were able to foster learning.

The courtier, however, in addition to being a scholar,
should also be a soldier.   As such his very conduct in
war was outlined for him.   In battle, for instance, he
ought to separate himself from the crowd and undertake
his feats alone, or with as few around him as possible.
He was thought a fool if he exposed himself in such
undertakings as capturing a flock of sheep, or even to
be the first to scale the walls of a battered town.   His
deeds of valor he ought to perform in the presence of
superiors, and if possible, before the eyes of the king,
— for while it was wrong to seek undeserved praise, it
should yet be looked for when due.[3]

There was, however, a quite different side to the
Italian military influence in England.   The Italians of
the Renaissance have not commonly been regarded as
a martial nation.   Their achievements in other directions obscured their feats in arms ; on the one hand,

[1] Guazzo, f. 104.

[2] *Cf.* Muzio, *Il Gentilhuomo*, and Mora, *Il Cavaliere*.

[3] Castiglione, p. 113.

an outlet for their military zeal was found in foreign service, while on the other, the comparative unimportance of results achieved in their own wars has made these live chiefly in the memories of historians. Yet in the sixteenth century there was scarcely an army in all Europe which had not in it Italian officers and soldiers. Among commanders also, the Duke of Parma was considered the greatest general of the age, while the Trivulzi, Caraccioli, San Severini, and other famous captains in the French service were all Italians. Even in England, Italian soldiers of fortune could be found ; Petruccio Ubaldini served in the wars of Henry the Eighth and Edward the Sixth; in 1548 Captain Tiberio, with a force of Italians, garrisoned Haddington for Lord Grey de Wilton.[1] Still later, a certain Captain Sassetti was described as an Italian soldier serving in Ireland,[2] while Sir Horatio Pallavicino, in the days of the Armada, served as a volunteer on a ship he had himself equipped.

The especial importance of Italy in the warfare of the Renaissance came through its development of military science and military engineering. It was first in Italy that war was looked upon as an art, and furthermore, as a fitting occasion for the employment of the keenest intellects. Thus the first suggestion of a change in tactics can be found in Machiavelli's *Art of War*, while with Leonardo da Vinci began the study of modern artillery.[3] It is therefore not surprising

---

[1] M. Hume, *Chronicle of Henry VIII*, p. 200.
[2] Hist. Ms. Com., Hatfield House, II, 169.
[3] M. J. D. Cockle, *Bibliography of Military Books*, p. xix *et seq.*

that Italian engineers should be found in England at a comparatively early date. Jerome of Trevisi, who lost his life in the French wars of Henry the Eighth, fighting for his adopted country, was an engineer as well as a painter, no uncommon thing in an age when Michelangelo designed the defences of Florence. Marco Savorgnano, one of the most distinguished military engineers of his time, visited the English court in 1531, under the guidance of Marco Rafael, a converted Venetian Jew, who was then high in favor with the king. Still another engineer, whose name appears frequently in matters of fortifications, was Sir John Portinari, for many years in the English royal service.

The few English military books of this time were likewise largely compilations from Italian sources,[1] but Italian books as well were often translated into English. One of the first of these was Whitehorne's rendering of Machiavelli's *Art of War*, which the translator dedicated to Elizabeth as " the first fruits of a poor soldier's study." This book, which had been translated by Whitehorne for soldiers rather than for scholars, was intended by him, as he said, to make his countrymen no less invincible in the knowledge of war than they had hitherto been in its practice.

Books such as Cataneo's *Military Tactics* and Count Giacomo Porcia's *Precepts of War* were also translated. Certain Italians condemned the practice of writing on fortifications, for the reason that foreigners,

[1] Cockle, p. viii.

if left untaught, would be obliged to employ Italian engineers.[1] Tartaglia, however, wrote a great work on gunnery, dedicated by him to Henry the Eighth, which treated both of practice and theory, entering deeply into problems of trajectory and ballistics. It was followed by another work compiled by Cyprian Lucar from the best authorities on the subject; and from the bibliography he gave of these, one can realize the extent to which England was indebted to Italy in all matters of military science.

VI

The knowledge of Italian possessed by Englishmen in the sixteenth century, and the means at the disposal of such as were anxious to learn the language, requires some consideration.

At the court of Henry the Eighth, that monarch, who was fond of foreigners, and especially of Italians,[2] set the example by himself understanding their tongue. Among his many courtiers who knew the language were Lord Rochford, Lord Morley the translator of Petrarch, and the Earl of Surrey, who, though he never set foot in Italy (in spite of the pretty story told by Nash and Drayton), is yet said to have affected its dress, and employed an Italian jester in his household. Others, too, such as the Earl of Wiltshire and Sir

[1] Cockle, p. xvi.
[2] *Cal. State Pap., Ven.*, IV, 287. "Il Re medesimo ha molti Italiani . . . al suo servitio, di ogni professione." — Ubaldini, Add. Mss. Brit. Mus. 10169, f. 116 *b*.

Thomas Wyatt, had travelled in Italy, and the Earl of
Bedford adopted *Che sarà sarà* for the motto of his
house after the battle of Pavia, at which he was present. The two princesses, Mary and Elizabeth, likewise both knew Italian. A knowledge of the language
spread rapidly among the upper classes, and increased
still further during the reign of Elizabeth; to address
one's sovereign with a few words of Italian was indeed
regarded as a mark of distinction.[1] Elizabeth herself
had learned the language as a child, and Roger Ascham
declared that she spoke it perfectly at sixteen. Several
of her Italian letters are still preserved, one to Catha-
rine Parr written in 1544, and another more than
twenty years later to the emperor. The testimony of
Italians bears further witness to her proficiency in the
language; Giovanni Antonio Ferrice, in a poem he
dedicated to her, praised her knowledge of the "soft
Tuscan."[2] Pietro Bizari, the historian, also spoke
favorably of her skill as a linguist, and especially of
her knowledge of Italian, which he said she had
learned from Battista Castiglione, a gentleman of the
privy chamber who was high in her favor.[3] A knowledge of Italian was then widespread at court, and
those who had not some smattering of it were the exceptions. Florio indeed remarked of it that "the best
speak it best, and her majesty none better;"[4] for she
"delights to speak to Italians."[5] Further illustra-

---

[1] L. Humphrey, *op. cit.*   [2] Ms. Bodleian.
[3] *Historia*, 1569, p. 206.   [4] *Second Fruites*, preface.
[5] *First Fruites*, ff. 11 *b*, and 18.

tions of the popularity of Italian might be given. Burleigh and Walsingham both made use of it frequently in their diplomatic correspondence. One of the Venetian envoys noted the fact that at a dinner given him by Cecil, where the entire Privy Council was present, the conversation was carried on chiefly in Italian, "almost all of them speaking our Italian tongue, or at least all understanding it." [1] Robert Cecil had travelled in Italy and was proficient in the language; so were the Earl of Rutland and Countess of Bedford; the Earl of Leicester had learned it in his youth, and even had Italian musicians in his employ.[2] Many others had Italians in their personal service; thus Virginio Orsini, a Roman baron, begged Lord Essex to allow him to be numbered among his servants.[3] Henry Wriothesley, Earl of Southampton, had John Florio in his pay and patronage, and, according to him, rapidly acquired a knowledge of Italian. On every side could be seen evidences of the same keen desire to learn the language. Hubert Languet, in a letter to Sidney, alluded jestingly to the craze : "It seems to me quite absurd that your countrymen should make such a point of speaking Italian well. . . . Perhaps you are afraid you will not persuade them to take your money unless you speak with perfect fluency." [4]

William Thomas, the author of the *History of Italy*,

[1] *Cal. State Pap. Ven.*, VII, 524 *et seq.*
[2] Cotton Ms. Titus, B. VII, Brit. Mus.
[3] Hist. Ms. Com., Hatfield House, VI, 534.
[4] Letter of Jan. 28, 1574.

wrote also the first English manual of Italian, which appeared in 1550. This was in the form of a grammar followed by a dictionary, the former containing the usual classifications, the latter consisting chiefly of a compilation taken from earlier Italian works. The purpose of the book was to enable the reader better to understand Italian writers. In the author's judgment, Italian was gradually coming to be considered on the same plane with Latin and Greek. If in Italy, he said, they would only continue for another ten years the same kind of work they had accomplished in the past ten, "surely their tongue will be as plentiful as any of the other." In support of these arguments he mentioned the various branches of science and history, eloquence and poetry, examples of which could be found in Italian.

Thomas's *Grammar*, while still in manuscript, fell into the hands of Sir Walter Mildmay, the Chancellor of the Exchequer, by whom it was printed for such as might be anxious to learn the language. Similar manuals were written, some of which were never published ; as, for instance, the *Regole della Lingua Toscana*,[1] by Michelangelo Florio, a Florentine refugee and teacher of Italian, whose son later became the great English apostle of Italian culture. New methods of instruction appeared from time to time : such as Lentulo's *Grammar*, "a very necessary book (in my concept) for all such as are studious of the Italian tongue."[2]

---

[1] Ms. Cambridge University Library.
[2] Preface by Granthan.

This was translated in 1575 by Henry Granthan and dedicated to the daughters of Lord Berkeley, who had been very anxious to learn the language. Even more significant testimony to the far-reaching knowledge of Italian can be found in a Latin method, translated by David Rowland, in 1578, from an Italian book. As he remarked in the preface, "Once every one knew Latin, and from that Italian was learned, and now the Italian is as widely spread."

In 1575 a Frenchman in London, called Desainliens, better known however as Claudius Hollyband, published an Italian method, which was subsequently reprinted in an enlarged form, under the title of the *Italian Schoolmaster*. This he dedicated to Master John Smith (probably the same Smith who later became a friend of Giordano Bruno) in gratitude for his having selected him to be his Italian teacher, from among so many in London. The book contained both a grammar with rules of conversation and a series of dialogues, referring for the most part to the commonplaces of life, and chiefly of use to the English traveller in Italy. Occasionally the conversation bordered unconsciously on the humorous. Thus an ardent lover was made to say, in both Italian and English : " Ho, fair maiden, will you take me for your lawful spouse and husband, and I will love and serve you faithfully? Say yea; defer not so long." In the later edition of this book, following the dialogues, speeches and phrases were printed, " taken out of the best Italian authors." The method by degrees led up to the main feature of the book, the *Novelle of Arnalt and Lucenda*, which, given in English and Italian, was held out as an inducement and reward to study the language. Hollyband wrote also the *Campo di Fior, or else the Flowery Field of Four Languages*, containing sentences and conversations in the form of more or less disconnected dialogues in Latin, French, Italian and English. The book, however, was of use only for beginners, and was in every way inferior to Florio's series of dialogues.

John Florio, the son of an Italian Protestant refugee, and the translator of Montaigne, was to be the best known by far of the Italian teachers in England. He was probably educated first on the Continent, and afterwards at Oxford. He called himself " an Englishman in Italian,"[1] and certainly appears to have combined the double training. From his first youth he lived in an atmosphere of teaching. Early in life, before entering the Earl of Southampton's household, he had been tutor in foreign languages to Robert Barnes, the son of the Bishop of Durham. Later, during the reign of James the First, he became Italian reader to the queen. His celebrity, however, apart from his translation of Montaigne, arose chiefly from his books which helped to popularize Italian among the young gallants of the court.

Florio made use of his books of instruction to give his own ideas on many subjects ; he thus combined the teaching of a foreign language with the expression of

[1] *Second Fruites*, preface.

IOANNES FLORIVS AVGVSTÆ ANNÆ ANGL: SCOT: FRANC: ET HIB: REGINÆ PRÆLECTOR LING: ITALICÆ

ÆT: 58. A.D: 1611.

CHI SI CONTENTA GODE

En virtute sua contentus, nobilis arte,
Italus ore, Anglus pectore, uterq; opere
Floret adhuc, et adhuc florebit; floreat ultra
FLORIVS, hac specie floridus, optat amans.

Gul. Hole sculp:

Tam felix utinam.

John Florio

personal opinions. The use of dialogue, the Italian and English being printed in parallel columns, aided him in this. Furthermore, he was able to say what he liked without fear of criticism. An instance of this freedom of speech will be found in his opinion of the English people: "a handicraftsman will be a merchant, a merchant will be a gentleman, a gentleman will be a lord, a lord a duke, a duke a king; so that every one seeks to overcome another in pride."[1] He had other remarks to make as well; the nobility, for instance, he found very courteous, but it was otherwise with the commons, especially toward strangers.[2] His advice to the English people was that they should teach their children several languages, and not do as so many who studied foreign tongues, and "when they have learned two words of Spanish, three words of French and four words of Italian, they think they have enough, they will study no more."[3] On another occasion, an Italian in England, asked to give his opinion of the language, replied that it was good enough in its own country, but worthless beyond Dover. "What a shame it is, therefore, that an Englishman, in the company of strangers, should be unable to speak to them, and should thus stand dumb, mocked of them and despised of all. . . . What a reproach to his parents; what a loss to him."[4]

In other dialogues the student could find expressed in Italian the ordinary conversations of the day; thus,

[1] *First Fruites*, f. 16 b.
[2] *Ibid.*, f. 9 b.
[3] *Ibid.*, f. 51 b.
[4] *Ibid.*, f. 62 b.

friends talked of going to see a comedy at the Bull, in spite of the sermons preached against theatres. A practical lesson in grammar was illustrated by a young man flirting with a girl, who went through the parts of the verb " to love " ; it ended by her accepting an invitation to the play ; or again a youth bearing viola and lute goes to serenade his lady ; court gossip, the amusements of the day and even the price of shirts and stockings, were all introduced into these dialogues.

Florio's first book, which had appeared in 1578, was followed by the *Second Fruites* in 1591. In this new work he boasted that, having " ransacked and rifled all the gardens of fame throughout Italy " to adorn English orchards, he had given the reader " a taste of the best Italian fruits."

The purpose of the book was to perfect one's knowledge of Italian, especially by making use of appropriate proverbs. These, it was said, both argued " a good conceit," and would prevent Italians from talking bookish, as they were inclined to do when conversing with strangers whose Italian had been learned out of Guazzo or Castiglione. The *Second Fruites* were intended likewise for the young gallants of the court, who had literary pretensions, " not unfit for those that embrace the language of the Muses."

Florio's second book, like its predecessor, was in dialogue form. Some of the names of the speakers, *Nolano* and *Torquato* for instance, were probably selected to add interest, Giordano Bruno, who had been in England but shortly before, being usually known by the former name, while he also had made use of *Torquato* as a speaker in his own dialogues. The conversations, however, were for the most part extremely commonplace, though answering their purpose in introducing an extended vocabulary. Quips and puns were of common occurrence all through the book. An imaginary journey to Italy was described, and doggerel rhymes on different cities, probably translated into English by Florio himself, were quoted. Thus of Rome it was said: —

> In Roman court no sheep may dwell:
> But such as are thrice fleeced well;
>
> Who goes to Rome, and hath good store of pence,
> May soon return a priest or bishop thence.[1]

Florio had announced in the preface to the *Second Fruites* that he intended shortly to publish an "exquisite" Italian and English dictionary, which was intended neither for scholars exclusively, nor beginners, nor even for advanced students who had run through Guarini and Ariosto, Tasso and Boccaccio. It was to be of use to "the most complete" doctor even though he had the memory of Scaliger. "Well to know Italian is a grace of all grace"; yet without knowing the language thoroughly, it was impossible to read Aretino or Doni, nor even understand Castelvetro or Caro, or any of the different Italian dialects. For all such purposes a dictionary was absolutely necessary. He compared his work to what Sir Thomas Elyot and

[1] *Second Fruites*, p. 109.

Bishop Cooper had accomplished in Latin, and the Estiennes in Greek; and lest any one might think that he had received too much assistance from the works of Alunno or Venuto, he bade his reader remember that a single letter in his dictionary contained more than twenty in theirs.

Of the dictionary itself, not much need be said. It was a careful work of over five hundred pages, each Italian word being given with several English equivalents. Florio's books, however, formed as a whole a series more or less indispensable to the English student of Italian. Their number attests their popularity, and the fact that so important a work as his dictionary should have been compiled at that time indicates a demand for similar work.

Italian proverbs were likewise popular in Elizabethan England. Close after the *Second Fruites*, followed the *Garden of Recreation*, a collection of six thousand proverbs, for the use of English students of Italian. Sometimes such proverbs were printed in books which had otherwise no bearing on the subject. Charles Merbury, for instance, to his *Discourse of Royal Monarchy*, published in 1581, added a "collection of Italian proverbs in benefit of such as were studious of that language, with an Italian preface to all courtiers and other gentlemen conversant in Italian." He maintained that a knowledge of proverbs would aid them greatly in conversation, and teach them foreign customs; if his readers would only learn a few of them, in a short time it would seem as if they had suddenly been transferred to Italy and had returned thence, although in fact they had passed over neither seas nor mountains.

VII

The theoretical expression of the courtier has chiefly been noticed hitherto. His actions and accomplishments, his tastes and conduct, as laid down by various writers in the Renaissance, have all been considered. The facts here brought together have been selected from the contemporary English translations of Italian books. The question may therefore well be asked : What was the effect of these books, and did they bring into England any new ideals of manners and education ?

The translation and publication of numerous Italian manuals of courtesy and conversation, was more conclusive in the sixteenth century in England of a demand for such books than it would have been in any subsequent age when printing was widely spread. It is by no means necessary, however, to remain satisfied with that. One has only to notice the numerous references in contemporary English literature to such translations and search for their influence in the English books themselves. Lastly, this influence can be observed in many English men and women who discovered in culture a new ideal to be striven for.

The mention of Italian courtesy books in Elizabethan literature would suffice for a study in itself. The *Cortegiano*, the *Galateo*, and Guazzo's *Conversa-*

tions especially were frequently referred to. Gabriel
Harvey alluded to their great popularity at Cambridge,
where every one had read them.[1] In recognition of the
author of the *Courtier*, the names of *Castilio* and
Balthazar came to mean in the English language the
perfection of courtesy; Marston, Guilpin and Ben
Jonson all employed the words in this sense. Thomas
Lupton called the book a manual of true gentlemanliness;[2] and Roger Ascham, the puritanical opponent
of Italian influence, said in his recommendation of the
work: "to join learning with comely exercises, Conte
Baldessar Castiglione in his book *Cortegiano* doth
trimly teach ; which book advisedly read and dili-
gently followed but one year at home in England,
would do a young gentleman more good, I wiss, than
three years travel abroad spent in Italy."[3] So late as
the eighteenth century, it was regarded by Dr. Johnson
as the best work on good breeding ever written.[4]

Courtesy books written in English were not very
numerous in Tudor England. Even in such early works
as Sir Thomas Elyot's *Governour*, Laurence Humphrey's *The Nobles* and the *Institution of a Gentleman*, the influence of certain Italian writers is plainly
evident, though not always acknowledged. Boccaccio
and Patrizi, from whom the above mentioned writers
borrowed, were, however, of a different type from the
true writers of courtesy, whose influence became later

---

[1] *Letter-Book*, p. 79.   [2] T. Lupton, *Civil and Uncivil Life.*
[3] *Scholemaster*, p. 66.
[4] Boswell, *Life of Johnson*, ed. G. B. Hill, V, 314.

so noticeable in England. In William Segar, for instance, the influence and example of these Italian courtesy writers was apparent. In the *Book of Honor and Arms*, he decided a question of etiquette, by quoting as eminent authority the Duke of Urbino ; his subsequent work contained numerous allusions to Italian practices of chivalry and even made use of Italian expressions. His argument on virtue as essential to nobility followed closely the example of Italian writers ; although himself garter king-of-arms, he further imitated them by maintaining that the pursuit of learning was in no way inferior to a military career ; no state, indeed, could be well governed " unless the governors thereof had studied philosophy." [1]

George Pettie, in the preface to his translation of Guazzo's *Conversations*, was even more emphatic on the same subject. A soldier himself, he said that he ought not to be condemned for spending his time in writing, since learning was necessary to the military man. " Those which mislike study or learning in a gentleman are some fresh water soldiers, who think that in war it is the body which only must bear the brunt of all, not knowing that the body is ruled by the mind, and that in all doubtful and dangerous matters it is the mind only which is the man. . . . Therefore (gentlemen) never deny yourselves to be scholars, never be ashamed to show your learning . . . it is only it which maketh you gentlemen, and seeing that the only way to win immortality is either to

[1] *Honor, Military and Civil*, p. 200 *et seq.*

do things worth the writing, or write things worth the reading."

If one idea could be picked out as the dominant thought in Italian courtesy books, it was that the outward graces of man should all be cultivated by education. Such education, however, was to be something more than a narrow book learning, and to rest on a broad basis of life. The courtier should be learned, said Pettie, in order that he might be able to properly advise his prince in the government of the state.[1] It was for this reason also that Castiglione wished his courtier to be accomplished in so many things. The courtier, however, was to be a soldier as well, and thus the new education was grafted on to the military ideal. Many Englishmen were to exemplify it; Sidney and Raleigh were both scholars and soldiers; so too were Gascoigne, Turbervile, Pettie, Whitehorne, Bedingfield and Hitchcock, to mention only some of the names of English poets and translators, who were to prove that the Italian idea of the soldier as a man of cultivation had likewise taken root in England.

In the Renaissance, when the encouragement of learned men was almost a matter of state policy, the numerous small Italian courts formed centres of patronage for the needy scholar and poet. In England, on the other hand, where similar centres did not exist, and the royal court did not entirely fill their place, this patronage was effected rather by the nobility, who in the sixteenth century began to regard them-

[1] Guazzo, preface.

The Earl of Leicester by Zuccaro.

selves as the protectors of learning and the arts. Their travels abroad had both familiarized them with the Italian example, and at the same time destroyed their prejudices against foreigners which existed among other classes in England. Without mentioning the numerous literary men in the time of Shakespeare who lived under the friendly protection of great noblemen, among Italians in England, Pietro Bizari dedicated his *History* to the Earl of Bedford, Saviolo his *Practise* to the Earl of Essex, " whose encouragement of letters has won for him the title of *the Students' Mæcenas.*" Among Florio's patrons likewise were the Earls of Rutland and Southampton, and Lucy, Countess of Bedford, while he in his praise of Leicester, his first protector, called him thrice fortunate in having had such a herald of his virtues as Edmund Spenser. " Courteous Lord, Courteous Spenser, I know not which hath purchased more fame, either he in deserving well of so famous a scholar, or so famous a scholar in being so thankful without hope of requital to so famous a lord." [1]

In other ways as well Italian examples were followed in England. The English courtier, in the sixteenth century, like his Italian brother, desired to shine in the cultivation of letters. It is only necessary to glance at the names of those who then wrote verse and were in fact known as " courtly makers." The Earl of Surrey, Sir Thomas Wyatt, Lord Rochford, Lord Morley, Lord Oxford, Sir Thomas Sackville, Sir Philip

[1] *Second Fruites*, preface.

Sidney and Sir Walter Raleigh were only some of the better known courtier poets. What deserves especially to be noticed is not so much the poetical faculty, possessed by a few imitators for the most part of Italian models, as the vast spread of education among the classes who previously had despised it. A literary taste had been awakened in them by the study of foreign models, and they now endeavored to accomplish in England what had already been done in Italy.

The rapid spread of education in the Renaissance, no less than its transformation, deserves to rank among the most marked features of the age. Especially in Italy, a universality of knowledge had characterized the greater minds of the sixteenth century. Later, in England, this same broad ideal of cultivation can also be found in such men as Crichton and Raleigh. The new humanism in all its breadth, no longer confined to any narrow group of scholars, left its mark in the education of Italian women. In England, as well, women, no longer satisfied to remain in their former sphere and anxious to follow the example of their Italian sisters, desired to shine in the pursuit of letters. Lady Jane Grey still passes for a wonder of erudition, and Queen Elizabeth is said to have known eight languages. Women like the Countesses of Bedford and Pembroke were the friends and patrons of literary men. In many ways the great change which had come over womanhood in the Renaissance was apparent. To give a single illustration. In 1550, Anne Cooke, who later became the mother of Francis Bacon, translated into English some of the sermons of the famous Sienese preacher, Bernardino Ochino, then a refugee in England. Her mother, it appeared, had often reproved her for her pursuit of Italian, considering it a godless study, and, therefore, a waste of time. This book was intended to prove the contrary, in revealing the spiritual side of the Italian nature. It showed, however, another side as well, — a touch of conscious pride in the idea that it was by a woman's work that the book had been translated. Although it were more fitting, she wrote, for " doctors of divinity " to meddle with such matters than young girls, yet now, " through the honest travail of a well-occupied gentlewoman and virtuous maiden, they speak in English. . . . If ought be erred in the translation, remember 'tis a woman's, yea, a gentlewoman's, who commonly are wonted to live idly, a maiden who never gadded farther than her father's house to learn the language."

In the age of Elizabeth men and women alike were to receive the benefit of Italian humanism as it spread through Europe. The olden days, when the upper classes could afford to live in ignorance, had given way to a new age, when learning was taught from childhood. Even in the sixteenth century, merit meant more and birth less than is commonly supposed. Cardinal Wolsey, Thomas Cromwell Earl of Essex, and Lord Burleigh were all of ordinary extraction. Education, however, often took the place of genius, in raising those of low descent to the highest places in the land. At one time even the king complained that positions of great responsibility had to be intrusted to those of low origin, who alone were fitted for them, on account of the lack of education on the part of the nobles. It was to remedy this and preserve their former ascendency that noblemen sought its benefits; while to the commoner, who obtained an education, it went far to remove differences of rank, to level class distinctions, and place him on an equality with those who were his superiors by position. In England, as in Italy, it came to be acknowledged that scholarship was a noble profession, and that by virtue of it scholars were gentlemen.[1] Every one was now interested in learning. There was a time, wrote Richard Willes, when logic and astrology so wearied the minds of scholars that true philosophy was almost forgotten, eloquence defaced, the languages exiled; that time was past. Not long since, happy was he who had any skill in Greek; while if he could make a Greek verse, he was thought a great scholar. "Nowadays who studieth not rather the Hebrew language?"[2] All ranks and classes bore witness to this new zeal for education, which had swept over the English nation and placed side by side with the old feudal distinctions a new field of honor in learning.

[1] Segar, *Honor and Arms*, p. 36.
[2] Anglerius, *History of Travel*, 1577, preface.

CHAPTER III

THE TRAVELLER

I

THE first recorded description of Italy by an English-man is in Sir Richard Guylforde's diary of 1506.[1] This was written entirely in the spirit of the Middle Ages and failed to take into account the new Renaissance civilization. Its author passed through Verona and Mantua on his way to Palestine, scarcely making a comment on what he saw. In Venice he was most impressed by the munitions of war stored in the arsenal. He went on excursions to *Moryan* [Murano] where he remarked that glass was made, and saw "many houses of religion that stand in the sea." He was present, moreover, at the Doge's marriage to the Adriatic, which he described very briefly. "And so they rowed in to the sea with the assistance of their Patriarch, and there spoused the sea with a ring. . . . The Duke let fall the ring into the sea, the process and the ceremonies whereof were too long to write." He expressed some surprise, it is true, at the beauty of Venetian buildings, but failed altogether to observe any differ-ence between the life of Italy and that of England, still half in the Middle Ages.

[1] *Camden Society*, 1851.

A very similar account was written some ten years after by Sir Richard Torkington,[1] who also passed through Italy on his way to the Holy Land. He saw Milan and Padua, and later Naples and Rome, but almost the only thing which impressed him was a banquet in Venice, where there was music and dancing, and the guests had basins and ewers in which to wash. The charm of Italy was thus felt neither by Torkington nor Guylforde. It was to be otherwise with the travellers of the next generation, when the new ideas brought in by the Renaissance had had time to develop.

There were several reasons why Englishmen should wish to visit Italy. In former years the numerous churchmen and diplomats, pilgrims and soldiers of fortune, who passed to and fro between the two countries, brought back with them admiring recollections of their travels. The scholars also, on their return, could give glowing accounts of Italian universities, then far in advance of their own. Moreover, the growth of the Renaissance in England developed the new taste for travel. With it there went a keen desire to see the country, which was celebrated no less for containing the treasures of former ages than for the splendor of its actual life. A knowledge of Italy having once spread from university to court the desire to share its culture drew across the Alps the cultivated classes of all Europe. Pious Catholics still went there, and eager students, attracted by its

[1] *Oldest Diary of English Travel.*

institutions of learning. The new type of traveller, however, who was neither diplomat, scholar nor pilgrim, now found his way in increasing numbers to Italy.

Sir Thomas Hoby and William Thomas, two English-men who were in Italy shortly before the middle of the sixteenth century, were both typical of this move-ment, and can be singled out from among so many by the records of their travels, written entirely from this new point of view. Italy itself was their goal, its sights the object of their visit. They were travellers for a purpose, who looked forward to the education and experience they should acquire which might be of service to them in their future careers. Unlike their English predecessors, they took interest in everything they saw, noting carefully the sights and customs of the strange country. William Thomas' observations are hardly in any way inferior to those of the Italian travellers of the age, from whose accounts he had profited. His keenness of penetration and ready sympathy with a foreign culture fitted him peculiarly for the work he undertook. The avowed purpose of his *History of Italy*, written after five years of residence there, and first published in 1549, was by a selection of examples from Italian history to enable Englishmen to see how a nation had been enriched through peace and concord and made poor by strife. The histori-cal portion of the work was, however, the least impor-tant. Its real interest and merit lay in the fact of its being a guide to Italy, full of antiquarian and political information, and containing, moreover, the impressions and experiences of one of the most cultivated men of the age. It was unquestionably the best English account of any foreign nation written before the seventeenth century; and its popularity, to judge only from the editions it passed through, points it out as an important channel by which a knowledge of Italy filtered into England.

Sir Thomas Hoby had gone to Italy after having been at Cambridge, in order both to complete his education and prepare himself for public life, since "the Italian nation which seemeth to flourish in civility most of all others at this date"[1] then offered the greatest opportunities to the student of politics as well as of culture. Hoby kept a record of his foreign travels in a diary, intended, however, only for private use, and which has never been published.[2] In shrewdness of observation it certainly does not begin to compare with Thomas' work. It is of considerable interest, nevertheless, in presenting without literary artifice the Italian experiences of an English gentleman of culture, in the middle of the sixteenth century. Hoby's purpose in travelling was to see what he could of Italy. With this in mind, he described the different Italian cities one after the other, with more repetition than variety. The ruins and antiquities of the ancient world chiefly attracted his curiosity; unlike Thomas, he never moralized on such sights, and rarely con-

[1] Thomas, *History of Italy*, preface.
[2] British Museum, Egerton Mss., 2148.

cerned himself with objects of merely historic interest. One would almost judge from his impressions
that he was satisfied rather with outward appearances
than the inner character of things. Some of the chief
elements of interest in Hoby's diary can be found in
his own personal experiences, which afford glimpses
of Italian life in the Renaissance. The celebrated
Hurtado de Mendoza, the Spanish governor of Siena,
showed him great courtesy while there, as did, on
another occasion, the young Marquis of Capistrano at
Amalfi. The important influence Italy had on Hoby
was thus the impression he derived from its courtly
life, which led him later to undertake his famous translation of the *Courtier*. With William Thomas, on the
other hand, the influence had been mainly political;
he typified in some degree the serious traveller, while
in Hoby there was something of the dilettante, who
travelled because to do so was the fashion.

The tide of foreign travel in Italy began in the reign
of Henry the Eighth. Hoby remarked the numbers
of Englishmen he met in every Italian city, while
Thomas wrote that in no region of the world were
"half so many strangers as in Italy, specially of
gentlemen, whose resort thither is principally under
pretence of study."[1] At this time, however, the
English travellers came almost exclusively from the
gentry and the court circle. A common impress of
class appears to animate them; all alike seem to
have passed through one mould. Even Thomas, who

[1] *Op. cit.*, p. 2.

was above most prejudices, contrasted the Italian universities, whose students were nearly all gentlemen, with the English colleges, with their " mean men's children set to school in hope to live upon hired learning."[1]

The desire to travel, however, had not as yet penetrated very deeply in England, beyond the narrow circle who then alone were conscious of the attraction of Italy. The English travellers of this period represent, for this reason, a unity of type never afterwards attained. They ought, moreover, to be judged not as travellers alone : often the traveller and the courtier were only different aspects of the same man, who looked upon travel as a necessary element in the perfection of the courtly type. Travel was thus intended solely for the upper classes, who would bring back with them on their return the new foreign culture. More than any other element, it familiarized England with the achievements of the Renaissance.

With the vast diffusion of Italian influence in the second half of the sixteenth century, a gradual evolution took place in the whole idea of travel. Already, with Thomas and Hoby, the type of traveller had begun to differentiate, and these differences were later to widen still more. One type was that of the dilettante pleasure-seeker, who travelled because it was fashionable, and returned to England with all the affectations and vices of the foreign country. The

[1] *Op. cit.*, p. 3.

other regarded travel almost entirely from an educational point of view, showing in his character an inclination toward puritanism, and in his work a tendency to specialization. There were many gentlemen in England whom all the "siren songs of Italy" could never turn aside,[1] while the books on Italy which now appeared in England, as translations or otherwise, were not so much general accounts as detailed descriptions of different parts of the country. Such, for instance, were Turler's *Naples*, Lewkenor's *Venice*, Marlianus' *Rome*, and Dallington's *Tuscany*.[2] In reading these later works, one is able to realize the extent to which Italy had degenerated. Venice alone remained comparatively pure amid degradation and servility elsewhere. Dallington especially wrote from this new point of view, which regarded the Italians as having little more to teach Englishmen. Even their learning was a thing of the past, and in their universities, "ye shall scarcely find two that are good Grecians."[3]

The same reasons which once induced men to cross the Alps no longer held good. Only the arts continued to draw the foreign student. Architecture and music were then in their prime, and serious minded

[1] Ascham, *Scholemaster*, p. 74 *et seq.*

[2] The Grand Duke of Tuscany complained of this book to King James, who gave orders for it to be publicly burned in the cemetery of St. Paul's, and for its author to be imprisoned at the Grand Duke's pleasure (Archivio Mediceo, Florence, 4185).

[3] Dallington, *Tuscany*, p. 62.

men like Inigo Jones and John Dowland were still able to learn new lessons in Italy. It was quite different with the ordinary traveller. The purely educational value of travel had, by degrees, been slighted, but the growing appreciation of art, no less than the ruins of antiquity, now influenced him. His point of view had changed, however. In place of the unqualified admiration of former years, there had arisen, especially in political matters, a conscious superiority in the Englishman, which often governed his judgment.

The dilettante, on the other hand, regarded travel in a somewhat different light, and was soon to bring ridicule on himself in his affectation of foreign fashions, which he carried back with him to England. "A great number of us never thought in ourselves why we went (on travels) but a certain tickling humour to do as other men had done. . . . I think ere it be long, like the mountebanks of Italy, we travellers shall be made sport of in comedies," wrote Sir Philip Sidney to his brother. The "nice travellers who return home with such queasy stomachs, that nothing will down with them but French, Italian or Spanish,"[1] were condemned by many. Especially censured were those " who having gotten a fond affected phrase of speech, or some conceited togs in their habit, would be accounted great travellers."[2] The dilettante traveller abroad became the " Italianate Englishman " at home, who was responsible for bringing the idea of

[1] Guazzo, preface by G. Pettie.
[2] Lewkenor, *Venice*, preface.

travel into disfavor, and largely for causing the reaction against Italy.   He is of interest not only in himself as a type, but as the last creation in the evolution of English travel in the sixteenth century.

II

English books on the art of travel were a somewhat late development in the literature of the sixteenth century.   In this as in many other things practice had preceded theory.   After it had finally been accepted that travelling was necessary as the finishing touch to an education, its philosophical justification was sought for, and advice in plenty was given as how best to profit from it.   The whole theory of travel was discussed in this rational spirit of inquiry, and certain definite results arrived at.

One of the greatest effects of the Renaissance had been to magnify the importance of the central power of government to a degree unknown since the days of the Roman Empire.   This resulted more and more in making the welfare of the state a final test in everything.   The important question at issue in regard to travel was with respect to its advantage to one's country.   Its apologists tried naturally to prove it of positive benefit to the state.   " If there be anything in the world that will bring a man into consideration of his own state, surely it is travel." [1]   It was shown, first of all, that the desire to travel was characteristic of "noble and virtuous natures."   The baser sort might

[1] Turler, *Traveller*, p. 38.

be satisfied to remain in their own country; nobler natures were only contented when they imitated the heavens, which were in continual motion.[1]   This rather curious idea was frequently expressed by others as well.[2] Another argument was based on the antiquity of travel. It was said that Homer had tried to portray in Ulysses " the most perfect and accomplished gentleman of Greece," that he praised him chiefly because he had travelled in foreign lands, and noted their customs.[3] One writer even mentioned a long list of names, beginning with Noah and Jupiter, and selected impartially from sacred and profane history, to prove that the heroes of every nation in all times had been travellers. " These men think it a great stain, and dishonor to the liberty which nature hath given them (to be cosmopolites, that is, citizens of the whole world), and yet to be restrained within the narrow precincts of a little country."[4]

The distinguished ancestry and noble motives of the traveller having thus been demonstrated, it was no less easy to prove his utility to the state.   He had to make up his mind that the purpose of his travels was to ripen his knowledge, the object of which was the service of his country.[5]   In travelling abroad, he ought for that very reason, to seek only profit, and

[1] *Direction for Travailers.*

[2] Cf. Dallington, *Method for Travel.*

[3] Lewkenor, *Venice,* preface.   [4] *Direction for Travailers.*

[5] Dallington, *Method for Travel;* Sidney, *Letter to his Brother.*

after he had well spent his time, to be ready at his
country's service, whenever the occasion demanded.[1]
It was generally recognized that travelling without
some definite purpose in view was useless. On the
other hand, " those who for a good cause depart their
country, are as men of a singular and divine quality." [2]
The necessary qualifications of the traveller were laid
down without difficulty. Women were debarred as
bringing suspicion upon themselves.[3] Young men likewise were considered too frivolous. The proper age
was said to be between forty and sixty.[4]

The general theory of travel was thus mapped out
for the prospective traveller. This was contained at first
in letters of advice, but it later became systematized in
books, till with Dallington and Palmer [5] an entire analysis was presented in the form of diagrams, in which
all possible methods and objects of travel were sub-
divided into classes. Travellers, for instance, were said
to be both regular and irregular, and the first were
either voluntary, involuntary or non-voluntary.   To
mention only the last class, this included ambassadors,
messengers and spies, and soldiers in time of war. The
many subdivisions are, however, far too numerous to describe. The writer elaborated at length each separate
heading, working out his plan from the diagrams.   In
similar fashion the different kinds of knowledge the

---

[1] *Direction for Travailers;* Lewkenor, *op. cit.*
[2] F. Meres, *Palladis Tamia,* p. 237.   [3] Turler, *op. cit.,* p. 9.
[4] W. Bourne, *Treasure for Travellers.*
[5] *Essay on Travel.*

traveller should possess before beginning his journey were presented in tabular form. He should try to perfect himself in the sciences, in virtues " moral and divine," and in the ornamental qualities, not only languages, but skill at arms, music, dancing and portraiture.[1]

The important question was with regard to what the traveller should observe, and the advantages he ought to derive from his travels. The first was easily answered. The traveller ought to acquire while abroad both facts and ideas. Whoever wished to hold public office should study the characteristics of different nations, to enable him to see their good and avoid their bad sides ;[2] a knowledge of facts which included a general acquaintance with the country, its products and trade, its armed strength, and political alliances and also its revenues and taxes, was useful. A knowledge of ideas was far more difficult to obtain, since it dealt with the religion, laws and education of foreign countries.[3] While any one could travel abroad, few only were capable of searching the deep meanings of things, and comparing the customs and governments of different nations.[4]

That the educational value of travel was more than mere talk and idle theory can be seen from contemporary letters. Francis Davison, for instance, carried with

[1] Palmer, *op. cit.*, p. 37 *et seq.*
[2] *Relation of Petruccio Ubaldini*, Ms. cit., f. 1.
[3] Sidney, *Letter to his Brother ;* cf. Bacon, *Essay on Travel*
[4] *Direction for Travailers.*

him on his continental tour over sixty "relations" or descriptions of foreign countries, all of which were in Italian, with the exception of one in Latin.[1]   Later, in writing to his father the Secretary, to whom he explained that his time had been occupied in reading the history and policy of nations, he said : " I am ashamed of myself that I have no new relation or discourse ready of some of these parts of Italy. . . . My promised relation of Tuscany your last letter hath so dashed as I am resolved not to proceed withal. . . . In the meantime I go on with my studies, contenting myself with the profit and use I make, without displaying it to others."   And again — " Touching giving some proof to yourself and others, whether I have made the same use of our travel in Italy that it pleased you to think I did in Germany, [a relation of Saxony], I have gathered and observed divers particulars both in Tuscany, and some other places, which I forbear to reduce into an absolute discourse before I hear how my Lord accepted of my other."

The chief advantage to be derived from travel was the acquisition of knowledge, and the fact that the information obtained would fit a man to be of service to his state, and give good advice to his prince.[3]   This last idea was especially popular in the sixteenth century.   It can be found in Sidney and Lewkenor, who

[1] Harleian Ms., Brit. Mus., 298, f. 154.

[2] Add. Mss., Brit. Mus., 4121, f. 265; 4122, ff. 111, 139.   Also cited in Davison's *Works*, edited by Harris Nicolas, 1826.

[3] Bourne, *op. cit.*

regarded it almost as the final justification of travel. It was, in a way, another side to Castiglione's belief that the ultimate purpose of the courtier was to advise his prince.

In spite of the many advantages offered by travel, it was useless to try and conceal its dangers. "Such is our nature, especially of us English, that as we admire and entertain strange artificers before our own, so we wonder at, and more willingly entreat of learning with the learned foreigners, than with our own native countrymen."[1] In another direction, this exposed the English traveller to the temptations of foreign countries, and especially of Italy, "for Italy moveth most of our travellers to go and visit it, of any other state in the world."[2] The danger of religion and morals should therefore be guarded against, the last especially, since "our [English] nature is prone to imitate outlandish vices."[3]

The extent to which the idea of travel, and its educational function, had been developed, may be judged from the numerous books on the subject. It was supposed to teach experience and wisdom, to refine manners, and give instruction in general conduct.[4] It was likewise intended to bring the traveller in contact with foreign scholars, with whom he was urged to maintain a correspondence after he had left their country.[5]

---

[1] *Direction for Travailers.*
[2] Palmer, *op. cit.*, p. 42.
[3] *Direction for Travailers.*
[4] *Ibid.*
[5] Bacon, *Essay on Travel.*

Regarding the part played by Italy in such books, it should be said that invariably reference was made to it as being the foreign country of greatest interest to Englishmen, while in addition, Italian examples were generally made use of as illustrations. Often, too, methods of travel preceded the guide-books. Turler's account of Naples followed his manual, while Lewkenor's advice on the subject was in the preface to his translation of Contarini's *Venice*.

The Elizabethan Age thus developed a theory of travel. It found in it an educational element of great value, and regarded it half as a science, half as an art. The different works on travel gave the criteria for the judging of foreign countries. The traveller of the Renaissance regarded himself as no teller of idle tales but as a skilled observer engaged almost in a solemn duty toward his country. In this high sense of public duty, and in its ethical and educational sides, the strength of the Renaissance theory of travel can at once be seen. At the same time, the very loftiness of the ideal aimed at was the cause of its one-sidedness. The traveller, in theory, was animated only by a stern sense of duty, which made of him almost a slave for the benefit of his country. There was no place in this conception for the pleasure-seeker, nor even for the most cultivated of dilettantes. In the ideas of the English Renaissance, travel was never regarded as a rational amusement.

III

The amount and variety of information given to the traveller about to set out on his journey was further evidence of the great popularity of travel in the Elizabethan Age. Instruction and advice was offered him in plenty. He was told where he ought to go, how he should act, and what he was especially to look for in Italy. For Italy was always the final goal in the *grand tour*. To Italy " all nations of christendom do flock." [1] Dallington for a similar reason advised his traveller to leave it for the last, since " we best remember the last impressions." The other countries traversed on the journey were of secondary consideration, if not in importance, at least in attraction. To follow the English traveller on his Italian journey, to note his qualifications, the advice given him, the sights he saw, and the benefits he derived from his travels ought, therefore, to present certain elements of interest.

He went abroad as a rule fresh from the university, where he had received a classical education. In rare cases did he possess more than a smattering of the modern languages.

It was to remedy this that the traveller's first care in Italy was usually to learn the language ; the testimony of all points to this ; thus Hoby studied Italian at Padua, and afterwards went alone on a journey through

---

[1] Sandys, *Speculum Europæ, a Relation of the State of Religion*, sig., M, 2 b.

southern Italy "to absent myself for a while out of Englishmen's company for the tongue's sake." Francis Davison likewise passed much of his time in "writing, speaking and reading Italian,"[1] and Robert Dallington, who placed the learning of languages among the great advantages to be derived, advised the traveller who did not care to settle in Florence to try either Prato or Siena, where the speech was as good and the expense far less.[2] Of all methods employed in studying the language, conversation was considered the best; the traveller was bidden to converse with all classes of people. With his master he ought to read preferably some modern comedy, and he should also attend lectures on the grammar of the language. "Privately he may for his pleasure read poetry, especially if at his return he mean to court it; but for his profit, if he be a man of means and likely hereafter to bear charge in his country, or if a man of endeavors and willing to prefer himself by service, I wish him to history."[3]

Rome was the principal place to be avoided on the journey. "Let them beware of Rome," wrote Thomas Palmer.[4] Dallington likewise advised against going there because of its being the seminary of English fugitives. He also warned his traveller of the Jesuits; "these men I would have my traveller never hear except in the pulpit, for, being eloquent, they speak excellent language." This was not the case with members of

---

[1] Add. Mss., Brit. Mus., 4122, f. 43.
[2] *Method for Travel.*   [3] *Ibid.*   [4] *Op. cit.*, p. 44.

other orders, who were often of use in improving one's knowledge of the language, and frequently proved to be pleasant companions. One last warning was to be careful not to carry books prohibited by the Inquisition, as they were likely to cause trouble when trunks were examined, which was done in every city.

The traveller was advised to follow the custom of the country as far as possible; whoever lived after his own fashion, it was said, made a laughing-stock of himself, and never improved his own barbarous manners.[1] "Nowhere more than in Italy do the three golden rules of *Frons aperta, Lingua parca, Mens clausa,* hold good. Be friendly to all, familiar to a few, and speak but seldom. In countenance be as courteous as you can . . . in talk as affable as you shall see cause; but keep your mind secret unto yourself, till you come to those whose hearts are as yours."[2]

Last of all advice was given regarding the amount of money needed by the traveller. A hundred and fifty pounds was considered by many to be ample for a year's travel; two hundred "were superfluous, and to his hurt."[3] Yet Edward Smyth, the tutor and companion of Francis Davison, in writing to the latter's father, the secretary of state, said that two hundred pounds would hardly suffice them, although he had never before endured so much hardship to save money. "I have hitherto gone to the market, and as frugally as I could, made our provision of all our necessaries;

---

[1] Turler, p. 21.   [2] *Direction for Travailers.*
[3] Dallington, *Method for Travel.*

and albeit we have not at any time more than one dish, and that not very costly neither, yet, with the rent of our chamber, our weekly expenses amount very nearly to forty shillings, besides apparel, books, and many other trifling charges which I see cannot be avoided, especially so long as we are in these parts, where in truth such are not fit to remain as cannot eat oil, roots, salad, cheese and such like cheap dishes, which Mr. Francis can in no wise digest, and any good thing else whatsoever is at very great rate ; we are nec-essarily compelled to spend the more, and yet not so much as other gentlemen of our nation in this town do make show of." [1] The traveller was advised to carry his money in four bills of exchange, "with letters of advice, to be paid him quarterly." Regarding the ordinary rates of expense, they would be about as fol-lows : ten gold crowns a month for his own board and lodging, eight at the most for his man, two crowns a month for his fencing, and the like amount for his dancing and reading ; his riding would cost him fif-teen crowns monthly, but he was to discontinue it during the heat of the year. The remainder of the money was to be given up to " apparel, books, trav-elling charges, tennis play, and other extraordinary expenses." [2]

The travelling itself was done almost entirely on horseback ; occasionally the litter was employed,[3] but it was unusual for men in good health to use it. Travel,

---

[1] Davison, *Works*, p. vii, and Harl. Ms., 296, f. 114.
[2] Dallington, *Method for Travel.*   [3] Cf. Hoby, Ms. cit., f. 28.

where possible, was often by water rather than by land, and there can be little doubt that many of the poorer Englishmen who visited Italy in the sixteenth century went there by sea; to give a single instance, one Nicholas Fluto, in his anxiety to see the country, embarked on a ship at Dartmouth, without passage-money; the condition being that if he deserved his food and drink by his labor, he should have it free; otherwise his father was to pay for it.[1] Travel then was never altogether safe from the danger of bandits and pirates. Hoby alluded to " the great corsair, Drag-out Rais," [2] and spoke also of receiving an escort of Spanish soldiers to protect him from the brigands, who " did great damage to the inhabitants of the country." [3] It was this presence of danger, as well as of personal inconvenience in travelling, which perhaps delayed for so long the appreciation of natural beauties. The interest in scenery and landscape on the part of the English travellers then in Italy was certainly not very pronounced. They noticed the general situation of each city, and at times made a few remarks on the beauty of the locality, but their observations on nature fell behind their other comments; the real attraction they found in Italy lay in other directions.

The great common bond which united each traveller in Italy was his love of antiquity. Classical training played so large a part in the education of the Renaissance that it seemed as if a realization of the

---

[1] Hist. Ms. Com., Hatfield House, IV, 581.
[2] Ms. cit., f. 79 *b*.   [3] *Ibid.*, f. 82.

ancient world, so to speak, could be seen in the Roman ruins, which were then far more numerous and in better preservation than at the present day. Whatever else the influence of Italy may have stood for, it was always classical.

The general attitude toward antiquity changed, however, with the progress of the century. Before the full breath of the Renaissance made itself felt in England, the interest taken in the ancient world had been very slight; Sir Richard Guylforde had barely mentioned the supposed tombs of Antenor of Troy and Livy the historian, which were pointed out to him at Padua; similarly, Robert Dallington, in his description of Tuscany in 1596, said very little about ancient ruins. The furor for antiquity had come, and had afterwards begun to decline in its relative importance, an interest in contemporary Italy having taken its place. It was rather about the middle of the sixteenth century that the greatest zeal for Roman remains existed. In both Hoby and Thomas, it is apparent at every step. Hoby's diary, for instance, is full of citations of classical interest; thus, when at Mantua he went on a pilgrimage to Virgil's birthplace, in the village of Pietole, and mentioned that " upon the hill there, there is a little brick house which the inhabitants of the country call *Casetta di Virgilio*, holding opinion that was his house." [1] Later, when at Naples, he likewise noted " a little old house where they say Virgil was buried," [2] and quoted from it the well-known epitaph, —

[1] Ms. cit., f. 17.   [2] *Ibid.*, f. 52 b.

Mantua me genuit, Calabri rapuere, tenet nunc
Parthenope, Cecini pascua rura, duces.

The ancient world, however, impressed itself on William Thomas in a quite different way. The sight of
the ruins of Rome brought out in him the Puritan and
moralist, no less than the classical scholar.

"When I came there and beheld the wonderful
majesty of buildings that the only roots thereof do yet
represent, the huge temples, the infinite great palaces,
the immeasurable pillars, most part of one piece, fine
marble and well wrought, the goodly arches of triumph,
the bains, the conduits of water, the images as well of
brass as of marble, the obelisks, and a number of
other like things not to be found again throughout an
whole world ; imagining withal, what majesty the city
might be of, when all these things flourished. Then
did it grieve me to see the only jewel mirror mistress
and beauty of this world that never had her like nor
(as I think) never shall, lie so desolate and dis-
figured. . . . Nevertheless when I remembered again
the occasions whereof these glorious things have grown,
what numbers of wars the Romans have maintained with
infinite blood shedding, destructions of whole countries, ravishments of chaste women, sack, spoil, trib-
utes, oppression of commonwealths, and a thousand
other tyrannies without the which the Romans could
never have achieved the perfection of so many
wonders as mine eye did there behold. Then per-
ceived I how just the judgment of God is, that hath
made those antiquities to remain as a foul spoil of the

Roman pride, and for a witness to the world's end of their tyranny, so that I wot not, whether of these two is greater, either the glory of that fame that the Romans purchased with their wonderful conquests ; or their present miserable estate with the deformity of their antiquities." [1]

In addition, however, to his moralizing on the decadence of the once great city, he described at length the Roman 'antiquities. In his account of them he wove a thread of mythical and historical anecdotes. He remarked of the great temples which once stood upon the Aventine, that nothing remained of them, not so much as a fragment of the aqueduct of Claudius. He made each of the seven hills tell its own story, and doing so, discussed the theories regarding the destruction of the great buildings of the ancient world. Some ascribed it to the barbarians, others to time, and still others to the stupid greed of the inhabitants themselves, who cared only for " those noble antiquities to garnish and beautify private buildings." In this manner he made the tour of pagan Rome, gaining from Frontinus, Cassiodorus and Vitruvius his insight into the life of the ancient world. He described in detail the sights of the Eternal City ; the Thermæ and the Coliseum, the triumphal arches and obelisks. His chief desire was to see " some of those ancient Romans that with their naked majesty durst pass through the power of their victorious enemies, as Livy writeth that Caius Fabius did when the French-

[1] *Op. cit.*, p. 22.

men [Gauls] had gotten Rome and besieged the Capital." [1]

The ruins of Rome made a deep impression on the visitor from the northern land; Joachim du Bellay had expressed their attraction in his sonnets, which were later translated by Spenser; their subtle charm was further described by many other travellers. The modern idea that the whole of Italy is one vast museum, was felt even then, though in a different sense. To the reader of the Roman historians it was only necessary to look around, to recall their pages, and see before his eyes the truth of their descriptions. Then "if he be not ravished with delight I shall take him, but for some stock or stone. . . . What a pleasure will it be to see the house where Pliny dwelt, the country wherein the famous Virgil, or the renowned Ovid was born." How delightful to behold so many ancient monuments and stately churches! "The mind of man begins to revive, and lift up himself above itself, and to affect and meditate on excellent and noble things at the very sight and consideration of these so great and glorious monuments of antiquity; neither can the remembrance of the valor, prowess and virtue of former men and ages, but engender brave and worthy thoughts in every gentle heart and noble blood." [2]

The effect of the remains of antiquity upon the traveller was thus supposed by some to elevate the

---

[1] *Op. cit.*, p. 32 *b*.
[2] *Direction for Travailers.*

mind, by others to point out moral lessons. In each
individual it varied to a certain degree, but a common element of interest yet existed. At times, however, it was rather archæological; thus, for instance,
Jerome Turler, in his *Traveller*, alluded to the delight
in discovering relics of classical times, and mentioned
as an example the unearthing in the Via Appia of the
embalmed body of a woman supposed to have been
Cicero's daughter. The interest taken in Latin epig-
raphy and classical quotations was also great. Hoby,
in his diary, copied a considerable number of inscrip-
tions from the ancient ruins, likewise quoting freely
from Latin poets; and William Barker, on his return
from Italy, even published a book of epitaphs he had
collected there.[1]

IV

The interest taken in antiquity, if it did not yield
entirely to that found in contemporary Italy, was
obliged, nevertheless, to share its attraction with it.
The contemplation of an entirely new world, differing
in almost every respect from England, aroused the
Elizabethan imagination. The novelty of the situation

---

[1] *Epitaphia et inscriptiones Lugubres a Gulielmo Berchero,
cum in Italia animi causa peregrinaretur collecta.* William
Barker, whom Hoby met at Siena in 1549 (Ms. cit., f. 25 *b*),
later became one of the secretaries to the Duke of Norfolk,
and was deeply implicated in his plot. He confessed his
share under torture, whereupon the duke, who had denied
everything, called him contemptuously an *Italianified Englishman.*

impressed itself on the visitor, and in many cases he described the smallest details as well as what was of real importance. The characteristics of the Italians were especially interesting to him; to note their traits and customs became, so to speak, an important object of every traveller.

William Thomas, in spite of his Puritan leanings, was a great admirer of the Italians and saw much to praise in their character. He himself had found the Italian gentlemen honorable, courteous and prudent, so that it seemed as if each one had received a princely training. They were, moreover, modest in dress, and neat at table. But above all they were sober of speech, enemies of slander, " and so tender over their own good name (which they call their honor) that whosoever speaketh ill of any one of them, shall die for it, if the party slandered may know it, and find time and place to do it. Whereof there is a use grown amongst them, that few gentlemen go abroad unarmed." [1] He and many others had, however, to censure the Italians for their sensuality and other vices. It is interesting to note that, as foreigners became more familiar with Italy, the censure increased; thus Turler noted that the Italians, although grave and learned, were crafty and jealous.[2] Languet, too, had written Sidney that while he could admire their keen wit, yet it was mostly on the surface, and they generally spoiled their attainments by undue display.[3] Still later, travellers found

---

[1] *Op. cit.*, p. 4.   [2] Turler, *op. cit.*, p. 40 *et seq.*
[3] Sidney and Languet, *Correspondence*, p. 12.

the Italians hypocritical, sensual and, worst of all, jealous to an absurd degree. They were called "inveigling underminers and deep dissemblers who when they have pried into your nature and are privy to your secrets will straight change their copy and show themselves in their colors."[1] The gravity and dignity of Italians were, however, admired by all,[2] even in after years, when the common idea of their treachery and sensuality had passed into a byword.

Regarding the division of classes in Italy, an observer like Thomas was greatly impressed by the fact that the leading merchants were for the most part gentlemen. If there are three or four brothers, he wrote, one or two of them go into a trade;[3] and in case they do not divide their father's patrimony, then the merchants work as well for their brothers' benefit as for their own. And inasmuch as their reputation does not suffer by reason of their trade, it follows that there are more wealthy men in Italy than in any other country, and there was nothing remarkable to find, in a single city, twenty people worth one hundred thousand crowns or more. Thomas admired the Italian artificers "as being the finest and most inventive workmen of all others;" although they often acquired great wealth, they rarely rose in the social scale. The peasants, on the other hand, he found were every-

---

[1] *Direction for Travailers.*

[2] Even Dallington in his *Method for Travel* alludes to it; cf. Sandys, *Speculum Europæ*, etc.

[3] *Op. cit.*, p. 5.

where oppressed, often not having enough to buy bread with. All wealthy people and gentlemen lived in the towns, renting their farms and pastures; but they had country houses, where they went in the heat of the summer, and there "under the fresh arbors, hedges, and boughs, amongst the delicate fruits, they triumph in as much pleasure as may be imagined . . . with some instrument of music and such other things as serve for his recreation. And if ever the tenant have good day, then licketh he his lips of his master's leavings."[1]

This contrast between the luxury and poverty of Italy greatly impressed Englishmen still unused to such extremes. Wealth in Italy was so unevenly divided that, while the rich people were the richest anywhere, the poor were likewise the poorest.[2] Dallington remarked, when at Prato, that one-quarter of the population were bare-legged, so "that we know all is not gold in Italy, though many travellers, gazing only on the beauty of their cities, and the painted surface of their houses, think it the only Paradise of Europe. But if they would come with me —

> Sordida rura
> Atque humiles intrare casas, et visere gentem —

they would surely grant that poverty and famine had not a greater kingdom."[3] On the other hand, fifty years earlier, Thomas was struck by the luxury of the Milan-

---

[1] *Op. cit.*, p. 6.   [2] Sandys, *op. cit.*
[3] Dallington, *Tuscany*, p. 16.

ese ; " there is almost no craftsman's wife in Milan, that hath not her gown of silk and her chain of gold ; " [1] Hoby was similarly impressed by the magnificence he saw around him in the Italian cities.

The characteristic traits of the inhabitants of the different cities of Italy were likewise noticed, and also the uniformity of speech on the part of the better classes who " are brought up in the courtesan [language] only ; " although between Florentines and Venetians there is as great a difference " as with us between a Londoner and a Yorkshireman." [2] Venice in particular aroused the admiration of all, and even Languet excepted its citizens from his almost universal condemnation of the country. What observers particularly admired was that " unweaponed men in gowns should with such happiness of success give direction and law to many mighty and warlike armies both by sea and land, and that a single city unwalled and alone should command and overtop mighty kingdoms . . . sued unto for entertainment by the greatest princes and peers of Italy ; amidst which infinite affluence of glory, and unmeasurable mightiness of power, of which there are in sovereignty partakers above three thousand gentlemen, yet is there not one among them to be found that doth aspire to any greater appellation of honor, or higher title of dignity than to be called ' A gentleman of Venice.' " [3] These lines were written at a time when all else in Italy was in decay ; but a half century before, when the contrast was not so sharp,

[1] *Op. cit.*, p. 188.   [2] *Ibid.*, p. 3.   [3] Lewkenor, *Venice*, preface.

Thomas remarked that if the Venetians had been men as were the Romans, and given as much to deeds on land as on water, " they might many years ago have subdued the world." As it was, their power had declined ever since the taking of Constantinople, and " they rather practise with money to buy and sell countries peace and war than to exercise deeds of arms ; . . . most Venetians are at these days become better merchants than men of war." [1]

Thomas, in his account of the private life of the Venetians, in spite of their alleged faults of sensuality, avarice and pride, observed many good qualities as well. He had met both old and young men who were all they ought to be. He tried to give both sides of their character, and allowed an imaginary Venetian to defend himself against his accusers ; to justify his pride, because he was " a prince, and no subject," his frugality, since the state allowed no pomp or display, and his lending money to the commonwealth because it was of advantage to both parties.[2] One other custom he noticed was the excessive liberty given to children. " One is no sooner out of the shell but he is hail fellow with father and friend." [3] Altogether, in spite of the faults alleged against them, one cannot but be impressed by the greater breadth of view of the Venetians over the other Italians of the late sixteenth century. The English traveller could not, however, foresee that a far greater colonial empire than the

[1] *Op. cit.*, p. 75.   [2] *Ibid.*, p. 84 *et seq.*
[3] *Ibid.*, p. 84.

one slipping from the Venetians' grasp would one day
be the heritage of his own descendants, and that its
possession would bring with it many of the qualities and
faults he had noted as especially belonging to Venice.

The ordinary impression made by the Florentines was
one of talkativeness and a great desire to appear eloquent. Thomas observed that "he is not reputed
a man among them that cannot play the orator in his
tale, as well in gesture as in word." [1] Dallington, fifty
years later, wrote that although he had heard much of
the great wit of the Florentines he was unable to find it
himself, whatever Machiavelli might say about it; the
Florentine was good enough for conversation on frivolous subjects, but for nothing deeper. And this, though
they "do all things *alla mostra* and speak always *alla
grande*, witness their great houses, and small furniture
of the one, their great words and small matter." [2]
Everything was done for show, — even their duels,
where each party was well armed under his garments.
He himself had seen "two gallants in Pisa fight thus
completely provided where after a very furious encounter, and a most merciless shredding and slashing
of their apparel, with a most desperate resolution to
cut one another out of his clothes, they were (to the
saving of many a stitch) parted and by mediation with
much ado made friends." [3]

To follow the English traveller through the cities of
Italy would be a study in itself. Each place excited

[1] *Op. cit.*, p. 139.   [2] Dallington, *Tuscany*, p. 61.
[3] *Ibid.*, p. 65.

some comment on his part.   Thus at Siena, Hoby noticed the hospitality of every one,[1] while at Naples,
Thomas remarked the politeness of the people, but
qualified it by saying that they could not be trusted.
In Genoa he was especially struck by the amorous
qualities of its inhabitants, who could indeed teach
Ovid " a dozen points . . . so that in mine opinion
the supreme court of love is nowhere to be found out
of Genoa." [2]

Although the English traveller in Italy no longer
went there purely to study, he was still interested in
culture ; while at Padua, for instance, Hoby alluded
to the great professors of classics, and mentioned later
that he passed the birthplace of " the famous clerk in
letters of humanity, Lazarus Bonamicus, stipended
reader in the schools of Padua." [3]   The learning of
the Italian women was also noticed,[4] especially that
of the Sienese who " wrote excellently well both in
prose and verse." [5]   What made a deep impression, however, was the Florentine Academy, of which Thomas
wrote probably the first English account, all the more
interesting in view of the Areopagus of Sidney, and
of Bolton's idea of a similar institution which was
never to take root in England.   The Academy seemed
to Thomas one of the most interesting of all the sights
he had seen.   He described how the learned Florentines met there, the duke being of their number.   The

[1] Ms. cit., f. 24 b.   [4] Turler, op. cit., p. 43.
[2] Thomas, op. cit., p. 162.   [5] Hoby, Ms. cit., f. 24 b.
[3] Ms. cit., f. 93.

one to whom the task had been assigned beforehand would ascend the tribune and deliver an oration, lasting an hour, on any subject of his choice, the orator of the occasion being seated higher than the duke himself. Thomas confessed to never having heard " reader in school nor preacher in pulpit handle themselves better."[1] Later on, Dallington presented the other side of the picture. In former days, he wrote, the Florentines may well have had wit, but like spendthrifts they had run through the fortune that was left them; if Machiavelli were still alive and could see those wont to rule a state pay toll for a few lettuce brought from their villa, " he would unsay that which he had formerly said, and swear they had no wit."

V

Architecture was then the only art really noticed by English travellers, perhaps because of its learned side. Thomas devoted considerable attention to it, and, following Vitruvius, he explained at some length the different classic orders and styles, probably for the first time in English. The ruins of antiquity were likewise often regarded from the point of view of their own intrinsic beauty. Frequently, too, the churches impressed the traveller. St. Peter's was briefly described by Thomas, who admired the grandeur of its dimensions, but said that most people were in doubt as to whether it would ever be finished.[2]

The great palaces of the Renaissance were also

[1] *Op. cit.*, p. 139.   [2] *Ibid.*, p. 40.

objects of the traveller's admiration. Thomas remarked of Venice that no place in all Europe was able
to compare with it in number of sumptuous houses,
and that there were over two hundred palaces there,
all able to lodge any king.[1] In Rome, too, he thought
the Palazzo Farnese one of the grandest buildings in
the world, and admired beyond measure the Belvedere, with the fountains and orange trees around it,
which made it look like another paradise.

The æsthetic appreciation of the Englishman in
the sixteenth century may be judged from the fact
that the only statues observed by him were antiques.
Classical education had not yet deigned to notice contemporary sculpture ; Hoby almost alone admired a
marble fountain representing the story of Actæon by
Giovan Angelo [Montorsoli] at Messina, " which to my
eyes is one of the fairest works of marble that ever I
saw."[2] But he passed the bronze gates of the Bap-
tistery in Florence without a remark of any kind. On
the other hand, such works as the marble horses on
the Monte Cavallo in Rome, supposed to have been by
Phidias and Praxiteles, were mentioned by nearly every
traveller. The statues of the Belvedere were also described by Thomas, who spoke of " the images of fine
marble, of Romulus and Remus playing with a wolf's
teats, of Apollo with his bow and arrows, of Laocöon
with his two children wrapped about with serpents, of
Venus beholding little Cupido, of the sorrowful Cleopatra [Ariadne] lying by the river side, and divers

[1] Turler, *op. cit.*, p. 74.   [2] Ms. cit., f. 69 *b*.

Adoration of the Magi.
Drawing by Isaac Oliver.

others too long to rehearse."[1] He noticed, also, the numerous headless statues he saw everywhere, which he ascribed to the zeal of collectors who cut off the heads to transport them home. Even the most cultivated Englishmen of the time were unable to appreciate the greatest of the Italian arts. At a time when painting had barely passed its zenith, Hoby and Thomas passed through Italy without even noticing its existence, and quite insensible to its charms. A little later, Sidney alluded, in a letter to his brother, to the Italian superiority in painting ; and he himself, it will be remembered, undecided at first whether to have his portrait painted by Tintoretto or Veronese, finally chose the latter. It was not, however, until toward the very end of the century that any appreciation of the Italian fine arts could be found in England. Lomazzo's treatise was then first translated, and Constable alluded in a sonnet to Michelangelo "the archpainter," and to Raphael's great skill.[2] Dallington likewise, who had previously praised Michelangelo as an " excellent painter," wrote that Italy generally excelled in that art as well as in poetry ; " and no marvel, when all their time is spent in amours, and all their churches decked with colors." [3]

One of the great causes which led Englishmen to travel in Italy was the supposed preparation it gave for court life. To see as much as possible of this was the object of most travellers. What particularly impressed them, however, was the luxury of the great

---

[1] *Op. cit.*, p. 40.   [2] Sonnet *to Mr. Hilliard.*
[3] Dallington, *Tuscany*, p. 62.

houses, while the Italian festivities and pageants were noticed by all. The former, especially, greatly struck Hoby, who wrote that when he stopped with the Marquis of Capistrano at Amalfi, he slept in " a chamber hanged with cloth of gold and velvet," while on the bed was silver work, and even the bolsters were of velvet.[1] Thomas had been similarly impressed with the luxury in other parts of Italy. The pageants and great spectacles were likewise sights to be seen by travellers. Perhaps the earliest existing record of these by any Englishman in Italy, was a letter written in 1458 by John Free, while a student at Ferrara, to his protector, William Grey, describing the celebrations, lasting four days, intended to celebrate the elevation of Æneas Sylvius to the papacy. A Virgilian song composed by the prince himself was sung and the *feux de joie* were lit in the evening. Youths and maidens sang through the whole night, and the rejoicings turned almost into frenzy as the populace rushed madly from one end of the town to the other to the ringing sound of trumpets. On the next day every one turned out to see the horse races and athletic games. Free described all this with the enthusiasm of the young student, who saw before him the realization of a world he had dreamed of.[2]

Other spectacles of similar nature were mentioned by later travellers : the ceremony of the Bucentaur, when the Doge went out to wed the Adriatic, was written of both by Torkington and Hoby. One last

[1] Ms. cit., f. 82 *b*.   [2] Ms. Bod., 587, f. 161.

description may be mentioned. The procession of Pope Paul the Third, on Christmas day, 1547, was narrated at length by William Thomas, who allowed all his Puritanism to appear in the account he gave. "O what a world it is to see the pride and abomination that the churchmen there maintain. What is a king? What is an emperor in his majesty? Anything like to the Roman bishop? No, surely, nor would I not wish them so to be." He described the salvo of cannon which greeted the cardinals as they crossed St. Angelo's bridge, and the guard of Switzers, all in white harness, marching out to meet them. "There was no cardinal that came without a great train of gentlemen and prelates, well horsed and appointed; some had forty, some fifty, and some sixty or mo[re]. And next, before every of them, rode two henchmen, the one carrying a cushion and a rich cloth and the other a pillar of silver, and the cardinals themselves appareled in robes of crimson chamlet, with red hats on their heads, rode on mules."

When they were all within the palace, the "bishop" (for Thomas never wrote of him as Pope) appeared with his "triple-crowned mitre and shoes of crimson velvet set with precious stones and all his other pontifical apparel." Then the prelates and officers passed before him "which are such a number as were able to make the muster of a battail, if they were well-ordered in the field. Dataries, Treasurers, Clerks of the Chamber, Penitentiaries, Prebendaries, Notaries, Protonotaries, and a thousand more, each order of them in his diverse devise of parliamentary robes, all in scarlet, and for the most part finely furred. Then came the double cross, the sword and the imperial hat, and after that the cardinals by two and two, and between every two a great rout of gentlemen. Then came the ambassadors, and next them the bishop himself blessing all the way, and carried in his chaise by eight men clothed in scarlet ; and on either side of him went his guard making room and crying, *Abasso abasso*, for they that will not kneel shall be made kneel by force." And the Pope, having been carried into a chapel behind the altar, on "a throne of wonderful majesty was set up as a god."[1]

Turning from the personal reminiscences of the traveller to the interest he took in matters which might later be of use to him in public life, besides the general descriptions of the country, there was also a considerable amount of historical and similar information. The first, in the case of Thomas, was usually compiled from the best authorities available, as he wrote in explanation of his own method : "Conferring the discourse of divers authors together, touching the Florentine histories and finding the effects of them all gathered in one by Nicholas Machiavegli, a notable learned man, and secretary of late days to the commonwealth there, I determined to take him for mine only author in that behalf."[2] In like manner, other historical accounts were given by him of the cities of Italy, for the purpose of teaching the English how from "little beginnings

[1] *Op. cit.*, p. 37 *et seq.*   [2] *Ibid.*, p. 140.

many great estates have arisen, and how they that have the power to rule, by using their authorities well and prudently, have merited immortal fame of honor and prize."[1] It was, however, not so much the historical portions which were of interest as those treating of the government, the laws and regulations of each state. In these were put in practice, so to speak, the advice given in the theories of travel. The methods of raising the revenue and the powers and duties of each office were all described. Thus, in Venice it was said of the Doge that "though in appearance he seemeth of great estate, yet in very deed his power is but small. . . . some of the Venetians themselves call him an honorable slave."[2] The privileges and duties of every office were discussed in this way. The great council was compared to the English Parliament, since matters of importance were submitted to it and its judgment was final on all subjects. In a similar manner the other institutions of the state were considered. The liberty enjoyed by strangers was greatly admired in Venice. "All men have so much liberty that they can say what they like about the Venetians so long as they attempt nothing." No man marks another's doings or meddles with his affairs. "If thou be a papist, then shalt thou want no kind of superstition to feed upon. If thou be a gospeller, no man shall ask why thou comest not to church. If thou be a Jew or a Turk, or believest in the devil (so thou spread not thy opinions abroad) thou art free from all controlment . . . and

[1] *Op. cit.*, p. I.   [2] *Ibid.*, p. 77.

generally of all other things, so thou offend no man
privately no man shall offend thee ; which undoubtedly is one principal cause that draweth so many
strangers thither." [1]   In a similar spirit, the institutions of the other states were discussed.   But they
offered few lessons to the English student of government.   Italy had without a doubt degenerated from its
former condition.   Sidney's and Languet's letters are
full of expressions of disgust at the servility found there.
Thomas long before had noted that the Romans, in
spite of the recollections of their former liberty, were
held in such subjection by the Pope that they dared
not stir.[2]   Last of all, Dallington spoke of the discon-
tent of the Tuscans, who found the yoke lie heavy on
their backs, and ended his book with the two-edged
saying, *Qui sub Medicis vivit, misere vivit.*

[1] *Op. cit.,* p. 85.   [2] *Ibid.,* p. 37.

CHAPTER IV

THE ITALIAN DANGER

I

A NEW era dawned in England with Elizabeth's accession to the throne. The long preparation of previous years was to bear its fruit during her reign, and amid the dangers which then threatened the nation, a generous enthusiasm swept over England, and made of those years an heroic period in its history. One of the main reasons, perhaps, of the greatness of the Elizabethan Age, lay in the growth of national consciousness. Kindred feelings and sentiments were infused into every class, while a new social structure was replacing the old distinctions of mediæval feudalism. The period was also characterized by the wide diffusion of Italian culture, and its spread from the powerful but necessarily narrow court circle to the educated middle classes. With the progress of the age, travel abroad, which meant especially Italy, became even more common, until it was regarded as a necessary complement to the education of a gentleman ; while in England, during this time, the Italian language was taught and Italian fashions extensively copied. A reaction, however, set in. The growth of Puritanism encouraged novelists to attack the "Circean Charms" of Italy and point out their pitfalls and perils. The "Italianate Englishman," as he was then known, became alike an object of satire and reproach.

The reaction against Italy was not altogether unexpected. There had always existed in England a dislike for anything foreign, noticed by all the early travellers. Italians had questioned William Thomas regarding the English incivility to strangers, and he replied that it was then a thing of the past,[1] yet Petruccio Ubaldini, writing later, thought it inadvisable for strangers to travel in England without a royal pass, as the inhabitants would find out how their own compatriots had been treated in the stranger's country, and if badly, the traveller would not be very secure.[2] Florio likewise complained that the masses were very discourteous toward strangers.[3] This hatred of everything foreign, existing in the minds of all untravelled Englishmen and running counter to the excessive imitation of Italian fashions, stirred up a feeling which found its outlet in the invectives launched against Italy and the "Italianate Englishman." The cry was joined in by others who, having been in Italy themselves, had been shocked by its open wickedness. Satirists, eager for new sensations, scholars and statesmen, pamphleteers and moralists all joined hands in condemning what had been the fashion of the age. Florio in vain attempted feebly to defend the Italians,

[1] *Pilgrim*, p. 6.   [2] Ms. cit., f. 230 *et seq.*
[3] *First Fruites*, ch. 12.

urging that great virtues flourished in Italy side by side with vice.[1] His was almost the only note raised in defence ; all else was invective and condemnation.

It must be said that there was justification for much of the anti-Italian feeling which then sprang up. Even Erasmus in his day had complained that many of the scholars who went to Italy in search of learning returned with a knowledge of evil practices they had acquired there.[2] As travel became more and more of an amusement, and as its educational value, while perhaps not entirely lost sight of, was yet slighted, it was pleasure alone which many travellers sought for abroad, where remoteness from criticism gave license to their desires. Temptations lay before them in Italy, which, even if found in England, were there, at least, kept within strict limits. The richness of Italian life had not departed in a day, and long after the downfall of its liberties in the very midst of political servitude faint glimmers of former splendor remained in its celebrations and festivals. Too often the young Englishman, travelling there for the experience which was to fit him for the service of his prince and state, saw little beyond vice of every kind. In many cases he was himself fresh from the university, for the first time, perhaps, his own master, with abundant money at his command ; and around him he found those willing to pander to him in all ways, and in case his conscience revolted, to ease his qualms with the sophistry of which they were masters. It was not so much

---

[1] *Second Fruites*, Introd.　　[2] *Epist.*, CCCLXIII.

that vice was more widely spread in Italy than before, but rather that the counterbalancing virtues had
departed, and it alone remained. Liberty, crushed
in Italy, left sensuality and treachery. Former virtues
might still remain, but they were beneath the surface.
The ordinary English traveller in Italian cities saw
only their worst side, often caring for no other. As
Ascham expressed it, he witnessed greater freedom to
sin in his nine days' stay in Venice than he had ever
heard of in nine years in London.

There can be no doubt that Italy had degenerated
from its former condition. The country which had
been the foster-mother of all Europe was at length
exhausted. Even among Italians this decay was noticeable. They deplored the past greatness of their
land; superfluous titles had alone increased; the
day for deeds had gone by.[1]   Italy, however, still
traded on its past fame, when first in Europe it had
discovered the ancient world. But its fate had been
sealed from the day when Rome was sacked and
pillaged, and the last stand for liberty had been made
on the walls of Florence. Venice might still·continue
in apparent magnificence to be queen of the Adriatic,
but even her life-blood had been sapped. The living
glory of Italy was soon to leave it. In the influence
of its teachings beyond the Alps, rather than in its own
deeds, its greatness was mainly to continue.

Foreign observers likewise commented on the degeneracy of Italy; some said that the long years of servi-

[1] Della Casa, *Galateo*, p. 42.

tude had subdued the minds of Italians, who were
ready to endure all kinds of indignities.[1] Edwin
Sandys thought their national faults to be sensuality,
malice and deceit. In spite of his having met good
men in Italy, he wrote, nevertheless, that "the whole
country is strongly overflown with wickedness."[2]
There can be little cause for surprise that moralists,
when they saw the best youth of England returning
from Italian travel, aping ridiculous customs and fashions and outwardly advocating immorality and atheism,
should have preached against the foreign influence.
"Our countrymen usually bring three things with
them out of Italy, a naughty conscience, an empty
purse, and a weak stomach."[3] The movement was
fostered by the growth of Puritanism, which looked
with suspicion on anything hailing from a Catholic
nation. At a time when the conflict arising from
the Reformation was still in its most deadly phase,
Italy, which to many Englishmen seemed the enemies'
country, was to be rigidly avoided in spite of its attractions. News of Englishmen imprisoned by the Inquisition was extensively circulated to frighten others away;
the fanatic Richard Atkins, who attempted to convert
the Pope, was made into a martyr and a hero. Travellers were especially warned against Jesuits, who would
make of men "bad Christians and worse subjects."[4]
On account of these dangers, Rome was not considered
a safe place to visit. Sidney, at Languet's request,

[1] Languet, *Epist.*, XXXIII. [3] Turler, *op. cit.*
[2] *Speculum Europæ.* [4] Dallington, *Method of Travel.*

refrained from going there, much as he would have liked to have done so. Others similarly recommended their readers to keep away from Rome, which was perilous both to conscience and conduct.[1] The whole of Italy was considered scarcely less dangerous. " I am convinced that this baneful Italy would so contaminate the very Turks, would so ensnare them with all its vile allurements, that they would soon fall down of themselves from their high place," Sidney wrote in a letter from Venice.[2] For similar reasons Lord Burleigh, in giving advice to his son Robert Cecil, urged him never to allow his sons to cross the Alps " for they shall learn nothing there but pride, blasphemy and atheism." [3]

Those supposedly best qualified to judge, who had written of travels in foreign countries, warned their compatriots of the physical as well as moral perils they would have to encounter. " O Italy academy of manslaughter, the sporting place of murder, the apothecary shop of all nations ! How many kinds of weapons has thou invented for malice ! " [4] George Gascoigne, in his lines to a friend about to travel in Italy, advised him to beware of poison when invited to dinners, never to drink before another had tasted the beverage, to be on the lookout for poisoned soap, and take care lest the tailor stuff his doublet with what might bring on a deadly sweat.[5] The Italian art of poisoning

---

[1] *Marlianus*, preface.   Dallington, *Method for Travel*.
[2] *Letters*, p. 48.   [3] Cited in Zouch, *Life of Sidney*, p. 373.
[4] Nash, *Piers Penniless*, p. 38.
[5] *Hundred Sundry Flowers*.

impressed itself especially on the Elizabethan imagination and furnished endless material to the dramatists.

Dangers of different kinds were thus alleged against the insidious influences of Italy. Travellers thence "bring home nothing but mere atheism, infidelity, vicious conversation," and returned to England far worse than they came.[1] Just as the young Athenian who, going to Corinth to hear the eloquence of Demosthenes, was seduced by the beauty of Lais, so the young Englishman who travelled to learn a strange language was "in short time transformed into so monstrous a shape, that he is fain to alter his mansion with his manners."[2] The zealous Protestant, after having been in Italy, would proclaim that faith and truth were to be kept only where there was no loss, and forgiveness should not be shown until full revenge had been exacted. Another would say on his return, that he was a fool who took account of any religion, but an even greater fool if he lost any of his wealth thereby; and if he were willing to give up his life for it, he must be stark mad. Still a third said he cared not for God, so long as he had the prince and the country's laws on his side.[3] It was said of the "Italianate Englishman" that he held in greater reverence the *Triumphs of Petrarch* than the book of *Genesis*, and preferred a tale of Boccaccio to a story in the Bible. The mysteries of religion he considered to be fables, and made

---

[1] Harrison, *England,* p. 129 *et seq.*
[2] F. Meres, *Palladis Tamia,* p. 237.
[3] Harrison, *loc. cit.*

M

"Christ and his Gospels only serve civil policy." If it suited his purpose, he would openly promote religion, and again scoff at it in private. He cared neither for scripture nor church, and when in the company of those who thought like him, he would mock the Pope and rail at Luther, explaining all the mysteries of religion with a half-verse of Horace, *Credat Judæus Apella*. An epicure in living, an atheist in doctrine, the only heaven he desired was that of his own pleasure.[1] In Italy itself the *Inglese Italianato è un Diavolo Incarnato* passed as a byword.

The Italianate Englishman was to be described, even more plainly, as one who, after living and travelling in Italy, brought back with him to England "the religion, the learning, the policy, the experience, the manners of Italy. . . . These be the enchantments of Circe brought out of Italia to mar men's manners in England, and which 'Our Italians' returned with."[2] A young man thus brought up, said Ascham, contemning all religion and honest living, would come back to England but ill taught to be either an honest man or a good subject of his prince or his God.

It was scarcely to be wondered at that educators and moralists looked with alarm on the effects of Italian travel on Englishmen. Roger Ascham, meeting Sir Richard Sackville in the queen's privy chamber at Windsor, had been asked his opinion regarding the desire of so many Englishmen to travel abroad, and especially to spend a long time in Italy. In

[1] Ascham, *Scholemaster*, p. 71 *et seq.*   [2] *Ibid.*

his reply he stated that he did not underrate the value of experiences acquired in foreign countries, nor disparage the Italian language which, after Latin and Greek, he loved above all other foreign tongues, nor did he bear personal malice toward Italy. Formerly it had been of the greatest benefit to the world at large, and had brought forth the worthiest men in all activities of public life. Times, however, had changed, and between the new and the old there was as great difference as between black and white. Virtue had once made Italy mistress of the world. Vice now compelled her to be a slave to all other nations, and made its inhabitants willing to bear the stranger's yoke. It was no longer the place where a man could learn either wisdom or proper conduct.[1] On similar grounds Harrison wrote that the usual sending of "noblemen's and mean gentlemen's sons into Italy" was to the detriment of England.[2] "England is indeed injured by the taste of the upper classes for foreign things alone," wrote Richard Mulcaster.[3] Everything learned in travel, he argued, could as readily be acquired at home, and with it, moreover, a love for one's native soil. Each country ought to develop its own individuality; foreign customs would not fit, and foreign ideas only distorted one's own. The things observed in travel were not in themselves valuable. It was rather the language and learning, which could as readily be studied at home, as in the

---

[1] Ascham, *op. cit.*, p. 72.   [2] Harrison, *loc. cit.*
[3] *Positions*, p. 210.

case of Queen Elizabeth, who had gathered in England the best fruits of the wisdom of other nations. The greatest danger Englishmen had to fear was their too great liking for what was foreign. The true lesson of patriotism was to be studied in one's native land. " I love Rome, but London better. I favor Italy, but England more. I honor the Latin, but I worship the English." [1]

II

The new type of Italianate Englishman who returned home, bringing with him foreign affectations and vices, with a smattering of learning and a pretence of worldly wisdom doubly irritating to sober Englishmen, was no rare exception. Marlowe represented him in *Piers Gaveston*, the royal favorite. Shakespeare portrayed him somewhat differently in *Jacques* [2] who, after a career of libertinage, returned from his travels abroad disappointed with life and with everything English. To him *Rosalind* says : " Farewell, Monsieur Traveller ; look you lisp and wear strange suits ; disable all the benefits of your own country ; be out of love with your nativity and almost chide God for making you that countenance you are, or I will scarce think you have swam in a gondola." In *Jack Wilton*, Nash wrote that Italy made the young man kiss his hand like an ape, and cringe his neck. " From thence he brings the art of atheism, the art of epicurising, the art of poisoning, lasciviousness," and

---

[1] *Elementary*, p. 254 *et seq.*
[2] *As You Like It*, IV, I, 32.

unnatural vices. The only benefit he acquired was that it made him a good courtier, an excellent "carpet knight." The young English "Italianate Signior," as Gabriel Harvey called him, in a letter to Spenser, would praise the Italian poets above all others, and denounce everything English, whether in apparel, language or behavior. Everything not outlandish, or which savored in any way of England, was thought vulgar and base. "O Italish England," he wrote, "what has become of your ancient fortitude and might; since Tuscanism has come in, Vanity is above all else, and next comes villainy; there is no one who is not a minion; grand words cover feeble deeds."[1] He drew a picture of the Italianate Englishman, which, according to Nash, was meant to be a satire on the Earl of Oxford, who, but lately returned from his Italian travels, had introduced from that country various articles of dress and toilet previously unknown in England : —

Indeed most frivolous: not a look but Italish always.
His cringing side neck, eyes gleaming, physiognomy smirking.
With forefinger kiss, and brave embrace to the footward.

*   *   *   *   *   *   *

A little apish hat, crushed fast to the pate like an oyster;
French cambric ruffs, deep with a witness starched to the purpose.
Every one *a per se a;* his terms and braveries in print.
Delicate in speech, quaint in array, conceited in all points.

*   *   *   *   *   *   *

In courtly guises, a passing singular odd man.
This nay more than this doth practice of Italy in one year.[2]

[1] *Letter-Book*, p. 65.   [2] *Ibid.*, p. 97.

There was much in the behavior of Englishmen fresh
from Italian travels, in their depreciation of their
own country and excessive admiration for everything
foreign, to irritate sensible men. George Pettie said
that he had himself heard them telling foreigners that
England was barbarous, that English manners were
rude, and English people uncivil; and if strangers
should think this true, he said it was owing to English travellers abroad, who ran down their own country,
and contemned one another, no less than they " apishly
imitate every outlandish ass, in their gestures, behavior,
and apparel." [1]

This affectation of everything Italian, noticed by
the Italians themselves,[2] offered the dramatists and
poets, but chiefly the pamphleteers, fine opportunities
for satires and jests. Shakespeare makes the Duke
of York say : —

> The open ear of youth doth always listen ;
> Report of fashions in proud Italy,
> Whose manners still our tardy apish nation
> Limps after in base imitation.[3]

Strangely enough the literary men, who were themselves most influenced by Italy, were the loudest in
their denunciations. John Marston, himself partly
Italian, spoke of the youth who abused their time in

---

[1] *Guazzo*, preface.

[2] "Costumi e maniere Italiane estimate et imitate da loro
[Inglesi] piu che quelli di altre nationi." — *Cal. St. Pap., Ven.*,
VI, 1080–81.   Vide also Cardan's Diary, etc.

[3] *Richard II*, II, 1, 20 *et seq.*

travel and came home "in clothes Italianate,"[1] returning with all kinds of half-devised villanies, of which the very beasts of the field would blush. Vice and the art of poisoning was what they brought back with them. Gabriel Harvey had accused Nash of having travelled in Italy " to fetch him twopenny worth of Tuscanism," quite renouncing his ordinary English intonation and gestures to adopt the Italian manner. Nash, however, in spite of being known as the " English Aretine," was full of condemnation for the " filthy Italianate," and described how he himself had hastened " out of the Sodom of Italy," where only lasciviousness could be learned.[2] And Robert Greene confessed regretfully that on his Italian travels he " saw and practised such villany as it is abominable to declare."[3]

The dramatists and pamphleteers, however, could not equal the ardor of the Puritans who thundered invectives in denouncing the Italian danger. " We have robbed Italy of wantonness," wrote Stephen Gosson ; " compare London to Rome, and England to Italy, you shall find the theatres of the one and the abuses of the other, to be rife among us."[4] He complained especially of the " many wanton books which, being translated into English, have poisoned the old manners of our country with foreign

---

[1] *Scourge of Villainy*, Bk. III, Sat. IX, l. 90; Vide Bk. I, Sat. II.

[2] Nash, III, 243; V, 146, etc., *passim*.

[3] *The Repentance.*   [4] *School of Abuse*, p. 34.

delights." [1]   Others likewise found a great source
of danger in the English translations of Italian
books.   It was thought a pity that they were
allowed to be printed.   Ten sermons at St. Paul's
did not so much good as a single one of these
books did harm in enticing men to wickedness,
corrupting honest living, and undermining religion.[2]
Although Ascham condemned the chivalric romance
of former years, where the noblest knights were
those who killed most men and committed the
foulest adulteries, he could not but feel that ten
Morte d'Arthurs did not do one-tenth as much
harm as the English translation of Italian books,
"sold in every shop in London, commended by
honest titles, the sooner to corrupt honest manners;
dedicated over boldly to virtuous and honest personages, the easier to beguile simple and innocent wits."
They taught such things and such wickedness "as
the simple head of an Englishman was unable to
invent, nor had, indeed, ever before been heard of in
England." [3]

A different side of the Italian danger was brought
out by the numerous Italian adventurers of every
description, who then overran all Europe, and were
regarded as the corrupters of nations.   A parliamentary
inquiry in 1559 had stated that the Italians, above all

---

[1] *Plays Confuted in Five Actions.*

[2] *Op. cit.*, p. 80.

[3] *Ibid.*   Ascham had probably in mind Fenton's translation of Bandello, dedicated to Lady Mary Sidney.

others, should be guarded against, since they passed to and fro everywhere, " serve all princes at once," and " with their perfumed gloves and wanton presents, and gold enough to boot if need be, work what they list, and lick the fat even from our beards." [1] From time to time many similar expressions of opinion can be found.[2] In a speech against Elizabeth's marrying a foreigner, particular reference was made to the immorality of the Italians.[3]

In France, where the power of the Italians was even greater than in England, a similar reaction of anti-Italian feeling had been going on. Jacques Grévin, Henri Estienne, Jacques Tahureau and Jean de la Taille, all satirized those who aped the Italian fashions, and were then trying to make the French language a servile copy of Italian. A special attack was made by Gentillet against Machiavelli, whose name, in consequence, passed into an English byword for tyranny and treachery. The Huguenot Languet, in a letter to Sidney, also called attention to the fact that the countries which made use of Italian counsels in their government had, in consequence, been involved in the greatest calamities.[4]

The most interesting, however, of all anti-Italian literature was a work on the subtlety of the Italians,

---

[1] Hist. Mss. Com., Hatfield House, I, 163.

[2] Vide Silver, *Paradoxes of Defence.*

[3] Strype, *Sir Thomas Smith,* p. 233.

[4] *Correspondence, Epist.* XXXIII, cited in Zouch's *Sidney,* p. 79.

which bade the nations of Europe rise up in common defence against Italy.[1] From internal evidence the book was probably written by a Frenchman. There was, however, nothing very unusual in this; Claudius Hollyband wrote in English, as did likewise the Italian Vincenzo Saviolo.

The writer traced the alleged cunning of the Italians from its earliest origin in Roman times. He found it even in Romulus, the murderer of Remus, in Numa Pompilius, "a most subtle inventer of a forged religion"; in Julius Cæsar, who had pillaged all Europe. He saw it continuing after the papacy had taken the place of paganism. Although intending neither to censure the Pope nor even the Church of Rome, he could not help noticing the fact that the subtle Italians borrowed the papal authority to mask their wiles. Whatever was done under the name of the Pope was in reality only "the counsel and invention of the Italians of Rome." In this manner, the clergy, fighting over the interpretation of biblical texts, fell into the traps laid for them by the wily Italians, who were always inventing new obscurities, so that their assistance might be summoned to show the way to heaven and salvation, that they might thus reap profit from the ruin of others.

If the Italians could only obtain a footing north of the Alps, the writer went on to say, by various shifts and subtleties they tore asunder all bonds of friend-

[1] *The Subtlety of the Italians*, by F. G. B. A., 1591.

ship, and set the different nations fighting among themselves, after which they would " fish for their riches and dignities." Their crafty and deceitful nature had, without difficulty, been able to dominate other people and obtain their money from them. In this manner, Catherine de' Medici, with her council of Italians, had disposed of all the affairs of France. " Like bloodsuckers, they sucked the blood of the poor people as dry as if it had been crushed out in a wine press," filling their own purses in the meantime, while they managed to throw the blame on other people's shoulders. If any one should ask what had become of all the money levied in France, he had only to go to Florence and see its sumptuous buildings and " the wondrous wealth, wherein many Florentines swim, which came like poor snakes into France."

The supposed method by which the Italians set out to ruin a country was described in detail. They would begin with one part or class, and then gradually work round to the others. One could not but admire their ingenuity, in reaping every advantage to the utmost. They used religion merely as a cloak to domination, caring for its truth only in so far as it was of use to them. In order to make the kings of the earth their vassals, they stirred up wars among them. "To fish money out of Judæa" they had brought about the Crusades. To blind the youth of other countries to their machinations, they made use of Jesuits to fill the chairs of universities. By every conceivable means, from ecclesiastical patronage to bestowing empty titles on monarchs, they secured the upper hand.[1]

It was only the Italian form of Catholicism which was so savagely attacked; of all other Catholics the writer spoke in the very highest terms of respect, even half suggesting that another Pope be established for the rest of Europe, who should be independent of Rome. His grievance was largely an economic one, as was Luther's, when he wrote that German money took wings to fly across the Alps but never returned.[2] The remedy proposed was to be of equal benefit to Catholic and Protestant nations. If men did only observe, they would see that God had set as protection for the rest of mankind, on one side the Alps and on the other the deep seas. The Italians ought, therefore, to be shut up from all access or entrance into other countries. If such means were adopted, " we no more shall be exposed to the lamentable miseries into which they were wont to bring us headlong at their own lust and pleasure."

III

It seems remarkable that one of the most curious types of Englishmen should be known by no account of himself, or of his own tastes and peculiarities, but

---

[1] To many the power of Rome seemed the centre of Italian schemes; Thomas Palmer declared it to be " the forge of every policy that setteth princes at odds." *Method of Travel*, p. 44.

[2] *Address to the German Nobility.* Ed. Wace and Buchheim, p. 32 *et seq.*

only by the satires and invectives written against him. The Italianate Englishman, who followed Italian ways in everything, who admired no wisdom which did not come from across the Alps, who regulated his life to imitate the Italians, wrote no defence of himself. He who was accused of corrupting his native land by introducing foreign vices, paid no attention to the popular voice. His own position at court was secure from the fumings of moralists and the bitter attacks of pamphleteers. Some were even afraid to attack him ; Harrison, for instance, in a rather general condemnation, ended abruptly by refusing to say more about Italianates, lest he should offend too much.[1] But although unaffected by popular clamor, it is noteworthy that his example was not followed, and the very name of Italianate Englishman passed into disuse, even though Bishop Hall, and much later James Howell, were still to warn their readers of the continuance of the Italian danger.

The great success of Italianism in England contributed to its final overthrow. Along with the ridiculous aping of Italian fashions on the part of the courtiers,[2] a freedom was professed by many from all moral and religious restraints, till the Englishman returning from Italy began to be looked upon as an enemy of society. The vices he flaunted so openly were turned against him and served to fan the flame of Puritanism. At the same time the Italianate Eng-

[1] Harrison, *op. cit.*, p. 129 *et seq.*
[2] Vide *The English Ape, the Italian Imitation*, 1588.

lishman cannot fairly be charged with being the only factor in the reaction which now made itself felt against Italy, nor were the dangers of immorality, of atheism and the power of the Roman church, the only charges which were brought up against Italy. A hatred for everything foreign had long existed in the English mind, and the competition of Italians in commerce and trade only increased the dislike. Along with it, too, there went a growing feeling of nationality, which stoutly rebelled at every sign of alien power; it penetrated even the scholarly world, where it brought about a strong movement against the introduction of foreign and learned words into the English language, protesting against both Italianisms and the so-called ink horn terms.[1]

In the century and a half which extended from the first beginnings of the English Renaissance to the time when with the death of Elizabeth it properly ended, much of what was good in Italy had been transplanted to England. In certain cases the work failed of result; the fine arts, for instance, can scarcely be said to have taken English root; but, generally speaking, whatever was suitable for the Northern Land had found its way there. Scholarship, literature, social life, and even statecraft, were all affected by the Italian influence. Toward the end of the sixteenth century, however, England, still growing in the fulness of its youth, had, as it were, little to learn from the aged Italy, which then lay helpless beneath the invader. The degeneracy of the country was apparent to all thoughtful

[1] Cf. Gascoigne, *Works.*

persons. Those who then combated its influence should for that reason not be thought blind Philistines, anxious only to destroy what they were themselves unable to understand, but stern-minded moralists, who saw the hollowness of what once was great, and realized the dangers which lay in its decay. With the beginning of the seventeenth century, moreover, the Italian influence was in many ways stationary, if not actually on the wane; the want of fresh vigor to reënforce its claims, perhaps no less than the attacks of moralists, had brought it to a standstill; but more than anything else was the fact that its place had been filled by Spain and France, then growing in their strength. Both countries, influenced by Italian traditions, contained beneath the surface the civilization and culture of Italy, which was often outwardly hidden from view. It was Italy transformed, passed through another mould, and bearing on its surface the stamp of France or Spain, — but it was Italy none the less, whose foster-children were now to continue her work. It is for this reason that the history of Italian influence in England after the death of Elizabeth has in one way little new to offer. For a time, indeed, the influence lingered at the court of the Stuarts; the poetry of Drummond, the masks of Ben Jonson and Inigo Jones, bore witness that it was not yet dead, while the mansions erected by the latter showed that the architecture of the Italian Renaissance could flourish in England as well; but its vitality in the life of the English people had departed once and for all.

PART SECOND

PART SECOND

CHAPTER V

THE ITALIANS IN ENGLAND: CHURCHMEN, ARTISTS AND TRAVELLERS

I

THE presence of Italians in England was by no means unusual, even before the conquest. The many ties with Rome caused papal legates and collectors, who were almost invariably Italians, to cross the channel frequently. Moreover they were often granted English benefices. Five successive bishops of Worcester were Italians, and Bishop Grosseteste, about the year 1250, refused to admit an Italian ignorant of English to a living in his diocese.[1] Cardinal Gualli, a little earlier, conferred Chesterton Rectory to the monastery of St. Andrews, which he had founded at Vercelli.[2] Italians likewise were found at Oxford from time to time. In the twelfth century, a certain Vicario had been called by the Archbishop of Canterbury to introduce the

---

[1] Vide *Calendars of entries in Papal Registers*, Bliss Series; the Marini *Vatican Transcripts* (Brit. Mus. Mss. Dept.); Stevenson and Bliss, *Roman Transcripts*, Record Office, London; J. Paton, *British History and Papal Claims*, for accounts of the relations existing in the Middle Ages between England and the papacy.

[2] Beckynton, II, 344. It was probably in this way that the Anglo-Saxon *Vercelli Book* found its way there.

new study of Roman law in the university,[1] and a little later, Francesco d' Accorso, a lecturer in civil law at Bologna, who had attached himself to Edward the First, and became his counsellor, also settled at Oxford. It has even been thought by some that Dante studied theology there. Strangers from foreign lands were often drawn to Oxford during the period when it was one of the great centres of mediæval learning. Specific reference was made to its Italian students in a letter of 1454, addressed to the Earl of Salisbury, chancellor of the university, complaining of the foreign students who came over during Lent, ostensibly to preach and shrive penitents, but in reality to receive the alms intended for such Italians as were regular students " to the injury of these last mentioned and discredit of our university."[2]

In addition to the Italian scholars sent for by Duke Humphrey, several others of distinction came, likewise, on different occasions. Poggio, for instance, searched English monasteries for rare manuscripts, but found nothing of interest. " Most of their libraries are full of foolishness," he wrote in disgust.[3] Although profoundly dissatisfied by his stay in London among the "Sarmatians and Scythians," and accusing the English of caring little for letters,[4] he formed, nevertheless, enduring friendships with several Englishmen, with whom he afterwards corresponded. Æneas Sylvius, whose visit to England was not dictated by the same motives, pre-

[1] Tiraboschi, *Storia della Letteratura Italiana*, III, 442.
[2] *Epist. Acad.*, I, 322.   [3] *Epist.*, I, 70.   [4] *Ibid.*, I, 43, 74.

served pleasanter remembrances of his stay there and of the learned men he met.   One of Guarino's former pupils, the Venetian, Piero del Monte, who had first come over as papal collector, made friends with Duke Humphrey, and later dedicated to him his philosophical dramas.[1]   It is only natural to suppose that the love of letters, then universal in Italy, caused Italian churchmen abroad to stimulate the latent zeal for learning they saw everywhere about them.

Toward the end of the fifteenth century a number of Italians were occupying important positions in England.   One of the most learned of these, Giovanni Gigli, better known as John of Sighs, had first been sent to England as papal collector; he was subsequently made Canon of Wells, and still later Bishop of Worcester.   He was in the service of both the Vatican and the king, being successively commissioner of papal indulgences, and Henry the Seventh's diplomatic agent and orator at Rome.   He showed there his friendship for Oxford, when the authorities requested his aid in obtaining certain favors from the Pope.   He had not forgotten, he said in his reply, that he was a member of the university, although an unworthy one.[2] Giovanni Gigli was a poet, as well, and on the occasion of Henry's marriage to Elizabeth of York, he composed a Latin epithalamium in the Virgilian style, in which Parliament was represented as entreating Henry to marry in order to ward off the evils of a civil war.

Peter Carmeliano, of Brescia, was another Italian

[1] Voigt, II, 257.   [2] *Epist. Acad.*, II, 564, 567.

poet of this period, in England.   His earliest work, on
the life of St. Mary the Egyptian, had praised Richard
the Third as a model king and pattern of virtue ; but
little more than a year after his death, in a poem
which celebrated Prince Arthur's birth, he denounced
him as a bloodthirsty monster ready to commit any
crime.   After describing his defeat, and the accession
of Henry to the throne, he bade Englishmen rejoice
over the birth of a royal heir.   This poem was written
in hexameters, in imitation of Virgil.   Carmeliano, who
was a kind of court poet, wrote considerable verse of
different kinds.   He was also Latin secretary to Henry
the Seventh and one of the king's chaplains.   As a
reward for his services various pensions were granted
him.[1]   Later, his poetic functions seem to have been
dispensed with.   He became lute player to Henry the
Eighth, but wrote one last poem on the death of the
Scottish king at Flodden Field.   His verse was not very
successful, while his false quantities furnished amusement for Erasmus.   It is noteworthy, however, that of
the very few contemporary narratives of the reign of
Henry the Seventh, three should have been written by
Italians, and a fourth writer, Johannes Opicius, was
probably likewise of Italian origin.   It is also remarkable that the Latin secretaries of the king, Carmeliano,
and then Ammonio and Peter Vannes, should all have
been Italians, as if to prove that polished Latin could
then properly be written by no one else.

[1] Campbell, *History of Henry VII*, II, 244, 289; J. Gairdner,
Memorials of Henry VII.

Several other Italian churchmen who were more or less connected with the English court during this period were likewise interested in the growth of humanism. It can scarcely be supposed that it was chance which led the shrewd, calculating nature of Henry the Seventh to cultivate their friendship, as he did in many instances. It was rather that he found his own ideas reflected in them, and was able to make use of their services and intelligence. Silvestro Gigli, who had been trained by his uncle in diplomacy, and succeeded him in the bishopric of Worcester, was appointed by the king his master of ceremonies,[1] and later resident ambassador at Rome. In after years he became Wolsey's chief diplomatic agent there, and was in constant correspondence with the king and cardinal. Like most other Italians of that age, he was a man of letters as well, corresponding with Erasmus. The example offered to English churchmen of Italian dignitaries who were patrons of the new learning and interested in humanism, might well have led them on in a similar direction, had such encouragement been necessary.

Adrian de Castello belonged also to the same group. After having been papal nuncio to Scotland, he had been sent by Pope Innocent as collector of Peter's pence in England. He became, however, an English citizen, and was employed by Henry the Seventh as his agent in Rome, and still later as ambassador to Alexander the Sixth, who conferred on him an English

[1] Bernard André, *Annales Henrici VII*, pp. 86, 122–123.

bishopric. He was also a man of the most cultivated tastes, and the author of a Latin poem published by Aldus.

By far the most interesting, however, of the Italian friends of Henry was Polydore Vergil, the historian. He was already an author of some reputation[1] when appointed papal sub-collector. In England he found his brother, who was there as a merchant, and his friend, Adrian de Castello. Although he himself was later to receive ecclesiastical preferment, and to hold several lucrative benefices in the church, his life was spent chiefly in literary and historical writing.

Having found, as he alleged, the English annals confused and unknown, even to natives, he had determined to write a short history of the country. The historical method of this work, compiled, it is said, at the request of Henry himself, was far in advance of anything England had known till then. In spite of many errors and prejudices, it was nevertheless the first history written along modern lines in which any attempt was made to weigh authorities. Its author, moreover, was a friend of Henry the Seventh, in complete sympathy with his task, and one who realized the rapid changes which had come over England, and marked the transition between the vanishing Middle Ages and the Renaissance now dawning on the land. It was a pity for his reputation that Polydore Vergil did not die before his friend and patron. Although he

[1] His *De Inventoribus Rerum* passed through 110 editions and was translated into English.

returned to Italy after his death, he came back once
more to be Adrian de Castello's factor in England.
Both, however, fell into disgrace on account of some
over-frank letters which had cast reflections on Wolsey
and Henry the Eighth.   One of these, containing im-
putations against both Pope and king, was intercepted,
probably by Adrian's enemy, Silvestro Gigli, the Bishop
of Worcester, who sent it to Andrea Ammonio, Polydore's rival.   It was shown to Wolsey, and a few days
later Vergil was a prisoner in the Tower, with his col-
lectorship forfeited.[1]   In his captivity he addressed the
most servile letters to Wolsey, stating he would like to
bow in worship before him, in order that his spirit might
rejoice in him " as in God my Saviour." He was released
in 1516, and took his revenge, when out of Wolsey's
reach, by abusing him in his history of England.

Henry the Eighth, who succeeded his father, likewise welcomed many Italians at the court. " He is
glad to see them, and especially Italians," wrote
Savorgnano.[2]   Ammonio, who had come to England as
the papal collector, was appointed his Latin secretary.
Ammonio had enjoyed a reputation for classical scholarship, even in Rome, and in later years he was known
for his Latin verse.   Like Polydore Vergil, he was also
a friend of Erasmus, to whom he confided occasional
grievances regarding the barbarism of the "inhospita-
ble Britons."[3]   He was a friend, however, of Linacre,

---

[1] Brewer, *Henry VIII*, I, 264 *et seq.*
[2] *Cal. St. Pap.*, *Ven.*, IV, 287.
[3] *Cal. St. Pap.*, *Foreign and Domestic, Henry VIII*, I, No. 1948.

Colet and More, and formed part of their small coterie in London. When afterwards he was appointed papal nuncio at the English court, he was succeeded in his secretaryship by Peter Vannes, another Italian. Vannes himself, who became Wolsey's secretary, was with him on many of his missions, and accompanied Sir Francis Bryan on his unsuccessful embassy to Rome, when it was intended that he should bribe the cardinals to declare the marriage of Henry the Eighth with Katherine invalid, and Pope Julius' brief a forgery.[1] Several other English diplomatic charges were intrusted to Vannes in the course of his long life.

It was especially in the matter of the king's divorce that Wolsey proposed to employ Italians, not only as more likely to secure aid at the Vatican, but also confessedly on the ground of their being more skilful diplomatists. Among his agents, besides the ones mentioned, were Ghinucci, Bishop of Worcester, Sir Thomas Spinelli, and the two Casales, John and Gregory, who was afterwards knighted.[2] By degrees, English diplomacy was able to dispense with the churchmen sent from Rome, on whom in former times it had relied so largely. With the rapid growth of international relations centring around the Italian apple of discord and the rise of the Spanish power, a new set of men had been found necessary in diplomacy. In part, they were humble, and often unknown, like the

[1] Vide Pocock, *Records of the Reformation*, I, 110 *et seq.*

[2] Vide Marini, *Vatican Transcripts*, Brit. Mus., Vol. XXXVII, *passim.*

numerous news agents employed by Thomas Cromwell, who made use of their services, just as Lord Burleigh did in after years. Many of these were Italian merchants, whose natural shrewdness, added to the facilities of communication they enjoyed, placed them in a peculiarly favorable position for the rapid forwarding of information. In the higher ranks of English diplomacy there were other Italians as well. Italy itself had offered the first examples of trained diplomats, while, moreover, the talented and pliable nature of the Italian of the Renaissance lent itself readily to all such work, especially if it had anything to do with the court.

A number of Italians from time to time visited England, either out of curiosity, or else engaged on some mission. Marco Savorgnano, the celebrated military engineer, was perhaps an example of the first kind ; Cardinal Campeggio, the papal legate and a protector of the new learning, of the second. Such missions, however, were not exclusively diplomatic. Baldessare Castiglione, the finest type of the Italian courtier, came over to acknowledge the Order of the Garter, conferred upon his master, the Duke of Urbino.[1] He himself, as he wrote his mother, was anxious to see the country, and looked forward to the company of his good friend Bishop Gigli, who "although a Florentine [Luccan], yet holds a rich bishopric in England and is the King's ambassador with the pope." He was accepted by Henry the Seventh as proxy to the

[1] Vide Dennistoun, *Memoirs of the Dukes of Urbino*, II, 443 *et seq.*

duke, and installed in his place a Knight of the Garter. The king, moreover, showed him every possible attention, knighted him personally, and made him presents of horses and dogs, and a gold chain bearing the royal badge.[1]

From time to time, during the sixteenth century, numerous Italians took up their residence at court, or were in the royal service. The musicians, for instance, were "almost all Italians."[2] The same thing was largely true of the court physicians. Henry the Eighth's surgeon was Antonio Ciabo; Battista de Boeria and Fernando de Vittoria were also his doctors, with Linacre and John Chamber, both of whom had studied in Italy. Later, Jerome Cardan, the greatest physician of his day, who was also a friend of Sir John Cheke's, was entreated to give an opinion on the health of Edward the Sixth. He cast his horoscope and predicted a long life, but in after years explained this by showing the influences he had to submit to, owing to the intrigues at the English court. Edward granted him an audience and gave him a hundred *scudi*, not so much as he had received from the Scottish king. A more liberal present would have been given, had he only acknowledged Edward's title as king; but as a prominent Catholic, who intended to return to Italy, he could not do so.[3] Cardan recorded his impressions of England in the *Dialogue on Death*.

---

[1] *Lettere del Conte B. Castiglione*, Letters XIII, XIV, XXVII.

[2] Florio, *First Fruites;* Ubaldini, Ms. cit., f. 43 *b*.

[3] Vide Cardan's *Vita;* Waters, *Jerome Cardan*, p. 132 *et seq.*

He spoke of the English imitating the Italians in habit, manner and dress as closely as they could. They also seemed similar to him in appearance. The difference in speech struck him chiefly, since he could not understand a word of the language. He thought them Italians gone mad: "The tongue is curved upon the palate; they turn about their words in the mouth, and make a hissing sound with their teeth."

Among other Italian physicians at the English court was Pietro Maria Adelmare, the father of Sir Julius Cæsar, the famous judge. He was the medical adviser of both Mary and Elizabeth, from whom he received fees of a hundred pounds for a single attendance. Giulio Borgarucci also, who first attended the Earl of Leicester, and distinguished himself in his treatment of plague sufferers by bleeding, later became the court physician; Elizabeth, moreover, held her Venetian doctor, Cæsar Scacco, in such high regard that she even wrote the doge, requesting that his stay in England might not prove prejudicial to his personal affairs in Italy.[1] Many other Italians at court enjoyed the protection of the Virgin Queen. "Doth she love Italians? Yes, sir, very well. Delighteth she to speak with them? Yes, sir, and she speaketh very eloquently," wrote Florio.[2] Even on the list of her New Years' gifts among those to whom perfumed gloves or gilt plate were given ap-

---

[1] *Cal. St. Pap., Ven.*, VII, 551.
[2] *First Fruites*, ch. 15.

peared such names as Bassano, Caliardi, Lupo and Ubaldini.[1] Petruccio Ubaldini was an example of the better type of Italian adventurers then to be found at every European court. He had first come over to England in the reign of Henry the Eighth, and having obtained government employ, had served in the war with Scotland. Shortly after this he wrote, probably for the Venetian Signory, an account of English manners, customs and institutions.[2] He found a patron in the Earl of Arundel, who presented him to the queen. The rest of his life he passed as one of the hangers-on at the court, engaged in teaching Italian, transcribing and illuminating manuscripts, rhyming and writing, or translating historical works. Twice he exchanged gifts with the queen, although never quite a courtier, nor yet a dependant. He was one of the many Italians who lived amid courtly surroundings, ready to turn hands and brains to any account. He tried to be historian, soldier, poet and artist, showing alike the many-sidedness and versatility of his nation and his century.

One of his books, a life of Charlemagne,[3] was dedicated by Ubaldini to the gentlemen of England in appreciation of their courtesy toward foreigners. In its preface he bade Englishmen rejoice, since Italian

[1] Add. Ms. Brit. Mus., 4827.

[2] Add. Ms. Brit. Mus., 10,169.   Several other transcripts exist of this interesting manuscript.

[3] *La Vita di Carlo Magno*, da Petruccio Ubaldini, Londra, 1581.

could be printed in England as well as in Italy. His own book he proclaimed had been the first so printed " by the diligence and effort of your citizen John Wolfe, and you will be able to have other such works from day to day, if you should give it that welcome, that I expect you will." Ubaldini's claim, however, was not strictly accurate. In 1545 already, a little work by John Clerk, on the resurrection of the dead,[1] had been printed in London, in Latin, English, French and Italian; and a few years later an Italian translation of a Latin catechism was published,[2] while another curious work also appeared not long afterward.[3] Ubaldini's history marked, however, a real beginning. Battista Castiglione, the queen's Italian master, in publishing a book by Accontio, which he dedicated to her,[4] stated that he had made up his mind to print it, owing to the fact that a young Londoner (John Wolfe) had just returned from Italy where he had learned the art, and was now able to print in Italian. Several books soon appeared from his press. Among these were the *Pastor Fido* of Guarini[5] and Tasso's *Aminta*, both published at Jacopo Castelvetri's expense, who said that, encouraged by friends, he was having them printed in London, on account of the great length of time necessary to obtain them from Italy. One edition

---

[1] *Opusculum Plane Divinum*, London, 1545.
[2] *Catechismo per amaestrare i fanciulli*, Londra (?), 1553(?).
[3] *Esposizione di Giovanbattista Agnello*, Londra, 1566.
[4] *Una Esortazione al Timor di Dio*, Londra, 1590 (?).
[5] *Il Pastor Fido; A spese di Jacopo Castelvetri*, Londra, 1591.

of the *Principe*, although bearing the press-mark of Palermo was probably also printed in England, as were likewise a number of Giordano Bruno's works, which first saw light on British soil.[1] Giordano Bruno was the greatest of all the Italians who came over to England in the sixteenth century; he was at the court of Elizabeth from 1583 to 1585, and came in contact with the best English minds of that age. Two of his dialogues were dedicated by him to Sir Philip Sidney, and in his *Supper of Ashes* he gave an account of a banquet at Fulke Greville's house, recording some very vivid impressions of the English people. His visit, however, left only doubtful traces on contemporary literature, and was barely noticed even by his English friends.

II

The genius of Italy in the Renaissance found its noblest expression in the fine arts. It was only natural, therefore, that some of the many Italian artists in an age of wandering should have found their way to England. It was really more remarkable that none of the first importance were attracted there. The arts, however, flourished in Italy, in the very midst of internal disturbances. Inducements to travel were not great, so long as reward awaited merit at home. Yet there were several Italians of note at the emperor's court, and Francis the First gathered round him such artists as Leonardo da Vinci, Benvenuto Cellini and Pri-

[1] Several bear other press-marks as well. Vide *Athenæum*, April 30, 1898.

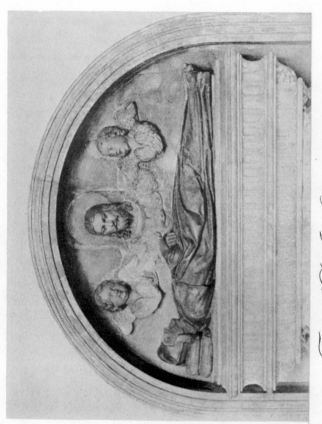

Tomb of Dr. John Yonge, by Torrigiano.

maticcio, although the greatest of the three, accomplished nothing in the land of exile.

Pietro Torrigiano was the best known of the Italian artists who came to seek their fortune in England. After leading a life of adventure, and having been a soldier of fortune, he was persuaded by some Florentine merchants to accompany them to London. The execution of the royal shrine in the chapel of Henry the Seventh at Westminster was entrusted to him in default of native workmen. During the years he was engaged on it, he executed many things in marble and bronze for the king, although one of his best works was the tomb of Dr. John Young, master of the Rolls.[1] His masterpiece, still preserved at Westminster, was the tomb of Lady Margaret of Richmond, which has been called "the most beautiful and venerable figure that the Abbey contains."[2] It seems strange, in contemplating it, to note the contrast between its Florentine Renaissance sculpture, and the mediæval architecture of the cathedral. It is more particularly in certain details that the Tuscan fancifulness and wealth of ornamentation show themselves even though the lightness of touch and joyousness of the school of Donatello were wanting in his chisel. He himself made use of Gothic shafts in the ornament, as if to reconcile to the Renaissance the spirit of the Middle Ages, long forgotten in his native city.

[1] Formerly in the Rolls Chapel, now in the Museum of the Record Office, London.

[2] Dean Stanley, *Memorials of Westminster Abbey*, p. 164.

Torrigiano's most important work, however, was to be the tomb of Henry the Seventh and his queen, also in the Abbey. The contract for this was drawn up in 1512. He entered into an agreement with the king's executors, " to make and work, or do to be made and wrought, well, surely, cleanly, workmanly, curiously, and substantially for the sum of £1500 sterling . . . a tomb or sepulture of white marble and of black touchstone, with images, figures, beasts, and other things of copper gilt . . . together with other diverse images, epitaphs and other things. . . . [This agreement to be entered upon] by Peter Torrysany of the city of Florence, painter." [1] The tomb itself, although differing from the conventional Florentine type, yet shows the Tuscan hand, in the fine bronze figures, the medallions of the base, and in many of the minor details. It is a significant proof of the lack of native talent and dependence on Italians, that the execution of royal tombs should have been intrusted to them. Another similar undertaking was, however, to fall through. This was the tomb Henry the Eighth wanted for himself and Queen Katherine. It was likewise to be of white marble and black touchstone, but "more greater by the fourth part," than his father's and to cost £2000. Wolsey, one of whose ideas it probably was, had charge of the financial arrangements. After prolonged negotiations with the king, who was unable to make up his mind to order it, Torrigiano left in great temper for Italy. It was on this occasion that Rinaldo de Ricasoli,

[1] Cited in *Archeologia*, XVI, 84.

consul of the Florentine nation in London, wrote to the signory in Florence, requesting them to see to it that he should get none of the money deposited by the king for the altar, since he had left England without his Majesty's permission and under dishonorable circumstances, perhaps to the detriment of the Florentine colony.[1] He returned to England, however, in 1519, possibly at the instance of the signory. It is significant of the manner in which artistic work was then conducted, that before his return he entered into an agreement with Antonio de Lorenzo, Antonio called Toto del Nunziata, a painter, and later with Giovanni Luigi da Verona, who bound themselves to work with him for four and a half years and to practise their arts in Italy, France, Flanders, England and Germany, or in any other part of the world, for a salary of three gold florins a month the first year, and forty ducats thereafter a year besides the cost of food, lodgings, and horse hire.[2] He himself told Benvenuto Cellini, whom he wanted to engage, that the king of England had intrusted him with a great undertaking, and he had in consequence gone to Florence to procure the aid of as many young men as possible. On his return to London he and his assistants completed the altar,[3] for which the king had previously advanced a thou-

---

[1] Cited in Milanesi's Vasari, IV, 262 note.

[2] *Ibid.*

[3] Like so many other works of art, it was destroyed during the civil wars. Three pieces of it were, however, preserved, and have been set up as an altar by Dean Stanley.

sand pounds. Torrigiano's irascible temperament did not long permit him to enjoy quiet among "those beasts the English" as he was wont to call them, and he left for Spain, where some of his best works are still preserved.

Other Italian artists also came over to seek service under a monarch whose overflowing coffers seemed to promise reward to all alike. Guido Mazzoni of Modena, whose sobriquet of Paganino was later anglicized into that of Pageny, had previously followed Charles the Eighth to Paris, and then crossed over to England where he designed a tomb for Henry the Seventh, which was, however, rejected.

Among the painters employed by Henry the Eighth were Vincent Volpe, Anthony Toto, Antonio Cavallari, Bartholomew Penni, and even a woman miniaturist, Alice Carmellian, a relative probably of Carmeliano, the court poet.[1] Little is known of Vincent Volpe, save that in 1514 he painted the streamers and banners for the great ship *Henry Grace à Dieu*. It is interesting to note among the causes which make the presence of foreigners in England often difficult to detect, that he anglicized his name to *Fox*.

Antonio Toto, likewise an architect and designer of masques, was considered the best of the Italian painters in England. He had studied under the younger Ghirlandajo, and had then been engaged by Torrigiano to accompany him to England, where he entered the royal service as "Sergeant painter,"

[1] *Archeologia*, XXXIX, 22.

his name being usually associated with that of Bartholomew Penni, another Florentine. The Italian frescoes
in one of the rooms of Cardinal Wolsey's apartment
at Hampton Court are almost certainly the work of
either Penni or Toto. The latter, who was naturalized
an Englishman, remained long in the service of Henry
the Eighth, and, according to Vasari, executed many
works for the king. It is remarkable that most of the
Italian artists were in some way connected with
Wolsey, whose orders were usually given in the name
of the king and who, amid the duties of state, found
time for the encouragement of art and learning.
Torrigiano's real successors in England were Benedetto
da Rovezzano and Giovanni da Majano. The former
was engaged by Wolsey through Cromwell, to prepare
his tomb. It was to be on a magnificent scale, worthy
of the tastes of a cardinal who was such a lover of
art, and far to surpass in splendor that of Henry the
Seventh.[1] The sculptor labored over it for five years.
But when Wolsey died in disgrace and was buried in
the Abbey Church at Leicester, the king tried to make
use of as much of the tomb as he could, although
according to Vasari, Baccio Bandinelli had prepared a
beautiful model in wood, with wax figures, which was intended for him. Rovezzano, however, was left in charge
of the royal monument, and cast it in metal. Among
the founders he employed were several other Italians,
Pietro Baldi, Giovanni Utrin, and two "engineers,"
Rinieri and Ambrogio. The monument, which Wolsey

[1] Vide *Arch. Journal*, September, 1894, pp. 1, 59, 203 *et seq.*

had begun was left unfinished at the king's death, in the Lady Chapel of Henry the Seventh at Windsor, and was never completed. Its subsequent history is not without interest. Charles the First, another lover of art, wished to be buried in it, but after his execution Parliament ordered the sale of all the bronze work on the monument. In the beginning of the last century, the marble sarcophagus was removed from Windsor to be used for Nelson's tomb, in the crypt of St. Pauls, and a little later the pavement it had rested on was taken up to build the royal vault for George the Third.[1]

The materials for the history of the Florentine sculptors in England during this period, are not very plentiful.[2] When all but the greatest artists were considered craftsmen, it is scarcely to be wondered that not much attention was given to the lives of the others. It can be said, however, that there was nothing unusual in the presence of Italian artists in England; the Bernardis for instance, settled at Chichester in 1519, at the invitation of Bishop Sherburne, and were probably the earliest decorative painters in England.[3] Only very little is really known of the English residence

---

[1] Blomfield, *Renaissance Architecture*, I, 13 *et seq.*

[2] Letters of Torrigiano, Rovezzano and Majano to Wolsey, the records of payments and inventories showing the work executed on Wolsey's tomb, and the accounts and records of the work done on Henry the Eighth's tomb from 1530 to 1536 are cited by Mr. Higgins, in his valuable article in the *Arch. Journal*, September, 1894.

[3] Digby Wyatt, *Foreign Artists in England*, p. 227.

of the sculptor Nicholas of Modena, who executed the royal effigy at the funeral of Henry the Eighth; likewise of John of Padua, who was both a musician and the "Devizor of his Majesty's buildings," entering afterward the service of the Protector Somerset, whose palace on the Strand he very likely built;[1] or of Jerome of Treviso, an imitator of Raphael,[2] who was architect, military engineer (*magister tormentorum*) and a favorite of Henry the Eighth. Their very names prove, however, that the great art of Italy had crossed the Alps to find new homes in distant lands.

The work of another Tuscan sculptor, Giovanni da Majano,[3] who assisted Rovezzano in the decoration of Hampton Court, can be seen there in the well-known terra-cotta roundels of Roman emperors.[4] The talents of the Italian artists were especially required in decoration, where their influence in England was then chiefly felt. In all matters of detail, ornamentation of surfaces, delicate arabesques, plaster modelling, terra-cotta medallions, and carving of every kind, they excelled. The German traveller, Braun, who was almost a contemporary, spoke of the numerous Italian artificers, sculptors, and architects in the service of Henry the Eighth. The royal palace of Nonesuch,

[1] Digby Wyatt, *op. cit.*, p. 234.

[2] A picture by him representing the Madonna and the Child with saints and angels is in the National Gallery, London.

[3] Often called John de Menns, or Demyans; Rovezzano's name was similarly anglicized into Rovesham or Rovesanne.

[4] For the terra-cotta busts he received the sum of £2 6s. 8d., and for three "histories of Hercules," £4 apiece.

the greatest building of that age in England, which was probably designed by Toto, contained numerous statues in plaster, and life-size reliefs representing the stories of pagan gods, said by Evelyn to have been the work of some celebrated Italian. Camden the antiquary also praised its splendor, and described the statuary as rivalling the monuments of ancient Rome.

The direct influence of Italy in the arts, or rather the work of Italians in England at this time, was largely confined to the southeastern counties, especially around Southampton and Winchester, where there were settlements of Italians. It was chiefly the product of small wandering handicraftsmen, who often carved their arabesques on the plain surfaces left by English masons. Another evidence of Italian influence can be seen in the use of terra-cotta, and plaster work in ceilings and friezes, of common occurrence toward the end of the sixteenth century. Although local tradition has usually assigned this to travelling companies of Italians, it was more likely inspired by the work of the Tuscan sculptors of the time of Henry the Eighth, from whom many Englishmen learned the new style.[1] Italian workmen, however, were probably employed at times, as, for instance, on the wooden screens and stalls in the chapel of King's College, Cambridge, where the mouldings show plainly the Renaissance design in all its beauty.

The Italian artists who centred around Wolsey and

[1] Blomfield, *op. cit.*, I, 23, mentions Richard Ridge's work at Hampton Court as an example of this.

Henry the Eighth disappeared as silently as they came. Excepting John of Padua, none seem to have remained in England after the king's death. The English lack of artistic interest and talent caused their places to remain unfilled, even though certain individuals were trying to encourage art. The first Earl of Bedford, who had been in Italy, was probably among its patrons. His tomb, dating from 1556, in the Russel Chapel at Chenies, is quite in the northern Italian style, bearing considerable resemblance to the Sforza monument by Solari at Pavia. The ideal treatment of the eyes, hair and beard all suggest a knowledge of the antique, unshared by any Englishmen of the time; the arabesque decoration of the cushion on which Lady Bedford's head rests is also characteristically Italian. The work on the base, which is of alabaster incrusted with black marble, may have been partly the labor of native artisans, but the statues themselves appear undoubtedly to be the work of an Italian, or at least of some thoroughly Italianated Fleming.

The indirect influence of the Italian artists in England proved of considerable importance. The example they set, their technical skill and ingenuity, the novelty of their designs and forms, must have come like a revelation to English craftsmen. The ancient Gothic architecture had degenerated, and the flamboyant style could not successfully oppose the Renaissance art with its new method of decoration. At the same time, the true Italian influence on English architecture was not to be felt for some time. Of exact copying from Italian buildings there was little or none. The Italian style was considerably modified by transmission through different lands, especially France and the Low Countries. When it once obtained a foothold in England, thousands of native artisans transformed it still further, until its original form could scarcely be recognized.[1] In the earlier buildings, however, numerous Italian traces can still be observed. Not only at Hampton Court, but at Sutton Place, Surrey, Layer Marney in Essex, Guildford, East Barsham and many other localities, there was considerable use made of terracotta for decorative purposes. At Sutton Place, for instance, it was utilized in the *amorini* above the hall door. The arabesque work in the mullions and the small mouldings were all of Italian design.[2]

There were no regular architects in England in the sixteenth century. The work was done by so-called "surveyors," who as a rule were English. Sometimes, as in the building of Wollaton Hall, master workmen were sent for from Italy. Most of the stone figures adorning the house were likewise Italian. Even the pilasters had gondola rings on their pedestals, which were copied from Venice. The circular panels contained busts of classic personages. Many of the niches are, however, empty, tradition ascribing the reason to the wrecking of the ship which was bringing their occupants from Italy.[3]

---

[1] J. Alfred Gotch, *Arch. of the Ren.*, I, xxii.
[2] F. Harrison, *Annals of an Old Manor House*, p. 126.
[3] Gotch, *op. cit.*, II, 62.

In numerous other buildings of the Elizabethan Age, the Italian influence was strongly marked ; Audley End showed it. Moreton Corbet, built in 1599, gave the effect of a *palazzo*. Longford Castle, constructed a year later, with its use of pilasters and columns, its open *loggia* effect and niches for statues, was quite in the Italian style. At Lyveden, the cornice of the new building was brought over from Italy. At Hatfield there was also use of fresco work, and of Italian columns and pilasters, and at Hardwick Hall an Italian portico.[1] When the queen went to Greenwich in 1583, Roger Manners wrote to the Earl of Rutland that " she was never in any place better pleased, and sure the house, garden, and walks may compare with any delicate place in Italy." [2] Gardens especially were imitated from the Italians.

The improvement in English architecture had not taken place over night. In 1550, John Shute, who, besides being a painter and miniaturist, was later to write one of the earliest English treatises on architecture, had been sent to Italy by the Duke of Northumberland to study there under the best architects. It was not, however, until the seventeenth century that, with Inigo Jones, the classic style of Palladio found a new home in England ; but his years of study had been in the reign of Elizabeth. " Being

---

[1] Vide J. A. Gotch, *Early Renaissance Architecture in England* and *Architecture of the Renaissance in England,* for accounts of the subject.

[2] *Hist. Ms. Com.*, Report 12, Appendix IV, p. 150.

naturally inclined," he wrote, "to study the arts of design, I passed into foreign parts to converse with the great masters thereof in Italy." The instruction he received was to bear its fruits in the time of James, but it would scarcely have been possible without the work of the Italians in England, in the first half of the sixteenth century, who prepared and smoothed the way, bridging over the transition between the Gothic and the new style of the Renaissance.

Hardly a single Italian artist of consequence came to England in the reign of Elizabeth ; the few who did come were all of minor importance. Valerio Belli, it is true, the celebrated engraver of gems, is supposed to have visited England and to have carved many portraits in cameo,[1] but even this is doubtful. The processes employed in the medallic art came, however, from Italy.[2] The first medallic portrait of an Englishman was made in Venice in 1480. Although considerably later the art was transplanted to England, it is very unlikely that either Jacopo Trezzo or Primavera, who executed the portraits of Mary, and Mary Queen of Scots, ever set foot on English soil.[3] A great number of paintings of all kinds, few of which have been authenticated, are ascribed to Frederick Zuccaro, who in his four years' residence in England painted Elizabeth and a number of her courtiers. His merit as an artist was

[1] Horace Walpole, *Anecdotes of Painting*, p. 188.

[2] Hawkins and Franks, *Medallic Illustrations of English History*, p. xii.

[3] *Ibid.*, p. 71.

Queen Mary by Trezzo.

Mary Queen of Scots by Primavera.

very slight, and it is scarcely remarkable that his influence was not more strongly felt. Petruccio Ubaldini, who has been mentioned before, was both an illuminator and painter of miniatures at the court. The English miniaturists, however, inclined rather to the French and Flemish schools, even where in other respects they felt the Italian influence. Isaac Oliver, for instance, one of whose drawings in the northern Italian style is reproduced, was quite un-Italian in his miniatures, and the same was true of his master, Nicholas Hilliard.

A taste for art was slowly growing in England, though not much proof of this now remains.[1] Sir Philip Hoby was counted by Titian among his friends. Constable also alluded to Raphael and Michelangelo in his sonnets.[2] Richard Haydocke, in his well-known translation of Lomazzo's *Art of Painting*, greatly deplored the English lack of artistic feeling and the alleged decay of the arts, the cause of which he ascribed largely to the fact that the purchaser would not pay well for the work of art, and in consequence the artist would not do his best. Haydocke's effort was to induce a cultivated class of patrons who might encourage art. From his words it is evident that the English were then beginning to appreciate painting. Previously there had been but few illustrations of this. In the reign of Henry the Seventh, it is true, the Duke of Urbino had sent over as a gift to that mon-

[1] For list of contemporary English painters, vide Francis Meres, *Palladis Tamia*, 1598, p. 287.
[2] Vide p. 143.

arch a small picture by Raphael[1] of St. George slay-
ing the dragon. Presents of similar nature were made
from time to time. The Grand Duke of Tuscany, for
instance, sent Queen Mary a miniature of the Three
Magi.[2] The zeal for collecting works of art, begun in
Italy, had spread to England — " In which point some
of our nobility and divers private gentlemen have very
well acquitted themselves ; as may appear by their
galleries, carefully furnished with the excellent monuments of sundry famous ancient masters, both Italian
and German."[3] Even the native painters were appreciated ; Richard Haydocke desired " the skilful pen of
George Vasari " to draw parallels between English
painters and Italian, and compare Nicholas Hilliard
" with the mild spirit of the late world's wonder,
Raphael Urbini."

It is significant of the interest which was beginning
to be taken in all works of art, especially by such
collectors as the Earl of Arundel, that a special in-
voice of bronzes by John Bologna was not long afterward sent on commission from Florence to London.[4]
Inigo Jones himself purchased works of art, when in

---

[1] Now at St. Petersburg.

[2] *Guardaroba Medicea*, Florence, filza 34.

[3] R. Haydocke, preface to Lomazzo, 1598.

[4] *Guardaroba Medicea*, 293, p. 81. Among other subjects
were represented a Hercules with a club in his hand (perhaps
the one now in the print room of the Fitzwilliam Museum,
Cambridge), a Hercules killing the Centaur, a woman with a
ball, a figure of Fortune, a Centaur carrying away Dejanira, etc.
In this consignment there were also several wax figures.

Italy, for the Earl of Arundel and Lords Pembroke and Danvers. The history of the collector's zeal in England rightly belongs, however, to a later period than the age of Elizabeth.

III

The Reformation has, until recently, been regarded almost as an exclusively Teutonic counterpart of the Italian Renaissance. As a result of this, the ethical and religious influence of Italy has been underrated, even when not entirely neglected. Toward the end of the sixteenth century it had become almost a fashion for moralists to see in Italy only a centre of vice and corruption. Partly, perhaps, on account of the survival of this idea, partly through ignorance, the sterner and more austere aspects of Italian life were generally overlooked. The religious enthusiasm of a Savonarola lay covered by the iniquity of the Borgias. The great crimes of the age, and not its virtues, alone struck the popular eye. It would, however, be a very one-sided estimate of the Italian Renaissance to regard it as an age when only the arts and learning flourished in an atmosphere of depravity. To deny the excesses committed, or the vice of the age, would be no less untrue than to blind one's eyes to its piety, which existed then, all the brighter, perhaps, for the evil which surrounded it. Too little attention has been given to the Italian religious influence in England, first noticeable in the effect of the humanist criticism of the Scriptures on Grocyn and Colet. The Italian reformers who found their way to England in the reign of Henry the Eighth showed a different side of the same influence.

Among the most eminent of these was Bernardino Ochino, a Capuchin monk of Siena, considered to be the most eloquent preacher of his time in all Italy. He had gradually drifted toward an attitude of dissent from Rome, and in consequence had been obliged to seek refuge elsewhere. His love of truth, it was said, led him to choose suffering and exile rather than wealth and honors. Because he followed " the true gospel," he had been persecuted by Paul the Third, who forced him to leave Italy.[1] In 1547 he went to England, at Cranmer's invitation. He received there a hearty welcome, was granted a crown pension, and appointed preacher of the Italian church in London. His presence in England attracted considerable attention, and his sermons were often translated, being among the most popular theological books of the time. In 1549, Bishop Ponet translated his *Tragedy*,[2] which had for its subject the rise of the papacy and contained a severe indictment directed against the Church of Rome. Ochino's sermons proved more popular, however, passing through several editions. The first appeared the year after his arrival in England, and was dedicated to the Duke of Somerset. In the address to the reader, the printer mentioned the

[1] Preface to the *Sermons of Ochino*, 1548.
[2] *The Tragedy by Bernardino Ochino*, 1549. A remarkable parallel between it and *Paradise Lost* has been pointed out by Dr. Garnett.

translations of the Scriptures, then beginning to be widely known. The prophets and patriarchs, it was said, were now familiar to all having " become English men. . . . God himself in our own tongue speaketh to us . . . and Paul being a Hebrew born hath changed his tongue, and is become ours, as though he had been bred and brought up all the days of his life amongst us." In consequence of the evil conditions in England, God had sent prophets out of strange countries. " Amongst the which, Bernardinus Ochinus and Petrus Martyr, men of great learning which are now come unto us." Inasmuch as Ochino's sermons had been preached in Italian, a selection of six were at first translated, with the intention of publishing the others, should the first meet with favor. In this way, it was hoped, " his native tongue thereby may be made ours." The chief object of the sermons was to show the benefits of making proper use of the Scriptures to attain knowledge of the Deity. Their further popularity was attested by an enlarged edition, printed not long afterward by a different publisher.

Another translation of Ochino's sermons [1] by Anne Cooke was more interesting. It was intended to show the spiritual side of the Italians and prove that a study of the language need by no means be fruitless from the religious point of view, although the object of this edition was to make Ochino's doctrines accessible to those ignorant of Italian. To defend the book seemed, however, unnecessary to the translator, since the author

[1] *Fourteen Sermons of Barnadine Ochyne* (1550 ?).

lived in England — "A man whose life without words would be sufficient protection to his work." As late, indeed, as 1580 a new edition appeared of Ochino's sermons[1] which praised the spiritual wisdom of the author and the "pure and perfect godliness of his works."

Peter Martyr Vermigli, the friend and contemporary of Ochino, was born in Florence, where his father had been a follower of Savonarola. He himself had studied for eight years at Padua, and came under the influence of the Spanish reformer, Juan de Valdes. In 1547, with Ochino, he had been invited by Cranmer to come to England. Together they were placed in the charge of John Abell, an English merchant, who escorted them from Basle to London, where Peter Martyr lived for some time with Cranmer. He was given a crown pension, was soon afterward made Regius professor of divinity at Oxford and later appointed to the first canonry of Christ Church. Peter Martyr was one of the three persons whom Cranmer associated with himself in revising the ecclesiastical laws. Cranmer selected him also to aid him in defending the Book of Common Prayer, established under Edward the Sixth when, at the beginning of Mary's reign, he challenged the Romanists to a public disputation. The two were on terms of cordial intimacy and friendship; the archbishop made particular use of him in the different steps of the Reformation, and

[1] *Certain Godly Sermons*, translated by William Phiston, 1580.

whenever he could be spared from his public readings at Oxford would send for him,[1] it was said, to confer on matters of importance.

Peter Martyr was also a prolific writer, and many of his works were translated into English. While few are of interest to the layman, they yet show the influence of an Italian in shaping the course of the English Reformation. His Puritanism appeared, for instance, in his tract on the *Abuse of Dancing*, in which he proved its wickedness by the Scriptures. One of his many religious treatises was translated by Nicholas Udall for the benefit of such curates and other good people " who in default of sufficient learning are unable thoroughly to instruct their flocks, nor to stop the mouths of malicious people, and of Papists." His most important writings, however, were the commentaries on the Scriptures; in his great book of *Commonplaces*, later translated by Anthony Martin,[2] were contained his ideas on the subject, and many inquiries on predestination, justification by faith, and the salvation of man through Christ. The work was especially praised for reproving the errors and heresies of Rome, and its author was eulogized for having devoted his life to preaching Protestantism in England. To accomplish this, it was said, he had left his own wealth and repose. His letters were also published, but contain little of general interest save his sorrows for Italy, and complaints of the penury in England " of the word of

[1] Strype, *Thomas Cranmer*, I, 593.
[2] *The Commonplaces of Peter Martyr*, 1583.

God." Like his other writings, the letters were full of an intense zeal and a deep religious enthusiasm not commonly associated with the Italians of the Renaissance.

The religious influence Italy exerted on Protestant England was by no means confined to the few reformers who came over. Even then a devotional and religious literature flourished south of the Alps which was known in England. Edward Courtenay, Earl of Devon, during his long imprisonment in the Tower, translated, in 1548, Aonio Paleario's book on the *Benefit of Christ's Death*,[1] a work of such extraordinary popularity in the sixteenth century that, until condemned by the Inquisition, it was admired alike by pious Catholics and those who favored the Reformation.

England then became a home and refuge for Italian reformers, just as in the nineteenth century it was one for political refugees. Jacopo Calco was another Italian theologian who came over for religious reasons.[2] Giulio Terenziano, better known in England as Julius, followed Peter Martyr, and in later years came such men as Jacopo Acontio, author of *Satan's Stratagems*, Alessandro Cittolini[3] and Giulio Borgarucci, who, arriving a Protestant refugee, later became court physician. Francesco Pucci was also one whose

[1] *Trattato Utilissimo*, by Antonio della Paglia, known as Aonio Paleario. Another English rendering of this book was made by Arthur Golding from its French translation.

[2] Bale, *Scriptorium Illustrium*, 1557, II, 140.

[3] Vide Roger Ascham, *Epistolæ, passim*.

reforming zeal led him to London and Oxford, where he delivered a course of lectures in theology. Still another was Pietro Bizari of Perugia, an historian and poet who described himself as " an exile from Italy his native country by reason of his confession of the doctrine of the Gospel." Michael Angelo Florio, a Florentine Protestant who had come over to England, in addition to being a teacher of Italian, became, in 1550, preacher to the congregation of Italian Protestants in London. This had been established chiefly through the influence of Archbishop Cranmer and Sir William Cecil. The archbishop obtained certain privileges for the members of the congregation, who were to be treated like free denizens, and given permission to reside and do business in London, with as much freedom as native-born Englishmen. The only obligation they were under was to swear fidelity and allegiance. Other requests were granted them from time to time, and many joined the church for worldly reasons. In spite of these advantages, quite a few returned to the Roman service. Florio complained of this to Cecil, then secretary of state, who bade him prepare a list of the apostates' names, which he did. The secretary sent for these, and informed them that, since they were citizens, and in consequence subject to English law, they ought to be punished the same as other Englishmen who heard the mass.[1] Florio, whose morals were not of the best, subsequently lost the favor of Cecil, who had before been his friend;

[1] Strype, *Memorials*, p. 343 *et seq.*

Jerome Zerlito later became the pastor of this church. Its existence for many years is perhaps the best proof of the Italian colony in London. Roger Ascham alluded to it, in condemning the courtiers who went there to hear the language and not for the service; "Italianated Englishmen," he called them,[1] who were unable to abide the godly Italian church at home and attended it only to listen to the Italian tongue naturally spoken.

The Italian reformers in England prove how one-sided any judgment would be, which laid down absolutely the nature of the Italian influence in England, condemning it for the same reasons which once acted on moralists like Ascham. The Italian spiritual nature, though less on the surface than its carnal side, was yet to be found by those who sought it. There were many besides John Colet who felt the Italian influences of piety and austerity.

IV

The Italians of the Renaissance were the first modern people to take note of the traits and characteristics of other nations. Beginning with Poggio and Æneas Sylvius, they recorded at length their impressions of foreign countries. During the sixteenth century a series of deep and accurate studies of national character was written by the Venetian ambassadors, one of whose duties it was to keep their government posted

[1] *Scholemaster*, p. 82.

on the condition of the countries with whom they had diplomatic relations. This had been the custom since the early years of the republic. The Grand Council decreed, in 1268, that all Venetian ambassadors on their return should report in full their proceedings to the signory, being supplied with a clerk to write out the narrative. By degrees it became usual to add descriptions of the country visited, and these were often elaborated at considerable length. The Venetian reports became celebrated as models of what such work should be, and copies were eagerly sought for in other countries as well.[1]

The Italian accounts of England in the sixteenth century were of several different kinds. Without considering the numerous letters containing information on many subjects, or the sharp but scattered impressions which Bruno recorded in the *Supper of Ashes*, partial descriptions of England can be found in such diaries as that of the Milanese merchant, who travelled there in 1518,[2] and in Jerome Cardan's experiences in the reign of Edward the Sixth; also in Paolus Jovius' and Botero's general histories and geographies.

The Venetian relations, however, were by far the most important. Although diplomatic intercourse, centring mainly on commercial questions, had existed for some time between the two states, yet Andrea Trevisani's embassy to the English court, in 1497, was really the first. During the sixteenth century, the Venetian

---

[1] *Cal. St. Pap., Ven.*, I, xliii *et seq.*
[2] Add. Ms. 24,180, Brit. Mus.

ambassadors in England numbered twenty-three in all. Diplomatic intercourse ceased almost entirely in the reign of Elizabeth, owing to the religious differences.[1]

The reports of the different ambassadors have many elements in common. The model the writers employed was the same, and they saw things through similar eyes. At the same time the outward panorama was continually changing. For this reason, while each " relation " serves in one way to corroborate the others, it adds also a certain amount of fresh material.

Almost invariably in the sixteenth century the first desire of any one who wished to relate the experiences of his travels was to preface these with a general account of the country he had visited. England was still too remote and distant a nation, and accurate knowledge too scarce, for its physical characteristics not to be of interest. This is scarcely the place, how- ever, to dwell on such matters. The government of the country, the crown revenues, parliament and judi- ciary can be passed over likewise, although naturally of the greatest interest to the signory for whose benefit these accounts were written. It may briefly be said that the liberties enjoyed by Englishmen and their freedom from oppressive taxes especially impressed the shrewd Italian observer.

Although the English characteristics noticed would be too numerous to mention here, the general im- pression derived from reading these accounts is one of keen and accurate observation. The religious trans-

---

[1] Baschet, *Diplomatie Venitienne*, p. 106.

formation of the country was naturally of great interest to the intelligent foreigner, and one writer, at least, described in detail the new prayer book of 1549 which made use of the English language, and the new church ceremonies and regulations.[1] England, especially in the first half of the sixteenth century, was passing through a period of transition, and the numerous changes of faith undergone perhaps almost justified one critic's remarks, that the English used religion merely as a cloak; that they believed what the king believed, and if he were to turn Mahometan or Jew, they would follow suit.[2]

The great effort of the kings of Spain ever since the Reformation had been directed to bringing England back to the Roman faith, accomplishing thereby both a political and a religious end. The military resources of England were consequently a matter of considerable interest, even to states which were neutral. Foreigners' opinions on English soldiers varied considerably, although certain of the traits then noticed still continue to hold true at the present day.

One of the least favorable of military critics was a certain Giovanni Sovico, who had lived many years in England, and gave as his opinion that ten or twelve thousand Spanish or Italian infantry and two thousand cavalry would be sufficient to restore the Catholic religion.[3] Petruccio Ubaldini, who had served in the Scotch war, thought it to be the general impression that if a

---

[1] Relazione Ubaldini, f. 93.   [2] Relazione Michele, f. 22 *et seq.*
[3] Arch. Med. Flor., 4185, *Letter to Father Panigarola.*

foreign prince were only able to land an army on English soil, and win the first battle, he would encounter no further difficulties, since, owing to the inability of the people to endure fatigue, and their nature, they would no longer oppose him. He went on to explain that this was not so easy as it seemed at first sight. All similar attempts since the Conquest had failed, and William only succeeded on account of the weakness of the opposing army.[1] Italian critics, generally, agreed on the English inability to withstand fatigue, and their need of an abundant meat diet. Without a great supply of food they were able to endure but little exertion.[2] "When war was raging most furiously, they would look for good eating and all their other comforts without thinking of what harm might befall them."[3] Although they showed great aptitude for sport, and readiness in times of danger, it could not be said that they cared much for arms. Their only opportunity to make use of them was in war, and once that was over they forgot all about them.[4] English soldiers enjoyed, however, a high reputation, and from the fear the French held them in, it was believed to have been justly acquired.[5] The critics singled out for especial praise the English proficiency in the use of the long bow.[6]

---

[1] Ubaldini, f. 83.

[2] *Ibid.*, f. 112 *b.*   Rel. Soranzo, 1554, ed. Alberi, Pt. II, p. 53.

[3] *Relation of England*, 1500, p. 22 *et seq.*

[4] Soranzo, p. 52.   [5] *Rel. of England, loc. cit.*

[6] Rel. Raviglio, Ms. Siena, Libreria comunale K., X, 29, f. 64, and *Cal. St. Pap., Ven.*, IV, 285–289.

It was easily recognized that the natural strength of the country lay in its insular position. Long before the Armada, the Italians appreciated the fact that the strong point of the English was in naval warfare, where they succeeded much better and were far braver than on land. They placed reliance in their ships, and, utterly regardless of death, performed prodigies of valor with them. The courage of English sailors in their attack was wonderful, wrote another writer. "These people fight to the death; and it is their habit before they sail, to swear to one another that they will fire the ship rather than yield themselves prisoners. So resolute is this race in battle."[1] This courage was admired in other respects as well. It was noticed especially that Englishmen had often been seen laughing while on their way to the stake or gibbet, ridiculing, as it were, such martyrdom.[2]

To the foreign diplomatist, especially, whose glimpses of national life were largely obtained at court, the reigning prince was always a subject of great interest. His relatives and favorites, his accomplishments, and even his most trivial wishes were all mentioned.[3] Surrounding Henry the Eighth, it was said, were many Spaniards and Italians of every profession, who in turn had a company of courtiers running after them, anxious to learn foreign languages.[4] The etiquette of the court,

---

[1] *Cal. St. Pap.*, *Ven.*, IX, 239.
[2] Litolfi, *Epist. cit.*, *Cal. St. Pap.*, *Ven.*, VI, 1668–73.
[3] Rel. Falier, 1531, ed. Alberi, Pt. II, p. 10 *et seq.*
[4] *Cal. St. Pap.*, *Ven.*, IV, 285–289.

and the continual use of ceremonies on the slightest occasion, seemed almost ridiculous to the Italian observer. Whether the king was present or absent there existed the same formalities.[1] It was the duty of the president of the royal council, the highest official in all England, to serve the sovereign at table.[2] Ubaldini had seen the Princess Elizabeth kneel five times in succession to the king, her father, before sitting down. It was even customary for the children of Henry the Eighth to address him on bended knees.

The daily life of Edward the Sixth was similarly described. Cardan, who saw the young king when still in his fifteenth year, wrote that he was skilled in seven languages. His tennis, horsemanship and archery were noticed, as well as the fact that his riding and dancing master, and many of his musicians, were Italians.[3] The attention of later travellers centred naturally on Queen Elizabeth, who was to become the most conspicuous figure of her age. In her youth, report had it that she lived a life of such splendor as could hardly be imagined. Much of her time was occupied by balls and banquets, hunting, and similar amusements, all of which were conducted with the greatest possible display. She insisted, however, that far greater respect be shown her than the late queen had exacted; and although she had summoned Parliament, she gave orders that her commands be executed, even if contrary to its will.[4]

---

[1] Rel. Raviglio, Ms. cit., f. 70.   [3] Ubaldini, f. 43 *b*.
[2] *Ibid.*, f. 64.   [4] *Cal. St. Pap., Ven.*, VII, 659.

Shortly after her accession, one envoy wrote regarding the likelihood of any foreigner ascending the throne. "During the last twenty years three princes of the blood, four dukes, forty earls, and more than three thousand other persons have died by violent death. It may therefore be easily imagined that no foreigner could rule this kind of people, when even their own countrymen are not safe. . . . Queen Elizabeth, who has succeeded to the throne . . . declines to rely upon any one save herself, although she is most gracious to all."[1] Her personal appearance was often described as well. Even in her seventieth year, it was said of her that she walked straight as a rod, *com' una canna*, clad all in white.[2]

Next in interest came the nobles directly after the sovereign. Poggio remarked in his day that they considered it disgraceful to live in towns, and judged the degree of a man's nobility by the extent of his estates. Their time was spent in agriculture, although they did not consider trading in wool and sheep to be beneath their dignity. He himself had known a wealthy merchant, who having invested his money in land became the founder of a noble race; and had likewise seen admitted into the highest circles many persons of low birth who had been ennobled on account of their warlike achievements.[3] Later in the sixteenth century, although very few of the old nobility remained, they yet

[1] *Cal. St. Pap., Ven.*, VII, 328 *et seq.*
[2] Arch. Med. Flor., 4185, July, 1599.
[3] Letter of Oct. 29th, 1420.

made use of almost royal ceremony, and were looked
upon with nearly as much respect as the monarch himself. They had their followers and retainers, who at
their lord's command would fight even against the king.
The people regarded them as their representatives, although the crown had often tried to break their power.
The nobles, except when at court, lived in the country
where they kept open house with great retinues of servants,[1] the Earl of Pembroke alone having more than
a thousand, who were all attired in his livery. Furthermore, there was not a lord in the land who did not
have foreign servants and gentlemen in his service.[2]

At the end of the fifteenth century, an Italian traveller in England had noticed that the common people
were held in but little higher regard than serfs.[3] Subsequent writers did not observe this, but many petty vex-
ations remained to indicate differences of rank. Thus,
even fifty years later, while commoners were forbidden
to go around at night without good reason, noblemen
might do so.[4] Another difference was that while the
nobility were extremely polite, especially to foreigners,
the populace were just as hostile.[5] The common people
had indeed many curious habits. Toward the infirm
they would show compassion in this way; if a man
were given up by the physicians and there was absolutely no hope, his nearest relatives would take a pil-
low, place it on his head, and then sit on it until he

---

[1] Soranzo, p. 52 *et seq.*
[2] Ubaldini, f. 116 *b.*
[3] *Rel. of England*, p. 34.
[4] Raviglio, Ms. cit., f. 71.
[5] Soranzo, *loc. cit.*

suffocated, a father doing this to his son, or a son to his own father; and they did it thinking that since there was no chance for his recovery, it was an act of charity to relieve him from his pain.[1] Another trait noticed was that when they fought, it was usually about some trifle, and after having exchanged a few thrusts with each other in the German fashion (*Coltellate alla Tedesca*), when one had wounded the other, they made peace instantly and went to drink together. They had not the point of honor of Italians, either as regards women or when the lie was given.[2]

The freedom allowed women was very puzzling to the Italians, who often misinterpreted it. It was in striking contrast to what a former traveller had alluded to when he said that the English kept very jealous guard over their wives.[3] Most writers agreed about the great attractiveness of English women; one proclaimed that in no respect were they inferior to the women of Siena or any of the most esteemed in Italy;[4] others, too, alluded to their handsome presence, fine complexions and ready wit, saying that only at Augsburg were their equals to be seen.[5] It was the liberty they enjoyed, however, which amazed the foreigners so much; no one inquired as to what they did either at home or abroad, and under pretence

[1] Relazione Daniele Barbaro, Ed. Alberi, 1551, Pt. I, p. 157.
[2] Letters of Annibale Litolfi to the Duke of Mantua, June 20, 1557, *Cal. St. Pap., Ven.,* VI, 1668-73.
[3] *Rel. of England,* p. 23.
[4] Ubaldini, Ms. cit., f. 114 *b.*   [5] Litolfi, *Epist. cit.*

of going out for meals, they could do what they liked. Married women especially, either alone or with a female companion, would accept invitations to dine, not only from an Englishman but a foreigner as well. It was said to be the custom, after having spoken once or twice to any woman, on meeting her again in the street " to take her to a tavern where all persons go without any reserve, or some other place, the husband not taking it amiss but remaining obliged to you and always thanking you, and if he sees you with her he departs."[1] Another curious custom mentioned was that if a man should give flowers to a lady, she had to wear them for three months (sic), when they were exchanged for others.

Great surprise was shown at the alleged want of affection displayed by Englishmen toward their children ; every one, however rich, sent his children away into the houses of others, receiving those of strangers in return ; the reason given for such severity was that they might learn better manners ; but one traveller,[2] at least, thought it was because they liked to enjoy all their comforts themselves, and that they were better served by strangers than they would be by their own children, since the English were great epicures and liked to indulge in the most delicate fare themselves, while the rest they gave to their household. The English fondness for food and long dinners was a trait always noticed by the more frugal Italians, who called

[1] Litolfi, *loc. cit.*
[2] *Rel. of England*, p. 25.

them gluttons,[1] and remarked that they ate five or six times a day.[2] Many years before Poggio had dreaded, while in England, the meals which sometimes lasted four hours, where he was obliged to wash his eyes with cold water to keep himself awake;[3] others, too, bore witness to similar conditions, and a century later this practice still continued, although conversation with ladies then accounted for part of the time spent. "The English thought no greater honor could be conferred or received than to invite others to eat with them or to be invited themselves; and they would sooner give five or six ducats to provide an entertainment for a person, than a groat to assist him in any distress."[4]

A characteristic noticed was their enjoyment of comfort. They loved their ease, and there was no peasant who did not ride on horseback; England was even called the land of comforts. Among the national traits observed was also their desire for novelty and change,[5] and their inconstancy, for which they were renowned in the sixteenth century. One day they did one thing in regard to religion, and the next day another.[6] An Italian, alluding to their fondness for novelty, says of them that they attempted to do anything that came into their heads, just as if what the imagination suggested could easily be executed; hence it was, he said, that a greater number of insurrections had broken out in England than in all the rest of the world. It

---

[1] Poggio, *Epist.*, I, 43.

[2] Litolfi, *Epist. cit.*, p. 1671. Vide Ubaldini, f. 112 *b*.

[3] Vespasiano, p. 420.   [5] Falier, p. 26.

[4] *Rel. of England*, p. 22 *et seq.*   [6] Barbaro, p. 18.

was perhaps on account of this that many people would boast of the members of their family who had been executed. "Lately a foreigner, having asked an English captain if any one of his family had been hanged and quartered, was answered, 'not that he knew of.' Another Englishman whispered to the foreigner, 'Don't be surprised, for he is not a gentleman.'"[1]

A certain arrogance and feeling of superiority over other nations was also noticed of the English. Litolfi remarked of it in a letter, "The man who said that England was a paradise inhabited by devils did not deceive himself."[2] Long before this it was said that the English were great lovers of themselves and of everything belonging to them; that they thought there were no other men as good as they were, and no other world but England. If they but shared some delicacy with a stranger they would ask him if such a thing was to be found in his country; and whenever they saw a handsome foreigner, they would say he looked like an Englishman, or that it was a pity he was not an Englishman.[3] They considered themselves handsomer than any other nation in the world.[4] Still another writer remarked that its inhabitants thought nothing existed outside England, from which they proceeded to such silly propositions that they aroused the laughter even of their own countrymen of better judgment.[5]

Many of the customs of the country were also

---

[1] Litolfi, *Epist. cit.* [2] *Ibid.* [3] *Rel. of England*, p. 20.
[4] Litolfi, *ibid.* [5] Ubaldini, Ms. cit., f. 115 *b.*

described by the writers on the subject. The fashion
in travelling was for gentlemen to be followed by their
servants, one of whom carried a valise containing his
master's cloak, hat and a book, while the others went
behind, bearing each a little round buckler and a
sword. Ladies travelled on horseback preceded by
footmen, and followed by their maids of honor, who
were usually of noble birth.[1]

The system of wards in chancery, a source of royal
revenue, by which the crown administered the estates
of orphans, and enjoyed the income until their coming of age, was described. The king enriched his
retainers by giving them wealthy wards in marriage,
to whom, if rejected, they were obliged to pay a
year's revenues. Matches were often purposely proposed, so that they might be refused, in order to gain
this money for the favorite of either sex.[2] Women, it
was noticed, were given but small dowries. Many
houses, however, such as the Arundels, had been enriched through the female line, the reason for this
being that, on a man's marriage, one-third of his estate
was settled on his wife, and in case of her remaining
a widow she could dispose of it as she liked, if there
were no children. The king, therefore, would often
try to marry one of his courtiers to a rich widow, and,
in case she refused her consent, he could seize her
estate pretending it was his intention to unite it to
another's. For fear of this many widows married
almost immediately after their husband's death.[3]

[1] Litolfi, *Epist. cit.*   [2] Raviglio, f. 62.   [3] Rel. Michele, f. 28.

It was said of the English that they were gifted with good understandings, and quick at anything they applied their mind to. In the beginning of the sixteenth century it was noticed that few except the clergy were given to study; later, however, one writer remarked that many of the women, and above all the nobility, were very learned in the classics. One curious bit of advice given by Ubaldini to his compatriots was for them to be careful not to offend Englishmen by a flat contradiction, but little by little to show them the truth, which they would then recognize.[1]

[1] Ms. cit., f. 116.

CHAPTER VI

THE ITALIAN MERCHANT IN ENGLAND

I

THE condition of commerce in England, through the long period of the Middle Ages, was in striking contrast to its importance in Italy. One country had remained to a great extent an agricultural community, the chief export of which was wool; the other, situated midway between Western Europe and the East, had developed a commercial life in its city republics far in advance of what was then known elsewhere. Coinciding with the first development of the Renaissance, there came a great expansion of trade. Long before this, however, the Venetians and Genoese in the Orient, and the Italian merchants in Western Europe, made of their country a central point in the commerce of the world. At a time when all the rest of Europe was still deep in the Middle Ages, the Italian city communities had realized the benefits which were to be derived from trade. A rapid accumulation of wealth followed the success of their undertakings. They were the first who introduced commercial life and ideas into the countries of Western Europe, teaching them banking and a knowledge of financial affairs. In commerce, as in literature and the arts, Italy led the way for the rest of Europe to follow.

In the great fairs that were held in Champagne, in the early Middle Ages, the Italian merchants had taken a prominent part. They had then gradually branched out, first going to Flanders, and then crossing the channel to England. They came over, likewise, in the trains of the Roman prelates sent to foreign countries, acting as their business men and bankers, and often too as the papal collectors of revenue.

Commercial relations of one nature or another had existed between Italy and England from very early times. Thus Otto degli Gherardini, a rich Florentine, was in England toward the end of the eleventh century, and acquired much landed property; his son, Walter Fitz Otto, became castellan of Windsor. A little later King John carried on negotiations with the *Mercatores Tuscie*, as they were then called, and even forbade them at one time to do business in England,[1] although he granted commercial privileges to a Venetian. On another occasion the great Florentine family of Bardi became impoverished, through having lent money to Prince Henry, the son of Henry the Second, which was never repaid. The Italian merchants, however, who had come over to England prior to 1229, were the exception, rather than the rule. In that year Master Stephen, chaplain and nuncio of the Pope, who had been charged to collect the tithes to

[1] Vide Davidsohn, *Geschichte von Florenz*, I, 798. Goldschmidt, *Universal Geschichte des Handelsrechts*, I, 186.

pay the expenses of the war which was to be waged against Frederick the Second, appeared with several of them in his retinue, who engaged in business under the papal protection.[1] The Pope, moreover, induced the unwary Henry the Third to accept for his second son, Edmund, the crown of Sicily. As security for the payment of the money he had expended, the Pope obtained a hold on English religious houses, and, in order to administer his affairs, numerous Italians were sent over. In the meantime more and more English money flowed into Sicily, till, at last, the barons, exasperated, rose in revolt to depose the king, while the Pope deprived the son of the empty title which had proved so ruinous to his father.[2]

The first half of the fourteenth century was a period of great commercial prosperity for the merchants and traders of Italy. The Italian bankers who accompanied the collectors of the papal tithes attended to forwarding, to the Curia, the sums they collected. From this time the names of Florentine, Sienese and Luccan bankers and money lenders appear on the English rolls, and in Italy, it was said, whoever had any ready money at his disposal became at once a banker.[3] The Italian merchants in England prospered greatly, and in very few years extended their enterprises throughout the kingdom;[4] the king and the

[1] Matthew Paris, *Chronica*, IV, 410.
[2] *Archæologia*, XXVIII, 237.
[3] Vide F. Patetta in *Bollettino Senese di Storia Patria*, IV, 320 *et seq.*   [4] Matthew Paris, *op. cit.*, III, 328 *et seq.*

clergy especially were in their debt for enormous amounts.

In 1240, a royal edict was issued expelling foreign merchants [1] on the ground of their iniquitous usury, but many of them managed to escape this decree by bribery. Some eleven years later, when they had once more settled comfortably in London, and were living under papal protection in the finest houses of the city, the king, perhaps because in need of money which they were unwilling to supply, accused them of being heretics and guilty of *lèse majesty*. They were charged with contaminating England by their usury, as well as with offending the royal conscience by practices which were contrary to the precepts of the church ; but this persecution ended, like others, in the payment of money. [2]

In spite of the many risks involved, England offered a profitable field for the enterprise of Italian bankers and merchants, and it is not surprising to find many of them, as, for instance, the Salimbeni family of Siena, returning to their native city and purchasing castles and estates in the neighborhood. In 1262, however, the Pope issued a bull against the Sienese, declaring them excommunicate, and furthermore decreeing that no debts be paid them until they had made their peace with the church. [3] Exceptions were soon made to this edict, and before long the Sienese were once again under the papal protection,

[1] Matthew Paris, *op. cit.*, IV, 8.   [2] Patetta, *op. cit.*, p. 331.
[3] *Ibid.*, p. 340.

although in the meantime they had suffered considerably. An incident which occurred about this time illustrates at once the jealousy which existed between the merchants of the different Italian cities, and the declining power of the Sienese as compared to the Florentines. Henry the Third, at the instigation of the latter, had expelled from England all Sienese bankers and merchants, who in consequence addressed a letter[1] to the king's brother, Richard, Duke of Cornwall, the newly elected emperor of the Holy Roman Empire, requesting his protection and defaming the Florentines as the enemies of mankind. From 1260 the Sienese yielded the palm to their rivals, who assumed the mastership. The Florentines long preserved the lead they had won. In 1375 Gregory the Eleventh issued his bull in which he declared them excommunicate. William Courtenay, Archbishop of Canterbury, published it in England, whereupon the Londoners pillaged the houses of all Florentine merchants. The king, in consequence of this, took them under his protection, and obtained thereby large sums of money, while on the other hand the archbishop was summoned to answer for his conduct.

The Italians at first had been merely trading merchants or agents of the Pope. They were, as a rule, members of established companies doing business in common. Thus, under Edward the First, there were four such companies of Sienese merchants known as *campsores Papæ*. As papal agents they had to remit

---

[1] Donati, *Boll. Stor. Pat. Sen.*, V, 257.

yearly to Rome one-tenth of the profits on ecclesiastical property. The king's connivance in this was often purchased by allowing him a share as well.[1] The Pope, moreover, was at first their protector, and interceded with the king in their behalf in case of trouble. Already before the end of Henry the Third's reign the Italians had obtained a firm footing in England. The facilities they enjoyed enabled them to issue letters of credit to ambassadors,[2] and bills of exchange were probably sold only by them. They also forwarded the money necessary to conduct the many English ecclesiastical lawsuits and cases, which were continually being pleaded in Rome.[3] In England, on the other hand, they purchased wool; the returns still exist of the quantity of wool in the possession of ten different companies of Italian merchants in the reign of Edward the First.[4] At a time, moreover, when it was extremely difficult to raise money on credit, princes like Henry the Third and the first three Edwards made use of their resources. Under Edward the First they enjoyed close connection with the throne, and the merchants of Lucca even remitted him from England the necessary sums for his expenses in Palestine,[5] and kept him informed of what went on at home. Later, when he became king, he fostered their trade and induced them to come over in considerable numbers, obtaining readily from them the money he could find nowhere else. Interest was rarely promised in the

---

[1] *Arch.*, XXVIII, 214 *et seq.*   [2] *Ibid.*, p. 218.
[3] *Ibid.*   [4] *Ibid.*, p. 220.   [5] *Ibid.*, p. 241.

royal loans from Italians, for interest meant usury, and usurers were liable to be treated as heretics; but charges of usury were often avoided by making loans gratuitous for a period. Instead of interest an additional amount was usually given as compensation for any losses or expenses incurred. Thus £10,000 was granted by Edward the First to the Frescobaldi of Florence [1] to reimburse them for the losses they had suffered, and similar premiums were often given. Later, however, as loans grew larger, interest began to be paid. Edward the Third, for instance, was obliged to grant it on 140,000 florins he had borrowed from a merchant of Lucca, and engage himself furthermore not to cross the seas until the sum advanced had been repaid. Security for loans was usually given by an assignment of a portion of the royal revenue for the amount received. Edward the Third surrendered all the customs of the kingdom for one year to the Bardi of Florence, who had undertaken to provide 1000 florins every month for the expenses of the royal household.[2] Often the great noblemen and sometimes the Italian merchants themselves would become the king's securities to other companies of their countrymen for sums advanced; Lord Derby was even confined in France for debts in which he had been the king's security, until he was released by the company of Leopardi who advanced the required sum.[3] Under Edward the First all the revenues of Ireland were assigned to the Frescobaldi in payment

[1] Vide *Arch.*, p. 229.   [2] *Ibid.*, p. 230.   [3] *Ibid.*

of a loan of £11,000;[1] for in Ireland the Italians were hardly less active than in England. The customs indeed came more often into their hands than into the royal treasury during the latter part of the first Edward's reign, and in the early years of Edward the Second all its receipts were made over to them.[2]

Another source of remuneration was obtained by means of the various commercial privileges granted them. If it had not been for the king's good will, the Italians could scarcely have been able to pursue their undertakings. By an ancient custom they were obliged to dispose of their cargo within forty days after landing, and so-called hosts were awarded them to watch and report on their dealings; but almost the only notices which occur of these restraints are in the petitions of English merchants regarding their infringement.[3] The offices to which they were appointed were another source of profit; they were often collectors of subsidies and customs, and the mint was generally in their charge, the coiners being principally Italians. But they held positions of greater trust as well; Amerigo de Frescobaldi was constable of Bordeaux under Edward the Second, and Alberto de' Medici was justice of the Jews of Agenois at the same time.[4] They seem also to have acted as royal agents and emissaries in foreign parts; under the second and third Edwards, Antonio Pessagno and Antonio Bache, merchants of Genoa, were frequently

1 *Arch.*, p. 290.
2 *Ibid.*, p. 231.
3 *Ibid.*, p. 232 *et seq.*
4 *Ibid.*, p. 233.

engaged abroad in the king's affairs.[1] The favor they enjoyed in England can be seen also in royal letters recommending them to the Pope and the king of France. The natural talents of the Italians fitted them peculiarly for all diplomatic work; as an illustration of this, it was said that, in 1244, there were no less than twelve Florentines at the Vatican acting as ambassadors from the different states of Europe.[2]

The great success enjoyed by the Italian merchants and money lenders in England roused native jealousy and hatred. At the death of Edward the First, the Frescobaldis alone obtained £56,500 out of his estate of £118,000, and much of the remainder went to pay other Italian creditors.[3] In the statutes of the Barons in the time of Edward the Second, several articles were directed especially against them: thus the customs were no longer to be trusted to aliens, and all who had received profits from them were to be arrested with their goods, and obliged to render account of their receipts. Amerigo de Frescobaldi, then constable of Bordeaux, was made a particular object of persecution in a special article directed against him. These measures checked the Italian money lenders for a time, and most of their loans after that were made to religious houses and private individuals,[4] with whom dealings were safer.

The greatest blow of all was to be received in

[1] *Arch.*, p. 234.

[2] *Delle eccelenze . . . della nazione Fiorentina*, p. 18.

[3] *Arch.*, p. 249 *et seq.*   [4] *Ibid.*, p. 257.

the reign of Edward the Third. The Bardi and Peruzzi of Florence had assisted that monarch to the full extent of their capital, and it was their money alone which enabled him to financier and carry on his wars with France. In spite of the successful ending of this war, the payment of the sums they had lent was constantly deferred. Although all the royal revenue and wool passed into their hands, yet their outlays were so much greater that, when the war was over, it was found that the king owed the Bardi 100,000 and the Peruzzi over 135,000 marks sterling. Much of this was not their own, but had been borrowed or received in trust from citizens and strangers. Unable finally to meet their obligations, they lost their credit and became bankrupt. In consequence of this, Florence received a great shock, and its wealth was perceptibly diminished, "for the Bardi and Peruzzi had held so large a share of the commerce of Christendom that upon their fall every other merchant was suspected and distrusted."[1]

In the beginning of the fourteenth century the Venetians began to make their appearance in England, coming over in their "Flanders Galleys," which were long the connecting link between the two states.[2] The first voyage made to the Low Countries was in 1317, and the first Venetian diplomatic agent, Gabriel Dandolo, captain of the galleys,[3] was also sent to England on this occasion. From that time on, some of the ves-

---

1 Villani, *Cronica*, Bk. XII, ch. LV.
2 *Cal. St. Pap., Ven.*, I, lxi.
3 *Ibid.*, I, cxxii.

sels were regularly diverted to Southampton, whither they carried the products of the East and brought back in return cloth and wool.

The English kings found, however, another use for the galleys. In 1340 Edward the Third wrote to the Doge of Venice,[1] requesting the hire of forty or more vessels for one year, to assist him in his war against France, and asked him furthermore to urge the Doge of Genoa not to give any subsidy to Philip of Valois. Characteristic of the chivalrous English monarch was his letter to the Doge in which he wrote that, in order to avoid further bloodshed, he had defied Philip either in single combat or with an equal number of knights, and had also challenged him to prove his kingship by placing himself in a lion's den, since in case he were a true king they would do him no harm. In his letter to the Doge, Edward likewise offered to place the Venetians in England on an equal footing with his own subjects, and requested that one or both of the Doge's sons be sent him to be educated at the English court, promising to confer on them every honor, including knighthood.

For two hundred years Southampton was the centre of Italian trade with England.[2] In 1379 a Genoese merchant who had promised the king[3] to make it the great port of Western Europe was assassinated by the merchants of London, for the English traders

---

[1] *Cal. St. Pap., Ven.*, I, 8.
[2] Mrs. J. R. Green, *Town Life in the Fifteenth Century*, II, 290.
[3] *Ibid.*, II, 293.

were extremely jealous of the Italians. The republic of Genoa, on another occasion, had made complaints of the depredations on its commerce by English privateers, and, as the outcome of this, in 1371, it ratified a treaty of commerce with England. The next year Geoffrey Chaucer was joined in a commission with two Genoese, James Pronan and John de Mari, to treat regarding the selection of a place on the English coast where the Genoese might locate a commercial establishment.

The English merchants, however, were bitterly hostile. They proposed a bill in Parliament to forbid the Venetians carrying any wares except those of their own manufacture, the effect of which would have been to destroy Venetian trade with England; and advocated another law forbidding sales of any kind to the Genoese, or even carrying anything to their port,[1] while an act of Parliament of 1439, still in force at the time of Polydore Vergil, prohibited strangers from selling merchandise to others than Englishmen, so that they should not get all the trade. This jealousy, however, was to some extent natural, as the carrying trade of England was then largely in the hands of the Italians; the Florentine society of the Alberti, for instance, carried all the wool from Southampton to Gascony.[2] Enough has been said to give some idea of the extent of the commercial relations existing in the Middle Ages between the two countries. The oft-cited name of Lombard Street still bears witness to

[1] Mrs. J. R. Green, *op. cit.*, I, 116.   [2] *Ibid.*, II, 290.

the time when the business of banking and exchange was in the hands of the Italians. The free commercial life of their city republics, their large shipping, their commanding position, situated between the Orient and Western Europe, all helped to make them the dominant factor in the trade of the Middle Ages. Long before the rest of Europe had awakened from its feudal dreams and the impracticable ideals of the age, the Italians had realized the benefits that were to be attained through commerce. Their success stirred the jealousy and hatred of the nations with whom they traded. But royal protection and court favor stood them in good stead, while those who were loudest in denouncing them learned the lessons which they taught.

II

No sudden transition separated the history of Italian commerce in the Renaissance from its course in the Middle Ages. Commercial development, although perhaps not quite orderly in its growth, yet remained constant. It is for this reason that the fifteenth century does not bear the same significance in its relation to Italian commerce in England as it did in the introduction of humanism. At the same time its end marked likewise the end of a certain stage in the commercial relations between England and Italy, when Italians no longer looked upon England as a country to be merely exploited, but as a land in which they could settle, acquire citizenship and justly take pride.

It may be of interest to enter into the composition
of an Italian banking house in London in the fifteenth
century; to show the manner in which such a firm
was established, the arrangements made between the
partners, regarding their shares of the profits, the
capital which was to be put in by each, and study
the details of management, the risks to be undertaken, the insurance to be paid on the shipping, and
the penalties for violation of rules; the whole organization, in a word, of a commercial firm in the fifteenth
century.

A typical instance can be found in the contract
drawn up on May 31, 1446, between Cosimo de'
Medici and Giovanni Benci on one hand, and Gierozo
de Pigli on the other, for the purpose of carrying
on a business in the city of London.[1] The arrangement made was for Gierozo de Pigli, a young man
with a limited capital, to be sent to England on a
four years' contract to engage in a business of exchange and general merchandise. The capital of the
company was to be £2500 sterling, of which Cosimo
and Giovanni were to supply £2166¾, and Gierozo the
balance, all of which was to be accounted for by the
first day of November. In case any money had not
been paid in by that time, twelve per cent interest was
to be charged on it. The said Gierozo was to go to
London and there manage in person the affairs of the
firm, nor was he to leave that city without writing for

[1] *Carteggio Mediceo avanti il Principato*, filza 94, Mss.
Archives Florence.

permission from his partners, except to go to Southampton or elsewhere in England on the firm's business. If he went anywhere without consent, it was at his own peril and expense, while otherwise the company assumed it.

Cosimo and Giovanni were each to get two-fifths of the profits, and Gierozo the other fifth; and the same arrangement was to hold good in case of loss, "which God forbid!" Nor were the profits to be removed from the business for the entire term of the agreement. Cosimo and Giovanni together, or even Cosimo alone, had, however, the privilege of terminating the four years' contract earlier in case they should see fit. Gierozo was to be allowed £33 10s. a year for necessary expenses. By the terms of the agreement, moreover, Gierozo was not to lend or give credit in any way to any *Signori*, but only to lend money to merchants and craftsmen of good reputation and credit. Since, however, it was often necessary to sell Roman exchange on credit to churchmen and pilgrims, and Venetian to knights of Rhodes and other gentlemen and pilgrims, and furthermore on account of favors at the court it was sometimes necessary to allow credit in different ways, he was to exercise his own judgment and discretion in all such matters, only securing himself sufficiently to cover risks.

Gierozo, moreover, was instructed not to purchase more than £500 worth of wool or cloth without the permission of Cosimo and Giovanni. He was not to forward cargo of a greater value than fifteen hundred ducats on Florentine and Venetian galleys; on any larger amount shipped he should obtain insurance. He was also to do this if the merchandise was sent on ships of any other nationality, otherwise it was to be at his own risk; moreover, he was not to insure any one else, except for his own personal account. He had to pledge himself not to engage, either directly or indirectly, during the length of this contract, in any other mercantile or exchange business without having first asked the permission of Cosimo and Giovanni and obtained it in writing from them; and if at any time he should violate this agreement, he was to pay a penalty of five hundred florins for each offence. He had also to promise not to gamble or play at dice; in case he did so, any winnings of over ten ducats were to go to the company, while any losses were to be out of his own pocket. Moreover, any gifts he might receive of over ten ducats in value were to be the property of the company.

Gierozo was to remit his balance sheets and accounts to Florence at least once a year, and at any other time Cosimo and Giovanni might demand. He was not to negotiate business of importance with any other firm without having previously consulted them. Nor was he to export gold from England or do anything else against the laws of the kingdom without first obtaining the permission of Cosimo and Giovanni, nor involve the firm in any way directly or indirectly under penalty of five hundred ducats for each offence.

The details of what was to happen at the expiration
of the contract, before anything new could be undertaken, were also given. Unless the agreement
were renewed, the signers bound themselves to settle
the affairs of the old firm, and wind up the business,
even if Gierozo should be obliged to remain in England an additional six months at the expense of the
company. The house in London as well as all the
books of the firm were to belong to Cosimo and Giovanni, but Gierozo was to have access to the latter.
All the creditors then unpaid, as well as the money
left to pay them, were to be looked after by the two
senior partners.

The above articles Cosimo, Giovanni and Gierozo
solemnly bound themselves to follow and observe,
submitting any difficulties which might arise before
the court of the *Mercanzia* in Florence, or any other
court, either in England, at Bruges, or elsewhere; in
recognition whereof they signed the agreement,
promising faithfully to obey it.

A second document in the same series[1] contains
the instructions given the same day the contract was
drawn, by Cosimo de' Medici and Giovanni Benci to
the said Gierozo, on his setting out to take charge of
the new firm in London. He was advised with regard
to his relations with other Italian merchants, and instructed further as to the nature of the loans he
should make, and the exchange he was to give. On

[1] *Carteggio Mediceo avanti il Principato*, filza 94, Archives
Florence.

account of his youth he was warned first of all to be careful of himself and also of the company he kept. His journey was also mapped out beforehand; in his partners' judgment it seemed best for him to travel by way of Milan and Geneva, through Burgundy to Bruges, and then on to London. He was given a letter of introduction to be presented in Milan to Alexander Castagniolo, who would give him further advice or aid if any were necessary, as well as furnish him with money, which he could also obtain at Geneva. He was told at the outset the amount of credit he could give certain firms, whose reputation had been good in the younger days of Cosimo and was still unchanged. In Milan he would be able to acquaint himself about other concerns. The next stopping place on the journey was Geneva, where he could stay at their own house, for the Medici possessed branch houses in many different cities. He was instructed to stir up the young men who conducted the firm's affairs in that city to do their best, and if necessary to advise them himself, as the head of that branch was absent on business; the youngsters, it was said, would obey any advice he saw fit to give them. Bruges was the next town where he could stay at the company's house; he was to urge the two agents, Simone Nori and Tomaso Portinari, to do their utmost, in order that they might give an account of themselves and of what they really were doing. He should report on this, as well as what his opinion of them really was; in the meantime Cosimo and Giovanni would write Nori to obey him and follow his instructions.

Arrived in London, he was told to occupy the same house he had taken there two years before, and make all necessary business arrangements in the name of the company. He had also a letter of introduction to a certain Angelo Tani; Tani was his subordinate, and to be directed by him as to what he should do; in the opinion of Cosimo he was best fitted to keep the accounts and attend to all the correspondence. Gerard Canigiani, another member of the firm, would probably be of most use behind the counter, while yet another who had learned English would do elsewhere; power was given him to dispose of them all as he saw fit. He was cautioned not to permit exchange or credit to be allowed nor loans made without his permission. In the places where the Medici and Benci had branches he was to do business with their houses and no others; at Bruges, for instance, they felt sure he could do better with Simone Nori than with any one else, and they thought he would be able to transact some profitable affairs with his assistance. In such places where they had no branch houses he was to select the best merchants, and be very careful to act in all honor toward those who treated him well. He would have to ship wool and cloth to the value of one thousand or fifteen hundred florins to the different houses of Medici in Rome, Florence, and Venice, the Benci in Geneva, and other allied firms at Avignon and Pisa, and he was to attend to any orders they might send him. Many firms as soon as they had heard of this new concern in London would forward goods on con-

signment.   For this reason he was advised, at the outset, with whom he should do business.   At Naples, for
instance, there was no one of sufficiently good standing for him to have dealings with; at Rome were the
Pazzi, whose credit was of the best; several other
firms, too, were mentioned where a limit of fifteen
hundred florins' credit was set down.   In Florence
there were also good concerns, such as the Serristori
and the Rucellai.   Cosimo confessed his ignorance of
mercantile houses in Venice, and advised him to be
very cautious and conservative in dealing with them,
but he mentioned houses of good standing at Genoa
and Avignon, Barcelona and Valencia.   He warned
Gierozo always to be on his guard and not pay more
than merchandise was worth; nor remit money or
exchange to any Genoese or Venetian merchants without special permission.   He was to have no business
relations with either Brittany or Gascony; but in case
good wines should be sent him on consignment, he
could keep them so long as it was not a matter of
any importance.   It was also thought best for him
to have nothing to do with Catalan merchants.   Regarding English traders who did business in the fairs
of Flanders, he must exercise his own judgment and
discretion.

Cosimo and Giovanni hoped he would enjoy the
favor of the king and queen; in case he should find
need for any letters of recommendation from King
Réné [of Provence, father of Margaret, the wife of
Henry the Sixth], if he would let them know, they

would send them to him very quickly. In London he was to have the direction of the entire concern, and the younger men were to follow his instructions and look up to him as their chief.

III

The animosity felt by the populace against the Italian merchants was difficult to overcome, and their very success in commerce only served to increase this hatred. The English dislike of everything foreign was long characteristic of the nation, and Voltaire himself was hooted and chased by a London mob for no other reason than being a foreigner. In earlier centuries popular indignation at the success of aliens took more violent forms in the frequent riots against them, when the king was obliged to take them under his protection. This hostility to all foreigners was well known on the continent. Italian gentlemen had asked its meaning of William Thomas,[1] who replied that it had existed at a time when there was no foreign commerce in England, and when ignorant people, seeing strangers resort thither for purposes of trade, imagined that they went there, not to buy commodities but to rob them, and that foreigners unable to make a living in their own country came to England to plunder the natives. But all that was a thing of the past, continued Thomas. Later travellers, however, did not cease to complain of the discourtesy shown them by the populace. Long before Thomas' day there had

[1] *Pilgrim*, p. 6.

been numerous complaints, and at Southampton there were frequent fights between Italians and English.[1] An Italian who travelled in England about the year 1500 noticed the general antipathy to foreigners, who were supposed, he said, never to go there but to make themselves masters of it and usurp English goods;[2] and a Milanese traveller in 1516 commented likewise on the hostility to strangers.[3]

Vexatious acts had several times already been aimed against them in Parliament. In 1455, however, a law was passed forbidding Italian merchants to buy wools or wool cloth of the producers in the country, or anywhere except in the cities of London, Southampton and Sandwich.[4] The disturbances leading up to this had begun some years earlier. Wool had frequently been seized on Venetian galleys, and the Doge had remonstrated on account of this, as well as about injurious trade regulations.[5] Many annoyances were suffered by Florentine merchants as well, and former favors were now refused, on account of an Englishman in the royal service who had some unsettled claims in Florence. The Florentines therefore came together, and selected, as their ambassador to the king, Bindo da Staggio, who was to request him to renew the safe-conducts and again allow the Floren-

---

[1] *Cal. St. Pap., Ven.*, I, 5.
[2] *Relation of England*, p. 21 *et seq.*
[3] Add. Ms. 24,180, Brit. Mus., f. 29.
[4] Mrs. J. R. Green, *op. cit.*, II, 293.
[5] Beckynton, II, 126.

tines to purchase English wool.[1] To procure these
favors required a considerable sum of money, and they
voted to allow Bindo five hundred and fifty ducats a
year for eight years; the cost of this was to be borne
by the galleys trading between England and Tuscany,
which were to pay a tax of one-half per cent in value
of the merchandise they carried. Any one violating
this agreement was to be fined five hundred florins.
All difficulties were to be submitted to the consuls of
the sea, whose duty it was to supervise the maritime
trade. A further tax of the same amount was also imposed on the merchandise carried by the galleys, in
order to pay off an English claim of forty-four hundred ducats, which had been the alleged cause of the
annoyances suffered by the Florentines in London.
Additional precautions were taken against possible
fraud, and further penalties assigned for violation of
the rules, the jurisdiction on all similar matters being
placed under the general direction of the consuls of
the sea. From these taxes, moreover, the expenses
of any Florentine who had been arrested in England
in consequence of the reprisals were to be paid provided the costs did not exceed five hundred florins.
It was also agreed that a syndic, or official, should be
selected in Florence, who was to have jurisdiction
over all Florentines residing in England, in order that
they might be properly organized. The two chosen for
this were Francesco Strozzi and Gierozo de Pigli, both

[1] *Filza Strozziana*, Archives Florence, 294 Cte., 135–136,
31st August 1448.

at that time residing in London, who were to arrange between themselves who should begin and who finish the term. In the Middle Ages the consul had been a magistrate elected by a colony of merchants at a foreign port to watch over their interests and govern them, being paid in fees fixed by the merchants themselves. The two before mentioned were thus the first consuls of the Florentine colony in London. Adversity was perhaps the cause which forced the other "nations" to organize in similar manner and plan measures of self-protection. In 1456 a popular riot drove the Italian merchants out of London, to seek refuge elsewhere. In consequence of this a mutual agreement was signed by the Florentines, Venetians, Genoese and Luccans residing there, in which they pledged themselves to remain away from London and have no business relations with any one in that city for the term of three years. The document itself will repay a closer examination.[1]

In the name of the Almighty, of the Most Holy Virgin, and the entire celestial court of Paradise, it began, the delegates representing the merchants of Venice, Genoa, Florence and Lucca, residing in London, bind other traders of their respective nations to observe the terms of the agreement here signed under a penalty of £200 sterling, which fine is to be inflicted by the consuls of his nation on any merchant breaking the agreement. And furthermore,

[1] *Filza Strozziana*, Archives Florence, 294 Cte., 138, 139, 22d June 1457.

in case the said consuls should neglect to enforce it, they themselves shall be held responsible and fined a like amount. In addition, the said merchants agree to leave London with all their possessions within six months (unless some good reason such as severe illness or imprisonment shall prevent them from so doing), and go to the city of Winchester, or any other place in the island, not within a radius of thirty miles from London. Those merchants only might stay who had wine or similar articles on hand, provided that on expiration of the six months they gave notice to their consuls, swearing that only such merchandise and no other was still for sale. But no merchant could import further goods from the first of July, eight days after the agreement had been signed, nor was he to receive any either directly or indirectly. After the first of January, which was six months from date, no business relations of any kind were to be conducted with any one in London, nor was exchange to be bought or sold there. Special provision was made, however, for goods shipped by way of Zealand which might be in transit at that time.

The signers furthermore bound themselves to do their best to dissuade all Italian, Sicilian, Catalan, or Spanish merchants from doing business either of money lending, importing, selling merchandise or exchange, or of any nature whatever, in London, during the same period, and in case they failed in this, such merchant was to be discriminated against by the rest and boycotted in every way possible, even to the extent of refusing to carry his goods in their ships. The same merchants signing this agreement were also to write to their respective governments requesting them to ratify the articles, and by inflicting suitable penalties see to it that they were observed by others of their community. This was acceded to very promptly, by the Venetian Senate at least.[1] The consuls were to notify all captains of merchantmen trading with England that they must observe the terms of the agreement; and the said captains were to certify before the consuls, within reasonable time from date, regarding the goods which had been shipped in their care.

The "nations" which signed this agreement bound themselves to stay away from the city of London for the term of three years, and not to return except by mutual agreement on the part of all four parties; at the end of that time a majority of three was to determine whether or not they should stay away from London for a longer time. Three months before the expiration of the agreement, each nation was to select two delegates, and on their coming together, a three-quarters vote should decide what was to be done. At the end of five years, in any case, they would be at liberty to do what they liked. Each nation, too, was to be permitted to send a representative to London, but only to collect outstanding debts.

These articles were thus signed and sealed by the delegates of the four nations, who swore on the sac-

[1] *Cal. St. Pap., Ven.,* I, 84.

rament to observe the agreement under the penalty of eternal damnation. Four copies of the compact were made, each nation preserving one. Last of all, they promised not to injure each other without good cause, through anything which might arise from these mutual obligations.

This agreement is of interest as showing the measures taken in self-defence by the Italian merchants against the hatred and violence of the London mob. That it was probably not without effect may be judged from the fact that they moved back before 1461.[1] The second term of absence was thus considered unnecessary, nor was any further self-imposed exile heard of from that time. The compact showed, also, the power of organization possessed by them; they were able to show their strength, and bind not only themselves but others as well who feared to incur their displeasure. Their consuls and *Massari* were the responsible officers of each community, through whom official relations with their respective republics could be maintained. A close connection existed between them and their native cities, and at no time in this early period did they make any decided attempt to identify themselves with those with whom they traded, nor break the ties which bound them to their own cities. There was then good reason for thinking that to be a citizen of Florence or Venice might well seem a nobler title of distinction than that of Englishman; the hatred, moreover, manifested toward foreigners also stood in the

[1] *Cal. St. Pap., Ven.,* I, 84.

way of any effort they might make toward seeking another allegiance.

In spite of certain disadvantages they labored under, the Italian merchants prospered in England. Soon after their return to London, in 1465, a new company was formed in Florence, to do business in England: this time Piero de' Medici and Tommaso Portinari provided most of the capital. Of this, too, the terms of contract and preliminary agreement are still preserved.[1] Without going into the details, which resemble in substance the contract already examined, in the present instance the conduct of affairs in England was assigned to two men, Gherardo Canigiani and Giovanni de Bardi. Its capital was to be two thousand pounds, of which Piero de' Medici alone put in nine hundred; instructions were given that all negotiations, exchanges and loans must be conducted in an honest and honorable manner. Moreover, a one-tenth share of the profits was to be distributed in charity, either in building churches, or in other pious works, to be disposed of by Piero de' Medici and Tommaso Portinari. The modern English traveller in Florence may find consolation in the thought that some of the money made from his forefathers went to construct the Renaissance churches of that city.

Each one of the junior partners had fifteen pounds granted him yearly for his living expenses in London, which gives a clew to the purchasing power of money at that time. They had to bind them-

---

[1] Arch. Flor., *filza* 99, *Mediceo Avanti il Principato*, 108.

selves not to undertake any other kind of business, either directly or indirectly. Other provisions were made regarding the rendering of accounts, their employees, leaves of absence, the final winding up of the business, and various contingencies. They were instructed regarding the risks which should be taken in shipping merchandise; while limited to fifty pounds on ordinary vessels, they had permission to go up to one hundred in the case of Venetian or Florentine galleys. They must do no insuring for others; and also pledged themselves not to involve the firm, either by their own actions or those of their friends or relatives. All gifts of greater value than two pounds must be handed over to the company, or else charged to their account. They promised also to do nothing against the laws of the country except at their own personal risk. This agreement they swore faithfully to abide by, leaving any points of dispute which might arise to be decided by the courts.

Such contracts as the two cited afford illustrations of the commercial life of the time, and the nature of the business relations existing between England and Italy. On the one hand, Italian merchants imported to their own country wool and wool cloth, for which England was then famous. On the other, they exported general merchandise, and especially the spices and products of the East,[1] for the Italians were then the intermediaries between the Orient and Western Europe. In addition to this they did a business of

[1] W. Heyd, *Geschichte des Levant Handels*, II, 715.

banking, money lending and exchange ; their excep-
tional facilities in different quarters of the civilized world
gave them almost a monopoly of such transactions; at
the same time their carrying trade was enormous for
that age, and Italian ships long enjoyed the supremacy
of the seas. Their success, however, in different commercial enterprises lent a spur to the English merchants and sailors who profited by their example.

Richard the Third, in 1483, issued an act regu-
lating the sales of Italian merchants. The fact that
they sold retail as well as wholesale, to the alleged
injury of native traders ; that their success was of
no benefit to England since they did not spend there
the money they had made ; and further, that they
played into each other's hands, — were the reasons
given for his restriction of their trade. Under the wise
legislation of Henry the Seventh, however, a commercial treaty was made with the Florentine Republic,[1]
in 1485, by which English merchants undertook to
carry every year to Florence sufficient wool to supply
all the Italian states save Venice, while the Florentines
promised to buy no wool unless carried on English
ships. In return for this and other privileges, corresponding ones were given to the Florentines. The
Venetians, also, had their charter to trade renewed by
Henry, in 1507,[2] but only on condition that they
do no more of the carrying trade between England
and Flanders, which was now left to the " Merchant
Adventurers."

[1] Mrs. T. R. Green, *op. cit.*, I, 117.   [2] *Ibid.*

The early years of the Renaissance in England were coincident with the growth and protection of trade. At a time when commercial life was still despised in feudal Europe, the Italians had realized its possibilities. Their methods and ideas were largely followed and imitated, in banking and exchange, as well as in other branches of industry. In many ways England was dependent upon Italy; to give but a trivial illustration, the famous cloth of Nottingham was long sent to Italy, to receive there the proper scarlet dye.[1] In commerce, as in other directions, England received from Italy a powerful and long-lasting stimulus. Through the possibilities of such intercourse, other streams of Italian influence were filtering in slowly. Perhaps, had commerce been alone, the others might have amounted to nothing, though John Free, it is said, was urged to study in Italy by some Italian merchants he had met in his native town of Bristol. The influence in commerce, however, was only a portion of that greater wave which had swept over all of Europe.

IV

There was no sharp dividing line in the history of Italian merchants in England during the Renaissance. At the same time, certain distinguishing points of view are clearly discernible at different times. In the early days, for instance, the feeling existed of the wide gulf between them and those with whom they traded.

[1] Mrs. T. R. Green, *op. cit.*, II, 326.

The years they spent in England were years almost of exile, undergone by needy ones, among people whom they considered barbarians, and among whom, it must be said, they lived in constant danger. The young men starting in life were sent out from Italy by wealthier merchants, who stayed at home, to establish commercial houses in England ; but at no time then did they endeavor to identify themselves with English life in any other than a business way. It was undoubtedly true that such an attempt, on their part, would have been much in the nature of a retrogression. To modern minds a sharp cleavage seems almost to separate the Middle Ages from the Renaissance. It is difficult to imagine the gradual change, when the shadows of one age slowly retreated before lights of the new era. But the separation was as distinct in place as in time, and the years which marked it varied with each nation, those who discerned it latest cherishing it the longest. In England, through the whole fifteenth century, the vitality of the Middle Ages was sinking, and there was nothing, as yet, to take its place. Faint glimmers of the new fire of Italy flickered above the Alps from time to time, while, at the same time, men bred in the surroundings of the early Italian Renaissance left their land to trade in foreign countries. Between London and Florence there was then almost a difference of two ages. However superior the Venetian and Florentine may have felt in his English mediæval environment, it seems likely that his example may, perhaps unconsciously, have done something to further the cause of the Renaissance in England, and hasten the coming of the new learning. The story of John Free is significant of what may well have taken place. It would be strange indeed if, in the leisure hours of the counting house, the merchants who, when at home, loved their Petrarch and Ovid failed to read them while absent in their foreign exile. It is easily conceivable that some of the early manuscripts of the Italian poets and humanists, still preserved in the college libraries of Oxford and Cambridge, were first brought over by Italian traders.

The Italian community in England, and especially in London, could not forever keep aloof from the native population. So long as centuries of culture may be said to have separated the two people, the gulf was a natural one; but after the first seeds of the Renaissance had taken root and the new spirit, transmitted in a dozen ways, had been planted in England, the chasm was to a great extent bridged over. What facilitated the friendlier intercourse between Italian merchants and Englishmen, more than anything else, was the growth of the centralized monarchy in the strong hands of the king. Henry the Seventh endeavored in every way to promote the commercial welfare of his people, and realized the advantages to be derived from Italian trade and friendlier relations with Italian merchants. Earlier ordinances had, it is true, been passed in their favor, such as a statute of Henry the Sixth, decreeing that no tin or lead be exported from England (except to Calais), save only by merchants of Genoa, Venice, and Florence, and burgesses of Berwick.[1] The court, it must be said, had always been least open to anti-foreign prejudices, and tried its best to shield and protect the Italians from the violence of the London mob; but it was not until the time of the Tudors that the crown tried to foster friendly relations, not only with Italian merchants, but with Italian commercial communities. In 1496, in the reign of Henry the Seventh, the diplomatic intercourse between Venice and England really began.[2] For the signory, it was transacted by Pietro Contarini and Luca Valatesso, two Venetian merchants established in London, who induced the king to join the Holy League.[3] The next year Andrea Trevisani was sent over as regular ambassador, and a few years later Francesco Capello, another Venetian envoy, was knighted by the king. The commercial treaties signed by Henry with Florence and Venice have been mentioned, as well as his relations with individual Italians and his fondness for them at the court. In various ways this was noticeable, and the first diplomatic

[1] *Hist. Ms. Com., Hatfield House*, V, 136.

[2] That is to say, regular relations between the two countries began then. Gabriel Dandolo was the first Venetian agent, in 1317. Another Venetian, Antonio Bembo, requested Henry the Fourth to force the Duke of Norfolk to repay a loan of 750 ducats borrowed of him for the duke's pilgrimage to the Holy Land in 1404. Michael Steno, then Doge, also interceded for Bembo with the king. (Cot. Mss., Brit. Mus., Nero B. VII, 5 and 6.)

[3] Rawdon Brown, *Four Years at the Court of Henry VIII*, I, xx, note.

correspondence [1] between England and Florence contained letters from Henry [2] requesting the Signoria to assist his equerry, Ambonio Spinola, to recover certain sums of money, and declared himself willing to execute similar demands against his own subjects. Another letter recommended his retainer, Antonio Corsi,[3] whom he was sending to Florence to purchase gold cloth and silks sufficient to load three mules, at the same time expressing his perfect willingness to reciprocate in any way he could.

Although the Italians were for long not permitted to have shops in London,[4] yet, after their return there, they began again to assume even greater importance than before, and had almost an established position at court. Henry the Eighth, for instance, granted letters of recommendation, addressed to the Pope and other dignitaries, to such merchants as Thomas Corbo and Giovanni Cavalcanti, who were among his favorites.[5] There can be but little doubt that the artisans and handicraftsmen who came over from Italy to England in the early years of the sixteenth century were largely encouraged to do so by merchants already there. In more ways than one Italians were now beginning to mingle with the community at large. Occasion-

---

[1] The magistrates of Florence had already interceded with Edward the Third in behalf of the Bardi (Cot. Mss., Brit. Mus., Nero B. VII, 4).

[2] Arch. Flor., *Atti Pub.*, 12th January 1498.

[3] *Ibid.*, 6th July 1502.

[4] Ubaldini, f. 236; also Add. Ms. 24,180, Brit. Mus., f. 27.

[5] *Marini Trans.*, Brit. Mus., XXXVII, ff. 128, 616.

ally one would marry a native and become an
Englishman to all intent; the grandfather of Nicholas
Grimald, the poet, for instance, was Giovanni Grim-
aldi, a merchant of Genoa, who became a denizen of
England in 1485. Usually the position enjoyed by
Italian merchants at home made them wish to retain
their nationality. Many of them, however, became
important personages in the early sixteenth century.
Leonardo Frescobaldi, the "Master Friskiball" of
Shakespeare, was well known in London and is mentioned in the *Life and Death of Cromwell*. Thomas
Cromwell was also said to have been befriended by
the Frescobaldis when as a youth he had to beg for
alms in Florence.[1] Frescobaldi was one of the great
merchants of the day and supplied the king with his
"damask gold," gilt axes, hand guns, and similar
merchandise.[2] The most prominent of the Italians
of that time, in England, was Antonio Bonvisi, the
friend of Sir Thomas More, Cardinal Pole, and other
well-known men. Stowe says of him that he came
over to England in 1505, and taught the English
people to spin with a distaff.[3] He acted also as
banker and news collector for the government, and
transmitted money and letters to ambassadors abroad.
He was, moreover, a patron and friend of learned men,
especially of those anxious to visit or study in Italy.

[1] This story of Bandello, though probably spurious, is yet
worth repeating.

[2] Stowe Mss., 1216, Brit. Mus.

[3] Burgon, *Sir Thomas Gresham*, II, 453.

Thomas Starkey, Thomas Winter, Florence Volusenus, were all his associates, and Sir Thomas More, from whom he purchased his residence of Crosby Place, in one of the last letters he wrote, spoke of himself not "as a guest but a continual nursling of the house of Bonvisi." Bonvisi was thus one of the links which then bound together the two countries; it is noteworthy that his family did not return to Italy, but settled in England. The old Italian idea of exile abroad was fast disappearing; England had caught up with rapid strides in the march of civilization, and the darkness beyond the Alps was giving away to a new dawn. Italians, too, could now feel that another home lay open to them. More and more from this time on they identified themselves with English life, and although the anti-foreign prejudices, especially of the populace, were not dispelled till long after, there were no longer unsurmountable obstacles separating the two people.

At the same time the Italians did not give up their almost inherited rights as foreign traders in a day. The household book of Henry the Eighth [1] is full of records of payments to such merchants as the Frescobaldi, the Corsi, the Cavalcanti, the Bardi, and so forth; and there were many other similar warrants, as one of the King, to pay " Charowchon," [2] Merchant of Florence, for " three pieces of cloth of gold." The same names recur time and time again, and would seem to show that the Italian bankers and merchants

[1] Brit. Mus., Mss. 2481 passim.   [2] Stowe, Ms. cit.

in London were in constant intercourse with the court, either as purveyors or money lenders. It was said that the king frequently lent money to the Florentine merchants in order to allow them to extend their trade ; they sometimes owed him as much as 300,000 ducats. The merchants were in this way able to obtain funds at a fair rate of interest, while the king often empowered his favorites to collect these debts for him, allowing them to keep the interest.[1] The Italian proclivities of Wolsey and Cromwell further encouraged the merchants. Wolsey in particular probably influenced the king to suppress the anti-foreign riots of 1517. Numerous complaints had been made at that time of foreigners bringing over ready-made goods to the injury of Englishmen whose work they took away : —

> Poor tradesmen had small dealings then;
> And who but strangers bore the bell?
> Which was a grief to Englishmen,
> To see them here in London dwell.[2]

The trouble had been stirred by a certain popular preacher, who abused the foreigners, accusing them not only of depriving Englishmen of the just earnings of their labor, but of debauching their families. He urged the people no longer to permit such a state of affairs to go on, and so inflamed them that from that day on they threatened to massacre the strangers and sack their houses. On the first day of May a mob of

---

[1] Sebastian Giustiniani, *Cal. St. Pap.*, *Ven.*, II, 562.
[2] Cited by Digby Wyatt, *op. cit.*, 222.

two thousand apprentices and a number of ruffians, after pillaging the French and Flemish quarters, proceeded to the Italian, shouting death to the cardinal for his foreign sympathies. But as the Italians were well armed the mob could do but little damage.[1] The king, however, had been warned of the intended massacre. Although at Richmond, he sent troops to London who seized all the rioters they found in the streets. Gibbets were then raised all over the town, and sixty of the mob were hanged, and many others executed in other ways. "Very great vengeance was taken on them, and his Majesty showed great love and good will to the strangers."[2]

Wolsey employed numerous Italian news collectors, among whom were Antonio Bonvisi and Antonio Grimaldi.[3] Cromwell, also, favored foreigners and the Venetian merchants addressed themselves to him when they requested him to obtain from the king a renewal of their license to trade in England;[4] the celebrated Aretino even recommended young men to his care.[5] It should not be supposed, however, that the Italian traders and bankers preserved the virtual monopoly they once enjoyed. Not only were the merchants of the Hanseatic League their rivals, although chiefly in other branches of trade; but Englishmen, too, had profited from the success of for-

[1] Brewer, *Letters and Papers, Henry VIII*, II, Pt. II, 1031.
[2] *Cal. St. Pap., Ven.*, II, 385.
[3] Cot. Mss., Brit. Mus., Vitellius, B. XIV, 173.
[4] *Ibid.*, Nero, B. VII, 21.   [5] *Ibid.*, Nero, B. VII, 123.

eigners and were rapidly learning from them. After the silent preparation in the fifteenth century, there had come a swift awakening in the next hundred years, and the same necessity for foreign enterprise to open up English commerce was no longer felt. Englishmen were now quite capable of looking after their own affairs and developing national industries, while judicious protection fostered the growth of their foreign trade. The sixteenth century also marked a relative decline in Italian commerce. Italian merchants were no longer undisputed masters of every field, but found new rivals springing up on all sides. Italy was fast approaching the downward path, and its importance was no longer the same. Although Italians during the age of Elizabeth occupied many positions of prominence in commercial and banking circles, their situation was yet a different one from what it once had been. Toward the end of the century they formed rather isolated instances, or seemed so at least when considered among the greater number of English competitors. On the other hand, they no longer assumed the entirely alien point of view which made their sojourn in England in former days seem temporary; although retaining their Italian character, they yet entered English life, sharing alike its privileges and responsibilities. Some became citizens, others married English women. One, the most prominent member of the Italian community of his day, in the time of national danger, equipped a vessel at his own cost in the fight against the Armada.

V

An English contemporary observer wrote of the Italian merchants that they "fly abroad in exceeding abundance to all places, and in wealth (wherever they come) overtop all other, such is their skill, their wit, their industry, their parsimony."[1] It will be sufficient to consider here certain of the Italian merchants in England during the sixteenth century, as illustrating phases of the commercial relations between the two countries, and showing their general character. Three types of men can be found: Sir Antonio Guidotti, the negotiator of loans between Henry the Eighth and Duke Cosimo of Florence, who was knighted by Edward the Sixth and later returned to Italy, leaving behind him in poverty an English wife and children; Ruberto Ridolfi, banker, conspirator and unofficial agent of the Pope, who plotted against Elizabeth; and Sir Horatio Pallavicino, merchant and political agent, who came to England in the service of the Vatican, and then identified himself in every way with the interests of the country he was to make his home.

Sir Antonio Guidotti belongs to the first half of the sixteenth century. In a letter to Cromwell, written in 1536, he offered to bring over to England some silk weavers from Messina;[2] what became of this project is unknown. He was one of the Florentine

---

[1] Sandys, *Speculum Europæ*, Sig. M. 2 b.
[2] Cot. Mss., Brit. Mus., Vitellius, B. XIV, 241.

merchants, however, whose trading ventures brought him into close relations with the king. He was the go-between and negotiator of a loan of £15,000 made by Duke Cosimo of Florence to Henry the Eighth, who wanted the money for his invasion of France. The duke seems to have been unwilling at first to lend the money, but was advised to do so by Guidotti, who argued that it would be to his advantage in Italy.

The amount borrowed was to be paid back in instalments extending over a period of thirty years;[1] the interest given was to be twelve per cent; Guidotti assured the duke that it was both a sound and profitable investment. His own share, he wanted him to understand, would come in only in the thanks he should receive from the duke and the king, which would compensate him amply for the trouble he had taken and the slander of his enemies. He informed the duke also that King Henry had given him plated money in exchange on which a profit could be made, as it was greatly in demand, particularly in Venice and Pisa. The royal treasurer, *Briam Tuck* [Sir Bryan Tuke], was a very intimate friend of his and he had arranged the loan with him. Guidotti himself had borrowed of him five thousand ducats, Cavalcanti and Giraldi, the duke's London correspondents, vouching for him.[2] From subsequent letters it would appear that Guidotti had a falling-out of some sort with the

---

[1] *Carteggio Universale Mediceo*, Arch. Flor., 341.
[2] Vide *Filza Med.*, 371 Cte., 3/4, 55.

London agents for he wrote the duke that he had been warned against them. He feared that if the affair fell through he would lose the king's consideration entirely ; but the loan, he felt sure, possessed too many advantages to fail. The thousand ducats profits which he acknowledged he expected to make on the negotiations, he hoped to give as dowry to his eighteen-year-old daughter, who was still in a convent, and whom he wanted to marry off as soon as possible. He assured the duke that the king bore him great good will, and held him in greater consideration than any of the other princes of Italy. This he could say without any flattery at all, as few knew the king better than he did. He had been about this affair for the last three years, and almost ruined himself over it. If it were to fall through now, it would break his heart, and he implored the duke to have pity on him and on his little children. There is a curious combination in all these letters of personal appeals and business considerations : at one time he proclaimed total disinterestedness in the matter, and then confessed that unless the loan should materialize he would be virtually a ruined man ; elsewhere again he brought in his own personal affairs, and tried to interest the duke in them ; it was a strange spectacle, however, to see a reigning prince occupied with business transactions and lending money at a remunerative rate of interest to another sovereign.

Guidotti at last wrote the duke that there was grave danger lest the king of Portugal might lend the money to Henry. This evidently settled matters, for in a letter to his agent in London[1] the duke wrote that he had definitely accepted the proposition. The payments were to be made by Bartholomew Fortini,[2] the agent of the firm of Cavalcanti and Giraldi in London. The instructions were given and explained in Latin letters to Sir Bryan Tuke, the royal treasurer.[3] Antonio Guidotti himself received a pension in 1550 for his services,[4] and was later knighted by Edward the Sixth.[5] On his return to Florence he is said to have been publicly welcomed, and to have received the congratulations of the entire city. He left his family in England, however, and a letter of Queen Mary to Cosimo[6] requested the duke to see to it that Guidotti, who had been given an ample pension, should provide for his wife, Dorothy Guidotti, and her three children, who were then living in great poverty. The later history of the loan can be quickly told. In 1558 Elizabeth wrote the duke that she wished to pay it.[7] No immediate steps seem at first to have been taken ; but a few years later she began payment of the loan, and made good the money her father had borrowed.[8] Elizabeth, it may be said, took good care to protect and foster English trade and shipping, which was still in its infancy. Many of her communications to the

---

[1] Arch. Flor., *Arch. Med. Minute del* 1545, *filza* No. 6.
[2] *Ibid.*   [7] *Ibid.*, f. 16.
[3] *Arch. Med.*, 372 Cte., 258 *et seq.*   [8] *Ibid.*
[4] *Lit. Rem. of Ed. VI*, II, 256.
[5] *Correspondence of Sir Thomas Copley*, p. 112.
[6] *Arch. Med.*, 4183, f. 9.

Grand Duke of Tuscany relate to commerce, and she tried to obtain special trading facilities for her subjects.[1]

Ruberto Ridolfi, banker and conspirator, belongs rather to the type of Italian who refused to identify himself with the interests of the country in which he had for so many years made his home. He used the position he had acquired in banking circles to plot against Queen Elizabeth, although he was shrewd enough to escape detection while his fellow conspirators perished on the scaffold. He was employed in various ways by Sir William Cecil and the crown, and at the same time supplied English information to the French and Spanish ambassadors, receiving pensions from both. Protestant England meant to him the enemy's country, and his life there was that of an intriguer and spy, shielding his own work behind that of nobler men who gave up their lives for the Catholic cause. Ridolfi's career in contrast with that of Pallavicino explains how difficult it is to draw generalizations. Of the two Italians, both prominent in England, the one refused to assimilate himself in any way, the other became to all purposes an Englishman.

Sir Horatio Pallavicino, a Genoese by birth, was one of the most interesting men of his time. He had first gone to England recommended to Mary, who was then queen. Having received an appointment as collector of papal taxes, he turned Protestant, kept what he had

[1] *Arch. Med.*, 4183, ff. 26, 54.

collected,[1] and became one of the great merchants of the day, lending money at usurious rates of interest to Elizabeth and Henry of Navarre. He was even said to have saved the English monarchs from ruin on one occasion. In addition to his banking business, he was a great collector of political intelligence. His many correspondents enabled him to secure information ahead of others, and he was often employed by the government to furnish foreign news.[2] He was naturalized an Englishman, and at the time of the Armada equipped a vessel at his own expense and was present as a volunteer. Anxious, as he wrote in a letter to Cecil, to show his devotion to the queen and to England, he decided that his best service could be done by sea; he was easily able to provide himself with what was necessary for a naval battle, and trusted the lord admiral would give him, as he had promised, one of the queen's ships to command.[3] In 1589 he tried political intrigue of his own, to upset the Spanish rule in the Netherlands;[4] and several of his cipher letters to Burghley on affairs of state are still preserved.[5] His chief occupation, however, was the negotiation of loans for the British and Dutch governments. At the time of his death the queen owed him £29,000,

---

[1] An epitaph written after his death read:—

 "Here lies Horatio Palavazene
  Who robbed the Pope to lend the queen."

[2] *Hist. Ms. Com., Hatfield House*, IV *passim*.

[3] *Ibid.*, IV, 563.

[4] Motley, *United Netherlands*, II, 539 *et seq.*

[5] *Hist. Ms. Com., Hatfield House*, III *passim*.

which was never fully repaid to his heirs by the government. Money from the queen had been due for some time, and there are many memoranda of such debts. Already, in 1593, she owed him £30,000; two years he begged for payment[1] which was not forthcoming. His brothers, he wrote, had suffered much in Italy for the sake of her Majesty, and the debt in question was the better part of their patrimony as well as the means of maintaining their dignity. Regarding the interest on the debt, although by no means small, he submitted himself entirely to the queen's pleasure, but begged that the loan might soon be settled, otherwise he feared that his brothers would seize as security the merchandise of English subjects and thereby incur her displeasure. In this letter he alluded to the bond of the City of London as "the first to-day in Europe."

Pallavicino throughout his life acted the part of a patriotic Englishman, and maintained his position with dignity and honor. He was on terms of friendship with Cecil, who reminded him in one letter[2] of the reputation he enjoyed at court; Lord Buckhurst also in a letter to Elizabeth's great minister spoke of him as his friend.[3] In the correspondence which passed between Pallavicino and Cecil, he told the latter that he would like his son Henry to pass under his guardianship,[4] and later sent him another son,[5] Edward, whom

---

[1] *Hist. Ms. Com., Hatfield House*, IV, 444. V, 462.
[2] *Ibid.*, IV, 609. [3] *Ibid.*, IV, 552. [4] *Ibid.*, V, 248.
[5] *Ibid.*, VI, 175.

he had promised to take into his service. He trusted that he would find use for his pen as well as for his body. He was evidently anxious to become Anglicized in every way, and even wrote Cecil[1] that he wanted to marry his sisters-in-law to Englishmen according to arrangements he had made, but that they were timid. His own family, by a rather remarkable series of alliances, married Cromwells, and broke away entirely from their Italian ties.

Pallavicino was a remarkable character in many ways. Not only was he banker and political agent, but Italian architect as well to Queen Elizabeth. At his death Theophilus Field wrote and edited *An Italian's Dead Body*, a book of elegies on the death of Sir Horatio Pallavicino, and Bishop Hall contributed verses to his memory. But he was remarkable in showing that, in spite of somewhat evil beginnings, he could become a loyal and patriotic Englishman, ready to do his duty to his adopted country. Ideas had greatly changed since the days of Antonio Bonvisi. Italy had retrograded, crushed by foreign oppression; and England had advanced, and asserted her place in the first rank of nations. She had destroyed the invincible Armada, and her sailors had singed the beard of the king of Spain. English gold and English arms on the Continent were now lending aid to the Protestants in France and the Low Countries. Italians therefore needed no longer to be ashamed to seek another nationality. Excepting

[1] *Hist. Ms. Com., Hatfield House*, V, 2.

Venice, which was even then in its decline, the other cities of Italy retained scarce a shadow of their former power. Their earlier commercial supremacy was a thing of the past; Elizabeth might still borrow huge sums from a Pallavicino or a Spinola,[1] but the crown was no longer dependent on Italian bankers alone, whose capital had been accumulated in former years. The growing resources of England were coming into play, and English industry and commerce, wisely encouraged, were forging to the front. It is therefore scarcely surprising that the Italians who settled in England should seek to identify themselves with the new nation, rather than cling to their own decaying cities. Fanatics and zealots like Ridolfi might still remain irreconcilably hostile, but the wiser, the more far-sighted among them saw that the old sun had set and a new star was above the horizon. They could throw in their lot with England, and of their English citizenship justly feel proud.

VI

There was another way in which Italians may be said to have influenced English trade and commerce. Not only did the example of Italian bankers and merchants give Englishmen a knowledge of commercial methods such as had hitherto been unknown to them, but Italian navigators and explorers, and Italian geographers and writers of travel, prepared the way for

[1] *Hist. Ms. Com., Hatfield House*, II, 356.

Englishmen to follow, and distinguish themselves in the deeds of daring which marked the closing years of the sixteenth century.

It would be idle to dwell here on the numerous Italian explorers and navigators. Columbus, who gave a new continent to Spain, was but the greatest of a long line of Italian navigators. In England, as is well known, the elder Cabot, who was Genoese by birth, Venetian by citizenship, English by adoption, sailed from Bristol to discover the American coast in his attempt to reach India. His daring son commanded the first English ship to visit the West Indies and South America, and he was later made life governor of the Company of Merchant Adventurers. But long before the Cabots first led English sailors on paths of adventure and exploration, Venetian and Genoese galleys between Southampton and other ports acted as carriers for English merchandise. There can be little doubt that this example, combined with the natural seafaring inclination of the race, led Englishmen to ply the trade which was so successful in enriching Italians. English shipping, moreover, was greatly encouraged by the wise regulations of Henry the Seventh, who tried to foster and protect the new source of national wealth.

But the influence and example here to be considered was rather a literary one, derived from the books of exploration and travels. It is well known that the Florentine, Amerigo Vespucci, whose name has been given to the new continent, wrote the first account of it. Italian geographers and cosmographers were then far ahead of those of other nations. It is scarcely to be wondered at, therefore, that some of the first English books of travel in the Renaissance were translations from Italian works. Already, in 1550–51, William Thomas dedicated to the king, as his New Year's gift, a translation of Josaphat Barbaro's *Account of his Voyages to the East*, published in Venice in 1543. A more interesting and important work, however, was to be published a few years later, *The Decades of the New World*, by Pietro Martire d'Anghiera,[1] one of the principal authorities on the settlement of America to this day.[2] A second and more complete edition (in spite of its omitting several of the earlier accounts) appeared some twenty years later.[3] The book was a general history of travel and exploration from the time of Columbus, compiled by Peter Martyr, an Italian by birth, who, like many of his compatriots, had gone into the service of the king of Spain, where he became president of the Royal Council for the West Indies, and collected narratives of the great explorers in the Spanish service. To the

[1] *The Decades of the New World*, by Peter Martyr of Angleria, translated into English by Richard Eden, 1555.

[2] Vide J. G. Underhill, *Spanish Literature in the England of the Tudors*, p. 124, for the Spanish influence in Elizabethan books of travel.

[3] *The History of Travel in the West and East Indies, and other countries. . . . With a discourse of the northwest passage. . . .* Translated by Richard Eden and by Richard Willes, 1577.

original edition, translated by Richard Eden, Willes added the travels of Luigi Vertomanno of Rome, in Arabia, Persia, Syria, and other countries of the Orient, and a description of *Northeast Frosty Seas* as related by the ambassador of the Duke of Muscovy to a learned gentleman of Italy named Galeatius Butrigarius, who had written them down. An account was added of the voyages "of that worthy old man, Sebastian Cabot," and several other translations as well from the Italian, as, for instance, a description of China by Galeotto Perera, who had been a prisoner there. One of the few English records in the book consisted of extracts from Anthony Jenkinson's *Journey to Persia* in 1561, where he had been sent as ambassador "With the Queen's Majesty's letters in the Latin, Italian, and Hebrew tongue to the great Sophy and King of Persia."

The most interesting portion of the work related to Columbus' discovery of America. A description was given of the new territories and their riches, well calculated to inflame the Elizabethan imagination. In the epistle to the reader, Willes bade him "consider the fruits, the drugs, the pearls, the treasure, the millions of gold and silver, the Spaniards have brought out of the West Indies since the first voyage of Columbus. . . . The north western voyage be it never so full of difficulties will become as plausible as any other journey, if our passengers may return with plenty of silver, silks and pearl. Let Columbus, Americus, Cortesius, be well set forth again and bountifully rewarded, you shall hear of other and new found lands yet altogether unknown."

Other books were translated from the Italian, such as the travels of Cesare Federici, a Venetian merchant in the Orient.[1] The author had spent eighteen years in the far East, and as he thought the subject new and never before treated, he gave an account of the princes of the Indies, their religious faith, rites, customs, and also a description of the products of the countries. Both the novelty and rarity of the subject attracted the translator, who apologized for his want of learning and use of the ordinary speech; his purpose had been that English merchants and his other countrymen might profit by the book, and he prophesied great wealth for those who travelled in these regions.

In Italy, long before the rest of Europe, geography had received the same stimulus as other arts and sciences, and the superiority of Italians in its study over all other nations was long maintained. Italy, in the Renaissance, continued to be the home of geographical literature, at a time when the discoverers themselves came almost exclusively from the countries of Western Europe. In the first half of the sixteenth century, Italian maps were in advance of any others, and even much later a portion of Botero's

[1] *The Voyage and Travel of M. Cesare Frederick, Merchant of Venice into the East India, the Indies, and beyond the Indies.* . . . Translated by T(homas) H(ickok), 1588.

great work on the geography of the world was translated into English.[1]

It would be too much to say that the accounts of the great Italian navigators and explorers led Elizabethan seamen to similar deeds of daring. At the same time, there can be little doubt that the example set by a Columbus or a Cabot, or the descriptions of a Vespucci, did much to fan their smouldering love of adventure. The venturesome tendencies of the nation could no longer be kept in, when once it had heard or read the deeds of others. In this, also, Italy led the way for Western Europe to follow. The art of Michael Angelo or Leonardo, the statecraft of Machiavelli, the poetry of Ariosto, the discoveries of Columbus, seem widely separated at first glance, looking back from modern times; yet they were but different phases of the same movement. The energy which could not be restrained, the daring which knew no bounds, the desire to tread still virgin soil, the striving toward perfection, were all characteristic of the Italian Renaissance.

In Italy, after the age of action was once over, there followed a more critical period when the adventures of former times were digested and studied, and geography, enriched by many discoveries, became a science. At a time when the countries of Western Europe were sending their expeditions to distant seas,

---

[1] *The Travellers' Breviat, or an historical description of the most famous kingdoms in the world.* Translated by Robert Johnson from Botero, 1601.

in search of gold, or to look for the western passage to Cathay, Italian activity of this sort had narrowed almost to a critical one alone. Their geographers were now supreme, where once their navigators had been.

This was, then, the period when Italian books of travel and adventure were translated into English, and inflamed the Elizabethan imagination with their tales of riches and conquest. Just as Italian bankers and merchants had first shown England the possibilities of commercial life, so too in exploration and adventure their example proved a powerful one. Even then, in the age of the hardy Elizabethan seamen, the trade of Italy was not dead. Venice was in many ways what England is to-day; her colonies formed a colonial empire governed by a merchant aristocracy. Although the trade of the Atlantic, and the new passage around the Cape of Good Hope, no longer left Venice the highway for direct intercourse with the East, the position she had taken centuries to build was not lost in a day. The knowledge of the Orient came first from Italy to England. It was through Venice that English ambassadors and merchants passed on their way to Constantinople and the Orient. It was Venice which brought East and West together in a common bond of trade.

The Italian influence in England through commerce was most important. The mere presence in a city such as London of a number of foreign merchants, trained in superior methods, possessing greater skill in commerce than had heretofore been known, could not but influence, by their example, the native community. Even to this day many Italian commercial terms have remained in English use : debtor and creditor, for instance ; cash from *cassa;* journal from *giornale;* bank and bankrupt, from *banco* and *bancorotto;* the abbreviations for *liri, soldi* and *denari,* and that of *company* on the Bank of England notes, and the oft-recurring *ditto,* which should be spelled with an *e* instead of an *i*.[1] When, toward the end of the sixteenth century, the English succeeded in freeing themselves from their foreign competitors, who had once enjoyed almost a monopoly of banking and the commerce of other countries, it was due as much to their growing technical and commercial capacity as to the trade regulations enforced by the government.[2] Alongside of the growth in native enterprise, and of commercial ideas in England, and running parallel with it, a great change had taken place in the Italian merchants in England. Coming over at first for a temporary sojourn in what they then regarded as a barbarous country, whose inhabitants, ignorant of the broader elements of commerce, hated them for their success, they gradually settled in the land, and many of them became English in their sentiments and devotion. At the same time, by their residence and example, they did much to teach ideas of trade to the English. They had been merchants when

[1] Burgon, *op. cit.,* I, 282, note.
[2] Vide *Hamburg und England in Zeitalter der Königin Elizabeth,* Richard Ehrenberg, 1896.

elsewhere in Europe trade was still despised. Their industry and enterprise in foreign parts had amassed wealth for them through the long years when other nations were still in the Middle Ages. In commerce, as in art and science, they discovered the new life, recognizing possibilities which lay open to them, and the new foundation for the work of nations as of men. Italian city republics first in modern times had grasped the idea of a navy necessary to protect their shipping and uphold their interests. The energy, the vigor, the daring and courage of the Italian Renaissance found itself reflected no less strongly in the history of its merchants and explorers, than in the works of its painters and poets. In commerce, as in the arts and sciences, Italy held up the guiding light for the rest of Europe to follow.

CHAPTER VII

ITALIAN POLITICAL AND HISTORICAL IDEAS IN ENGLAND

I

THE transition effected by the Wars of the Roses, which led to the firm foundation of the Tudor monarchy under Henry the Seventh, marked the transformation of England from a feudal state to a centralized government under a prince possessing practically absolute power. It was characteristic of the period that similar changes were taking place about the same time in both France and Spain, where the decaying ideas of the Middle Ages were gradually becoming obscured by new conceptions, whose theoretical foundation at least was made possible by the revival of classical antiquity.

One of the most significant changes in the history of civilization is that, while in modern times the study of antiquity has suggested rather the Athenian democracy and Roman republic, it was otherwise in past centuries, when, from the time of the revival of Roman law at Bologna and Padua, the memory of imperial Rome was always present to the mind of the student and political dreamer. It was perhaps for this reason, in part, that the new humanism obtained its first patrons among Italian despots, whose example was later imitated in other countries of Europe. Classical learning did not appear to them as a dangerous model which might incite their subjects to strike for liberty, but rather a justification, in an age of reason, of the same despotic power they were then endeavoring to wield. At a time when precedent and tradition counted for so much, they sought to find in the example of great men of former times the sanction, as it were, of the power which in many instances they had obtained by the most unscrupulous means. This was especially the case in Italy, where classical tradition was stronger than in any other country. It would, however, be a mistake to suppose that princes elsewhere were insensible to the advantages of a patronage of learned men, ready to find an ancient pedigree for their methods of government. The historical resemblances, which could in all cases be discovered between their own rule and that of the princes of classical antiquity, must naturally have appealed to them at a time when they were endeavoring to strip the nobility of their feudal power in order to centralize it in themselves. In such patronage, moreover, they could feel that they were following in the footsteps of an Augustus or a Hadrian, with whom the claims of an empire had not destroyed an appreciation of letters and the arts.

From another point of view, as well, it is apparent that Italian scholars and humanists could hope to find a ready welcome at foreign courts. Not only were they first in the field, but the encouragement received at the hands of a Montefeltro or a Malatesta must have spurred them on to similar conquests. Beyond the Alps the whole of Europe stretched before them, while the competition among learned men diminished where their numbers were few. The fact, moreover, that they were aliens, with no ties binding them to the soil, and dependent only on the good will of their patron, favored them with princes, who often did not dare trust their half-submissive noblemen.

Beginning about 1460, the new centralized power at the court encouraged the growth of letters. Edward the Fourth laid the foundation of the new monarchy in England; he practically discontinued Parliament and worked silently toward absolute power ; he introduced a system of spies, and even interfered with the pure administration of justice. But he also encouraged Caxton in the new art of printing, and gave directions that no hindrance be placed on any stranger who might import or sell books in the kingdom. He was the first in England of the new type of princes who broke loose from the feudal traditions of the Middle Ages, and endeavored to centralize power in the hands of the monarch alone, and make of him at once an absolute ruler and a patron of arts and letters, although like many of the Italian despots, he united utter unscrupulousness with cultivation. But stormy days were still at hand, and it was not until the accession of Henry the Seventh that the position of learning began to be secure. Although life gave Henry but little opportunity for culture, his tastes were all inclined toward the patronage of literature and art. What he did most successfully was to play in England the rôle of an Italian despot. The best contemporary appreciation of his methods and character has, perhaps, for this reason been written by the Italian, Polydore Vergil.

Edward the Fourth conferred the highest English distinction, the Order of the Garter, upon Duke Frederick of Urbino. The same honor was later granted by Henry the Seventh to Duke Guidobaldo. There were other evidences of his desire to be on a friendly footing with Italian princes, even though they could be of little direct advantage to him. His correspondence, for instance, with the Estensi of Ferrara, and the frequent employment of Italians in his service, would seem to indicate that they were sympathetic to his nature. His policy, moreover, in its steady direction toward an absolute despotism, had been made familiar by Italian examples. While it would be going too far to say that he held any Italian model consciously before him in his creation of the Tudor monarchy, it seems likely that the political methods and ideas of Italy were present in his mind as he labored to strengthen his rule.

Polydore Vergil, soon after he had taken up his residence in London, became intimate with Henry the Seventh, at whose request he is said to have written his history of England, on which he was to spend almost thirty years of his life. It was not the first English historical work by an Italian; Tito Livio of Forli, "poet and orator of the Duke of Gloucester," had long before written a life of Henry the Fifth.[1] Polydore Vergil, however, in spite of his poor reputation for veracity,[2] was the first to employ modern methods in English history, and attempt to weigh authorities, summarize character, and tell a connected story. The historical method he employed was far in advance of anything England had known. The first part of the book roused national prejudices; he discarded Brute, the reputed founder of England, as an imaginary character, and treated Geoffrey of Monmouth's history as a combination of fact and fable, on which but little reliance could be placed.[3] Vergil's history, however, recorded not only political events, but such facts as the introduction of the new learning into England. It was of especial value for its account of the reign of Henry the Seventh, with whose aims and character he sympathized. His work, in spite of numerous errors which can be excused by reason of his ignorance of English dialects and customs, was a contribution of real importance. A letter of his to James the Fourth of Scotland is significant as showing the method he employed in writing.[4] He had

[1] Voigt, II, 255.

[2] Cf. "Maro and Polydore bore Vergil's name;
One reaps a poet's, one a liar's fame."

[3] *Three Books of Vergil's English History*, Camden Society, 1844. Introduction.   [4] *Cal. St. Pap.*, *Henry VIII*, I, 105.

visited England, he said, largely to see the country and study its antiquities. He had been so surprised to find its history confused, and unknown even to Englishmen, that he determined, in consequence, to write a short chronicle, which was now finished. Very few references to Scotland had been made, since there was no good author to follow. He therefore requested King James to furnish him either with annals of the country, or with the names and lives of Scottish kings, his own amongst the number.

With all its blunders, the history enjoyed considerable influence. Vergil's personal animosity to Wolsey led him, however, to defame the great cardinal's character; his opinion was passed on from one English historian to another, Hall taking it from Vergil, Foxe from Hall, Burnet and Strype from Foxe, Hume from Burnet, and so on.[1] But English history owed a real debt to Polydore Vergil. In the dedication of his work to Henry the Eighth he compared the early chronicles of Bede and Gildas to meat without the salt, which it was his object to supply; but recognizing their value, he edited Gildas for the first time in 1525. Alike in his methods and in his use of material he ushered the new study of history into England.

II

The influence of Machiavelli first entered England with Thomas Cromwell. Like many other Englishmen of the age, Cromwell probably took part in the

[1] Brewer, *Henry VIII*, I, 264 *et seq.*

Italian wars and there learned the language. From soldiering he became a trader, and acted as commercial agent to a Venetian merchant. In after years, when he became minister, it appears to have been Italy that left its deepest stamp on him. Not only, it was said, "in the rapidity and unscrupulousness of his designs, but in their larger scope, their clearer purpose and admirable combination, the Italian statecraft entered with Cromwell into English politics."[1] He was the first English minister in whom there can be traced the steady working out of a great and definite aim to raise the king to absolute authority on the ruins of every rival power within the realm. His policy was closely modelled on the lines laid down by Machiavelli. While still in the employ of Wolsey, he advised Reginald Pole to read as his manual in politics *The Prince* which he possessed in manuscript even before it had been published in Italy, and which he described as a practical work on government far more useful than the dreams of Plato.[2] His own aim was to secure peace and order for England by centralizing all power in the crown, and strengthening the hands of the king. As the church alone stood in the way of the absolute rule of the king, the last check that had survived the Wars of the Roses, his unbending

[1] J. R. Green, *Short History of England*, p. 335. For the influence of Machiavelli on other English statesmen, vide W. Alison Phillips' article in the *Nineteenth Century*, December, 1896.

[2] For Pole's opinion of Machiavelli, vide *Epistolæ Reg. Pole*, 1744, p. 151.

efforts and energies were directed to destroying its authority. His interest for the present study lies, however, in his being the first great English disciple of Machiavelli.

Long before the writings of Machiavelli had as yet been read in England, or his influence had made itself felt in political philosophy, several other Italian thinkers were well known. Sir Thomas More, it will be remembered, was thoroughly familiar with the best Italian thought, and fondly cherished Pico della Mirandola as his one ideal. Sir Thomas Elyot was perhaps even more affected by Italian philosophy. The influence of Pontano, the elder Patrizi, Pico, and many minor writers, has been traced in his *Governour*,[1] a treatise on the education of statesmen, dedicated to Henry the Eighth; to this book Elyot owed his appointment as ambassador to Charles the Fifth. *The Governour* was one of the earliest treatises on moral philosophy in English, although similar works had been written by Fortescue in the fifteenth century, and in Italy, by Pontano and Beroaldo. To Pontano Elyot readily acknowledged his indebtedness; but the book which he really took as his model, and borrowed from to a great extent, was a work very popular at that time, by Francesco Patrizi.[2] Between it and *The Governour* a general similarity exists, and many passages are identical, translated word for word.

[1] Sir Thomas Elyot, *The Governour*, ed. H. H. S. Croft, p. lxiii *et seq.*

[2] *De Regno et Regio Institutione.*

Elyot showed his familiarity as well with the writings of several Italian humanists, such as Valla, Perotto, Calepino, and many others of less repute.[1]   The purpose he had in writing was that the children of the upper classes should be better educated in order that they too "may be deemed worthy to be Governours"; all this was thoroughly characteristic of the Renaissance. The influence of Machiavelli, however, had not as yet reached him, nor does he seem to have been aware of its existence.

Another English political thinker, somewhat later in date, was John Ponet (or Poynet), Bishop of Winchester, who was also familiar with Italian, and had himself translated the *Tragedy* of Ochino.   In his treatise on political power[2] he discussed the causes of its growth, the reasons which sanctioned it, and its proper use and duty.   He found a justification in the law of nature for all animals to be ruled by a superior creature.   Government he divided, like Aristotle, into monarchy, aristocracy and democracy; the state in which all three had power was in his judgment the best.   A discussion followed as to whether kings, princes and other governors possessed absolute power and authority over their subjects: should the prince be subject to the law of God and of his country?   The answer to this, that the prince must obey his own laws, he pretended to find in the Bible.   He considered the

[1] *The Governour*, p. cxxxv.
[2] *A Short Treatise of Politic Power and of the True Obedience which Subjects owe to Kings*, 1556.

question as to how far subjects were bound to obey
their princes. Furthermore, if the property of the subject belonged to the prince, might he not lawfully take
it as his own. In discussing the great question "whether
it be lawful to depose an evil governor and kill a tyrant," Ponet proved himself to be one of the earliest
English advocates of tyrannicide. In the examples
given as illustrations, he showed his familiarity with
Italian, and particularly Venetian, history.

Scattered through the pages of Elizabethan literature can be found hundreds of references to Machiavelli,[1] whose name passed as a synonym for treachery
and tyranny, used even by many who had never seen
his works. At the same time, in a less known direction, his influence made itself felt in English political
philosophy. His method and ideas were reflected
particularly in the writings of William Thomas, John
Leslie, Thomas Bedingfield and Charles Merbury,
while even Bacon was influenced by him.

The theory generally adopted by the English writers
of the sixteenth century, as to the form of government
which would present fewest dangers to the welfare of
the state, favored absolute monarchy. Machiavelli
had argued for this in *The Prince*. To the great Florentine, who elsewhere advocated a republic, the mere
form of government mattered little in comparison with
the methods employed for attaining and holding power.
Inasmuch as these means were best suited to abso-

---

[1] Vide E. Meyer, *Machiavelli and the Elizabethan Drama*,
Litterarhistorische Forschungen, 1897, *passim*.

lutism, his ideas seemed like the apology and defence of the absolute ruler. Friend and foe alike, then, regarded him, not in the modern light of an Italian patriot, but as the exponent and advocate of a strong rule, regardless of the methods employed to obtain power. Absolute government was the goal to which his ideas led; the Italian political philosophy of the age was all in the direction of absolutism.[1] This influence can be traced likewise in England, where it provided the theoretical foundation for the doctrine of the divine right of kings.

The English arguments in favor of the absolute monarchy were generally reached after supposedly impartial investigations into the different forms of government. Democracy and aristocracy were both discussed, and the advantages and disadvantages of each were weighed. In the ordinary division of every country between the nobility and commons, it was recognized that the desire of the one was always to rule, of the other not to be ruled. The question, therefore, at issue was whether the nobleman, endeavoring to maintain his position, or the commoner, seeking to attain power for himself, was the more prejudicial to the welfare of the state. Or, to describe it in another way, whose desire was the greater, he who feared to lose what he already possessed, or he who, having nothing, had everything to gain? The desire of both was thought equal, although the effects were unequal; for the man of property could easily obtain more, while

[1] *Cf.* Castiglione, *Courtier*, p. 312.

he who had nothing could not acquire more without much labor. If, however, the one could grow rich without toil and the other found no ease in his riches, the world would become barbarous through lack of work. In labor, therefore, lay the foundation of all "civil policy." It was necessary both to force the needy to labor, and maintain the rights of those possessing property. As long as neither nobleman nor commoner overstepped their bounds, so long were both of benefit to the state. If either should do so, the party of the commons would certainly prove the more dangerous on account of their ignorance and inconstancy. Moreover, it was impossible for many individuals long to preserve the same opinion. They might agree, but it would only be for a short time, and if once they lost their heads, no peril could be compared to the frenzy of the multitude. Their occasional success had come rather from good fortune than wisdom. In Thomas' mind, if the commons once attained power, they would destroy both the nobility and themselves.[1] Others likewise shared this view of democracy. Its advantages, however, were also considered. Democracy observed perfect equality and reduced the constitution of the state to the law of nature. Just as nature gave riches, honor and office to one man no more than to another, so popular government tended to make all men equal without privilege or prerogative. The avarice of the rich and the insolence of the great were supposed alike to be done

[1] *Works*, p. 157 *et seq.*

away with by democracy. It fostered friendship and equality in human society, and permitted every one to enjoy liberty and equal justice without fear of tyranny or oppression. In spite of all this the faults of democracy were said to outweigh its advantages. No true equality could be observed under any system of popular government, since it was contrary to the law of nature, which made certain men wiser than others, decreeing that some were to command and others to obey. General equality, moreover, seemed impossible so long as there were magistrates and forms of government.[1] The characteristic of a democracy was that "handicraftsmen" and the "baser sort" of people should manage public affairs. Its main drawback was that with it went envy of the rich, and an intense conceit accompanied the feeling it possessed of its own infallibility. To describe democracy in a sentence, it seemed a "horrible monster of many heads without reason."[2]

After the popular form of government had been removed from consideration, the question of aristocracy was approached. It was observed that the greed of the nobility resulted frequently in the oppression and suffering of the multitude. So long as the commons were in power, magistrates were careful to restrain the excesses of the nobility and advance public welfare. This condition would prove most beneficial if order

[1] Bedingfield, *Florentine History of Machiavelli*, preface, 1595.

[2] Merbury, *Brief Discourse*, 1581, p. 11.

could always be maintained, and laws remained inviolate. What popular state, however, could point to freedom from sedition, violence and faction for thirty years, during which time the state had never been in danger of overthrow?[1] The tendency to faction was among the greatest dangers of an aristocracy as well. The greater the number of rulers, the more factions and disputes there were,[2] while another peril lay in state secrets being often disclosed.

The idea of government by parties is a comparatively modern one. Even to the framers of the American Constitution the presence of party government appeared as one of the grave dangers which was to beset the young republic. Its presence in the mind of William Thomas made him incline toward possible tyranny in an absolute ruler, in preference to the danger of an overthrow of government through factional contests. His argument in favor of absolute monarchy was that a good prince, even though he diminished the power of the commons, preserved them, at the same time, from the tyranny of the nobility, acting toward the latter in the way they did to the multitude; he was as much interested in governing well one class as the other. Contrariwise, even if he were a tyrant, yet his tyranny was preferable to that of the nobility. In the one case there were many tyrants, while in the other a single one would suffer no one but himself. The prince's tyranny was, therefore, to be preferred to that of an aristocracy,

[1] Thomas, *op. cit.*, p. 166.   [2] Bedingfield, *loc. cit.*

and was infinitely better than the insolence of the multitude. The conclusion reached was that it was best for the prince to have supreme power. While he should not oppress the people, he ought to train them so that his very name would make them tremble.[1] They should not even be allowed to talk of his actions and laws, since contempt and disobedience, the mother of all errors, would follow such criticism.

John Leslie argued, likewise, in favor of the absolute power of one prince. " By the providence of one God, the whole world is ruled; so is the body of man by one soul governed; a ship by one master is guided." One king stood for peace and unity, which all good citizens should wish for.[2] Charles Merbury also tried to show that the rule of the lawful monarch was the best of all forms of government. His title should be by descent in blood royal. Election was open to many disadvantages, not only in the anarchy which necessarily existed before a new prince could be chosen, but in the fact that to satisfy his ambition in that direction a prince would even impoverish a country. Another drawback was the possible election of an alien. Italians, for instance, called all others barbarians, and it was readily conceivable that an Italian prince might try to change the language and customs of the country. The great advantage in a prince who had absolute power over all his subjects

---

[1] Thomas, p. 169.

[2] *Treatise touching the Right of Mary Queen of Scotland,* 1584, p. 65 *et seq.*

was in sovereignty, which was without other limitation of time than his own life, and after that passed to his sons and heirs. He was accountable to no one, since he received his power only from God. He was subject, therefore, to no other law than that of God. Whatever differed from the divine law he was not bound to obey. For the prince to be governed by the estates and peers of his realm would be most injurious to the whole idea of monarchy. Still less ought he to be subject to the common multitude, who, as they obtained greater authority, became both more insolent and disposed to rebellion. In all well-administered kingdoms, therefore, the commons had only the power of petition, the nobles of deliberation, and the prince alone of execution; for "our Prince, who is the image of God on Earth, and as it were, *Un Minor Esempio* of His almighty power, is not to acknowledge any greater than himself, nor any authority greater than his own."[1] The perfection of monarchy was therefore to be found in the absolute rule of the monarch. Thomas Bedingfield, likewise, in his translation of Machiavelli, congratulated his compatriots that they were destined by God to live in the obedience of an hereditary royal monarchy, where the prince submitted himself no less to the law of nature than he desired his subjects to be obedient to him. Following the idea expressed by Patrizi in his *Civil Policy*, which Richard Robinson had translated into English, and where an absolutism was declared to be the only

[1] *Op. cit.*, p. 43 *et seq.; cf.* Castiglione, p. 314.

logical form of government, Bedingfield argued in favor
of the monarch ruling alone, just as God ruled the
entire universe. It was the best state of affairs, and
all nations, it was said, were first so governed. Of all
forms it was "the most reasonable, most natural, most
honorable, and most necessary." [1] The power of the
king was of direct advantage to his subjects; witness
the haughtiness of the Spaniard, who, although he
might have no clothes on his back, was proud simply
because his master was king of Spain. On the other
hand, said Merbury, it was only necessary to look at
the Italian, who had lost "the light and dignity of
his nation." It was no small comfort for the English
gentleman abroad to be able to sit side by side, the
equal of the proudest Spaniard and most boastful
Frenchman.

Other writers also argued in favor of the absolute
power of the sovereign. John Leslie, who cited
Machiavelli, Contarini and Polydore Vergil, described
the great difference between the king's right and that
of all others: the king alone was not subject to the
common law of the realm; nor could any law bind
the crown. [2]

It is remarkable that the writers in favor of the absolute power of the king were all connected in some
way with Italy. William Thomas had been the greatest
English authority on everything Italian. Charles Merbury prefaced his book with an Italian dedication to
Queen Elizabeth, and added to it a collection of Italian

---

[1] Bedingfield, *loc. cit.*   [2] *Treatise*, p. 21 *b, et seq.*

proverbs. John Leslie quoted from several Italian authorities, while Thomas Bedingfield gave his ideas on the subject as an introduction to a translation of Machiavelli's History of Florence. Englishmen ignorant of Italian could even read in Patrizi, that as there was but one God for all creation, so there should be but one prince. All these arguments were constructed on similar plans. There was always the same rational, apparently unbiassed, historical examination into the different forms of government; and always the same preference toward absolutism as the most logical form, since it bestowed sovereignty on the most worthy. A growing tendency existed to establish its foundation on the divine right of kings. The ancient system of checks on the royal authority was disappearing from the political philosophy of the day; the sovereign was to be one and absolute in his power, accountable only to God.

The Italian political ideas of that age were in the direction of absolute monarchy. This influence can be traced in English legal thought in the work of Alberico Gentile, who came to England in 1580, and seven years later was appointed Regius professor of civil law at Oxford. Even before that, however, he was consulted by the government as to what course to pursue in the case of the Spanish ambassador who had been detected plotting against Elizabeth; it was by his advice that Mendoza was merely ordered to leave the country. He later took up his residence in London with a view to forensic practice. His work brought new life to the dead body of civil law,[1] and gave a fresh impulse to the study of Roman and international law, which, before Grotius, he attempted to establish on a non-theological basis.[2] His *De Jure Belli* combined for the first time, it is said, the practical discussions of Catholic theologians with the Protestant theory of natural law. It criticised and systematized the rules for the conduct of warfare, and has been called a legal commentary on the events of the sixteenth century. In addition to this he wrote an apology for Machiavelli,[3] and also a treatise favoring the supreme power of the prince, which he dedicated to James the First.[4] Herein he tried to prove the prince to be an absolute monarch, and have arbitrary power over the lives and estates of his people. Since the people had conferred on him all their rule and power, he need acknowledge no superior but God, whose will was sufficient reason, and whose reason was absolute law. The prince possessed and enjoyed dominion over everything; he was above the civil law, and only under the law of God, of nature and of nations. He was cautioned, however, to use his power justly, otherwise trouble would follow.

This book by Gentile was not many years later to call forth an indignant Puritan refutation.[5] " The author's

---

[1] Fulbeck, *Direction to the Study of Law*, 1620.

[2] *Il Principe*, Preface by Burd, p. 63.

[3] *De legationibus libri tres*, London, 1585.

[4] *Regales Disputationes Tres de Potestate Regis Absolutis*, 1605.

[5] *England's Monarch, or a conviction and refutation by the Common Law of those false principles and insinuating flatteries*

name is Albericus, . . . what countryman I know not, but his name as also his principles seem to speak him a stranger by birth." The ideas underlying absolute monarchy were not English; their root was foreign, and British soil did not prove congenial to their growth. In most cases Machiavelli was regarded as their promoter and prime mover; for his English readers of that time abstracted from his writings only the arguments favoring the absolute rule of the prince. To sixteenth century Europe, Machiavelli represented something entirely different from what we see in him to-day; to the men of the Renaissance, he seemed the apologist of tyranny, the teacher of subtle methods of how to enslave a free people. He was in fact known rather by the books of his opponents than his own writings, which were not translated till later. Innocent Gentillet, a French Huguenot, wrote the most celebrated of these denunciations, and fixed on Machiavelli the responsibility for the massacre of Saint Bartholomew, pointing out the supposed influence of the great Florentine on the politics and statecraft of the time. From this book, most subsequent denunciations were taken. In its English rendering[1] the translator referred to Machiavelli taking faith away from princes, authority and majesty from laws, and liberty

---

of Albericus. . . . Together with a general confutation . . . of all absolute monarchy, London, 1644.

[1] *A Discourse upon the means of well-governing a kingdom against Nicholas Machiavell the Florentine* (by I. Gentillet). Translated into the English by Simon Patericke, London, 1602.

from the people, and called his book " this deadly poison sent out of Italy." A like opinion of Machiavelli was then current in England. Contemporary literature was full of it. Men judged him rather from hearsay than by his actual writings, though they too were known. A whole school grew up, whose conception of statecraft, resting on a common basis of falsehood and fraud, exaggerated his ideas.[1] Carefully selected passages in Gentillet further convinced Englishmen of his wickedness. His influence with the dramatists, especially Greene and Marlowe, will be considered later, but in ordinary life and conversation his very name passed into a byword. Some idea of his general reputation may perhaps be obtained from a letter of advice written by a friend to a young Englishman in Italy[2] of how best to profit from his travels; after urging him to study the Italian language and civil law, he advised him to read the *Discourse on Livy*, by one whom he called the " vile, treacherous, devilish person whom you would call him devil is Machiavelli." He should remember, however, that to be called by his name was a disgrace and an infamy. Machiavelli's influence was thus, in part, an imaginary one, many things being attributed to him which he never advocated. At the same time, the new spirit of rational inquiry in state affairs, the historic sense and illustration, and even the leaning toward absolutism, can all be traced

[1] Janet, *Science Politique*, I, 542.
[2] All Souls Library (Oxford), Ms. CLV, f. 77 *b*, dated 27th February, 1599.

to the influence of his writings. His popularity in England was shown in other ways : Gabriel Harvey, fresh from Cambridge, asked for the books of " the great founder and master of policies," [1] claiming that his works had supplanted all others ; and the *Prince* and *Discourses*, it is said, were both printed in London at this time.[2]

III

Nannini's *Civil Considerations*, a treatise on practical government based on Guicciardini, was only one of the numerous Italian books then translated into English. More important than the problems it discussed, and the working side of the state it presented, in preference to its theoretical ideal, was its new method of treatment by historical illustrations. Questions were put in their relation to actual life, and not the ideal possibilities they might contain.

Another book of this period in which the influence of the Italian method can be found was Sir Thomas Smith's work on England, written on a plan similar to Contarini's *Venice*. Smith, it should be remembered, had studied under Alciati, the reformer of civil law, and listened to Accoramboni and Rubeo, at Padua, where he graduated a doctor of laws. The book he was later to write showed the power of systematic analysis so characteristic of the Italian treatises of the time. In discussing the merits of different

[1] *Letter-Book*, p. 174 *et seq.*
[2] *Nineteenth Century*, December, 1896, p. 915.

forms of government, he gave the qualities and defects of each, considering that state the best which was most in accordance with the nature of its people.

The actual influence of the Italian historical method was gathered not only from books but from men; Tito Livio of Forli and Polydore Vergil offered early instances of Italian historians in England, and later Pietro Bizari came over as well. On the other hand, Nicholas Sanders, an English controversialist and historian, remained long in Rome, where he lived under the protection of Cardinal Morone.

The Italian influence in William Thomas was evident in his historical work. In the *History of Italy*, before describing the sights of each city came an account of the place, written, as he frankly stated,[1] by comparing together the works of different authors; he borrowed especially from Machiavelli's account of Florence. Machiavelli's history was later translated by Bedingfield,[2] who prefaced the book with his arguments in favor of absolute monarchy. The history itself equalled or excelled, in his judgment, any hitherto written, not only in the method of presentation, but on account of the observations of the author, who left aside all partiality and flattery and tried only to arrive at the truth. His method of writing was to set forth the causes and effects of every action rather than to extoll or condemn the per-

[1] *Op. cit.*, p. 140.
[2] *The Florentine History*, translated by T[homas] B[edingfield], 1595.

sons of whom he wrote. Other Italian histories were also translated into English ; Guicciardini's *Wars of Italy*, by Geoffrey Fenton,[1] and histories of Portugal,[2] of the Low Countries,[3] and of the Turks and Persians.[4] Examples of the manner in which history should be written were presented in these works ; not only were they chronicles of events, but descriptions as well of the religion, military strength, government, colonies and revenues of the countries they described.

The Italian philosophy of history and method of historical writing was illustrated in a selection from the works of Francesco Patrizi and Jacopo Acontio,[5] the latter an Italian refugee in England, and one of Bacon's forerunners in the method of experimental research. This book, though almost unknown, was one of the

[1] *The History of Guicciardin. . . .* Reduced into English by Geoffrey Fenton, London, 1579.

[2] *The History of the Uniting of the Kingdom of Portugal to the Crown of Castile* . . . translated by Edward Blount (?) from the Italian of Girolamo Conestaggio, London, 1600.

[3] *The Description of the Low Countries* . . . out of the history of Lodovico Guicciardini by Th. Danett, London, 1593.

[4] *The History of the Wars between the Turks and the Persians*, written in Italian by John Thomas Minadoi, and translated into English by Abraham Hartwell, London, 1595. *The Ottoman of Lazaro Soranzo* . . . translated out of Italian into English by Abraham Hartwell, London, 1603.

[5] *The True Order and Method of writing and reading Histories according to the Precepts of Francisco Patricio and Accontio Tridentino, two Italian writers* . . . by Thomas Blundeville, London, 1574. The manuscript of Acontio, which has never been published, is preserved at the Record Office, London (Dom. Ser., Vol. XXXIV, Aug., 1564). It was dedicated by him to Robert Dudley, Earl of Leicester.

most remarkable of its kind in the sixteenth century, foreshadowing, in its ideas, so much of what is commonly thought the creation of our own times and the modern scientific method.   It was an analysis of history, the study of which was looked upon as a preparation for princes, to guard them against errors. History was treated from the point of view that everything had its cause, and every cause a beginning, early growth, climax, decline and end.   In considering any question, therefore, one ought to begin by noticing its relations. Four things especially should always be kept in mind, trade, public revenues, armament and the form of government.

The argument briefly stated was that history was made up of deeds done either by a state, or against a state, and such deeds arose in turn, either from some outward cause, as force or fortune, or inward cause, like reason or desire.   Every action was therefore done by some person, for some cause in time and place, with means and instruments. This was true regardless of the magnitude of the action.   There was always a principal doer, over and above the inferior doers ; likewise a principal cause ruling inferior causes, and a principal time, means and instrument. Such were the outward conditions of an action ; but within it, also, there existed possibility, occasion and success. Regarding the doer, both his position and his ability were to be considered, the first dependent upon his family and country, the second on his power, skill and industry.   No man ought for an instant to imagine he could achieve success unless he possessed some of these qualities. Even emotions had their final causes, for the object of wrath was revenge, and of mercy, help and comfort.

"Those whose lives ought to be chronicled" were also considered. In writing a biography one ought first to give the hero's family and country, and then search for the principle which moved him in his undertakings; whether an outward one, such as destiny or fortune; or inward, as by choice or nature. It was also necessary for the biographer to determine the origin of that principle — whether it was passion, custom, or reason. Such actions as were forced by outward circumstances deserved neither praise nor blame, and were indeed only to be mentioned so far as they brought out or hindered others springing from inward causes, which alone were worthy of description. The historian ought, therefore, to analyze the cause and reason of each action, if it was by choice, and to what extent education on the part of the doer had modified it; for education both confirmed a man in his bringing up, framed his inclinations, and trained his mind. The historian's aim should be to show the influence of environment and its exemplification through outward deeds. The hero's personality ought to be considered, however, not only for his deeds and speeches, which were, after all, only the result of the man, but in other respects as well.

All public actions everywhere depended on three things, peace, sedition and war. Peace existed both in outward action and inward frame of mind. It had for its proper foundation the contentment of citizens and was broken only by some inward cause, such as famine, the denial to classes of their just rights, or else by war. Analyses of revolutions and wars, with an account of the great conspiracies of the sixteenth century, further illustrated this discussion.

It was considered to be the duty of the historian to relate everything without either adding to it or taking away from it. Since every action resulted from some person's activity the doer ought to be mentioned, with the reasons which led him to undertake it; and when several had been engaged in it, the parts should be kept in such relation as to form together one simple action.

Regarding the order and method to be observed in reading history, those eager to learn ought to understand the object and purpose for which it was written. There were three principal causes: first, to acknowledge the providence of God; secondly, in order that wisdom might be learned from the example of the wise; and lastly, it was intended to lead men to greater good, and similarly to shun evil. Nothing, it was thought, removed one further from the desire of evil than to see the punishment of the wicked, and history exposed this clearly to the world. History made men wiser both to direct their own actions and to advise others. It was its proper fruit that it should be of benefit alike to the reader and to his country. Regarding those who, having spent their lifetime in study, knew nothing beyond the genealogies and pedigrees of kings and emperors, one knew not whether more to pity or deride them.

This historical method has fallen into undeserved oblivion. It was in many ways a remarkable work, clearly demonstrating the influence of environment on the individual, and of man as the product of his age. It showed, too, the analytical and systematizing tendency of the Italians in the sixteenth century. In history, as in other things, Italy gave the model, from which the other nations of Europe could build.

IV

In the sixteenth century Italians did much to teach Englishmen the writing of history, on a different plan from that of the mediæval chronicles. Polydore Vergil's *History of England* was especially influential and may be said to have been the first of the long chain of English histories which have since appeared. The translations of Guicciardini and Machiavelli gave to Elizabethan historians the best of models and examples, while Acontio and Patrizi's philosophy and critique furnished an analysis of the methods of writing history.

In considering the influence of Italy on England in the political thought of the Renaissance, it should be looked for in the intellectual substructure and theoretical foundation on which political action was based. The pendulum had far to swing from the direction of feudal ideas to that of absolute monarchy. Between the Plantagenets and the second of the Stuarts the line of the Tudors bridged the interval, and their rule prepared the way for the despotic attempt of Charles the First. The absolute power of the prince had begun to be wielded by Edward the Fourth in the earliest days of the Renaissance. In many ways Henry the Seventh laid the firm foundations for the monarchy. Its intellectual justification, however, was still lacking in England. It was this which was supplied by Italy and Italian thought. In practical life and in the world of action it was from Italy that Tiptoft brought the Paduan Law, and the ruthlessness of his methods was worthy of the example set by the Italian despots of the fifteenth century. It was an Italian, too, who could sympathize with his ideas and task in forming the new monarchy, that the first of the Tudors chose to be his friend and biographer. In his love of art and splendor, in his encouragement of learning, as in his methods, Wolsey had much in common with the great Italian cardinals of the Renaissance. A little later it was Thomas Cromwell, a reader of Machiavelli, who crushed the last power of the church that still dared assert itself in opposition to the authority of the king.

In the world of ideas at the same time Italy supplied the material for the apologists of the Tudor monarchy. Machiavelli offered, indeed, a ready reply to all who searched his works for arguments. His calm, dispassionate statements, his cool judgments, lent themselves to many constructions. While, in the sixteenth and seventeenth centuries at least, the great Florentine was a much maligned man, at the same time there can be little doubt that the men of the Renaissance found in his works a mine of arguments in behalf of the absolute power of the state ; and to Englishmen then the state meant the monarchy. Thomas, Leslie, Merbury and Bedingfield, students of Italian statecraft, all showed his influence in their writings in favor of the absolute power of the prince. His historical method, his balance and judgment, they adopted ; but after weighing all considerations, their inclinations led them toward absolute rule as the most perfect form of government. Other Italians, too, whose works were translated into English or written in England, all favored it. The revival of antiquity had brought with it the belief that the power of the sovereign should be absolute, and to Englishmen unused to the Italian city republics and other forms of government, sovereignty meant, therefore, the power of the prince. How alien and foreign this was, in fact, to their own ideas was not to be realized until the time of the English revolution.

CHAPTER VIII

THE ITALIAN INFLUENCE IN ENGLISH POETRY

I

THE Renaissance, in its first intention at least, was largely an effort to imitate the life and conditions of antiquity. That it became otherwise, that, far from being the servile imitation of another age, it was to embody a great force in remoulding the civilized world, from which almost every modern idea may be said to trace its origin, was largely due to the influence of Italy. The Renaissance in the countries beyond the Alps was often, in more ways than one, a continuation of the movement begun on Italian soil. Erasmus and Holbein, Lope de Vega and Montaigne, Camoens and even Shakespeare, owed each a debt of gratitude to the art, the letters and the civilization of Italy.

In English poetry this Italian influence was of a twofold nature. On the one hand, it taught new forms and stood for precision, balance and polish ; it brought in a greater consciousness of the poet's art and dignity, and demanded on his part a deeper learning and scholarship. On the other, it created a fresh atmosphere for the poet's life. The new spirit of the Renaissance in Italy, by removing existing barriers, enriched the life of man, while, by a similar process, his nature felt itself freed from all moral restraints. Italy was thus destined to teach measure and art in form, while in spirit it stood for unbridled license and excess. Its æsthetic side taught a new art of verse to English poets ; its life created a romantic atmosphere for English dramatists.

It is somewhat significant that the father of English poetry was the first to express the influence of Italy. Chaucer led his nation in realizing that a new age had dawned. He had been the first in England to read the Tuscan poets ; his writings, like Petrarch's, were the first to be freed from theological purpose. He foreshadowed, though long in advance of his age, the influence which was later to be felt. The glimmer of the new era he awakened disappeared once more after his death. His successors, Gower and Lydgate, and later the Scotch Chaucerians, although familiar with a few of the Italian writers, failed to appreciate their true spirit. Petrarch they regarded as a scholar, Boccaccio as a teacher. During the entire fifteenth century this condition prevailed, the Tuscan poets usually being valued for nothing else.[1] The real significance of the new poetry could not yet be grasped beyond the Alps. It was necessary for Englishmen to be educated to the point where the great Tuscan poets

[1] Although two English bishops, Hallam and Bubwith, meeting John of Serravalle at the Council of Constance, induced him to write a commentary on Dante's *Commedia.* — E. Moore, *Dante and his Early Biographers,* London, 1890, p. 65.

would be able to make an appeal to their taste and understanding. Neither Stephen Hawes nor Skelton ever really felt the spirit of the Renaissance, or saw Petrarch otherwise than as a "famous clerk."[1] Poetry remained backward when all else progressed. It was time for it, however, to leave the sterile traditions of the Middle Ages. At the court of Henry the Eighth, with its affectations of foreign fashions, its love of Italian learning, Italian music, and Italian art, it was scarcely conceivable that poets alone should repeat allegorical expressions then dead and meaningless. Latin humanistic poetry had already been cultivated by Flemming, Free and other English scholars, with fair success, while numerous Italian residents at the Tudor court also practised it. It was only natural that poetical forms more in harmony with the spirit of the age should be attempted. Italy, which in scholarship, art and courtly life offered the example to Europe, was to do so in poetry as well.

The cultivation of Latin verse had been among the earliest labors of Italian humanists. The more gifted and less pedantic among them, like Politian, wrote poetry also in the vernacular. English scholars, by no means so talented as their masters, left this for courtiers to do. At the court, therefore, the new poetry grew up, just as the new learning had prospered at the university. In each case the limited sphere of its surroundings was responsible for the slow development; scholarship, for instance, had

[1] Skelton, I, 377.

taken fully seventy-five years to succeed. Its final triumph was marked at the same time by the introduction of the Italian verse forms into English poetry, even though these were not to take firm hold until the reign of Elizabeth.

Navagero's famous conversation with Boscan remains unparalleled in the pages of English literature. A number of circumstances might lead one, however, to suppose that it was something more than chance which first induced Wyatt and Surrey to begin their work of poetical reform. The Italian humanist poets, resident at the English court, perhaps, encouraged it. Silvestro Gigli, Adrian de Castello and Andrea Ammonio, all of whom were poets, must have known Wyatt. Ammonio, especially, who lived for a time in More's household, was a member of a literary coterie in London, which included other Italians and several of the Oxford men who had studied abroad.[1] The new poetry was distinctively a product of the court in the beginning, flourishing there and nowhere else. In Italy, every courtier had been a poet, and every poet a courtier. Castiglione, who had himself visited England, laid it down as a rule for his courtier to cultivate and polish his native language. "Let him much exercise himself in poets . . . and also in writing both rhyme and prose, and especially in this our vulgar tongue."[2]

The new poetry in England was to be full of courtly feelings and ideas. It was essentially a literature not

[1] Giustiniani, II, 68. [2] *Courtier*, p. 85.

of the people at large, but of a narrow circle. A distinct connection existed, however, between scholars and poets. Several of the former had left Oxford for London, where a larger field awaited their activities. Sir Thomas More, himself a Latin poet of eminence, was high in favor with the king. Poets and scholars alike had similar ambitions, and in different ways accomplished the same task. John Leland, the royal antiquarian, linked together the two groups. Leland had known Wyatt ever since the two had been together at Cambridge, and on his death he wrote a threnody, dedicated to Surrey, in which he praised him especially for his use of the English language in poetry, regarding him as the equal of Dante and Petrarch.[1]

The task of the courtly poets was not an easy one. Vagueness and diffuseness, prolixity, tautology and lack of taste had been among the commonest errors of the earlier school. These faults were not corrected immediately. The followers of Skelton and Hawes did not cease to write after the new Italian forms had been introduced. Their importance, however, was greatly diminished, while at the same time the dignity of poetry was reestablished once more; the mere fact that it could flourish at court and be taken up by favorites of the king was to act power-

---

[1] *Næniæ in mortem Thomæ Viati*, 1542.

Anglus per Italis

" *Bella suum merito jactet Florentia Dantem,*
Regia Petrarchæ carmina Roma probet.
His non inferior patrio sermone Viatus
Eloquii secum qui decus omne tulit."

fully in its favor.   There sprang up, in England, "a new company of courtly-makers, of whom Sir Thomas Wyatt, the elder, and Henry, Earl of Surrey, were the two chieftains, who, having travelled into Italy and there tasted the sweet and stately measures and style of the Italian poesy, as novices newly crept out of the schools of Dante, Arioste, and Petrarch, they greatly polished our rude and homely manner of vulgar poesy, from that it had been before, and for that cause may justly be said to be the first reformers of our English metre and style."[1]

The great importance of Wyatt and Surrey was in being the first to make use in English of the new Italian poetic forms of the Renaissance.   Their task in literature was analogous to that of Grocyn and Linacre in scholarship.   Yet the positions of Wyatt and Surrey in poetry were by no means the same. There can be as little doubt that Wyatt was the innovator as that Surrey was the greater poet of the two. Wyatt was born in 1503, thirteen years before the Earl of Surrey.   It is scarcely likely that the older man should learn from the younger one.   Wyatt, moreover, had travelled in Italy,[2] Surrey never did.   In addition, John Leland, in some memorial verses on Wyatt, regarded Surrey in the light of his poetic successor.   He wrote of him : —

> *Perge Howarde precor, virtute referre Viatum,*
> *Discerisque tuæ, clarissima gloria stirpis.*

[1] Puttenham, p. 74.
[2] Vide article in *Gentleman's Magazine*, September, 1850.

Last of all, the technique of their poetry proves Wyatt's to have been the earlier. In every respect, Surrey's work marked a distinct advance on that of his predecessor and master. Wyatt was indeed the father of modern English poetry; Surrey, the greatest of his immediate successors. Wyatt was the master whose verse marked the beginning of the influence of Petrarch in the poetry of the English Renaissance.

II

One of the most remarkable things in the history of culture was that the influence of a single individual should endure through centuries, and yet change entirely in its nature. Petrarch to his contemporaries had been first and foremost a humanist. More than any one else he had brought into disfavor the old scholastic learning, and ushered in the new age, which revived the knowledge of the ancient world. Later generations, however, were to praise him chiefly for his sonnets which fitted in with the Platonic tendencies of the age. Petrarch, who laid his title to immortality on his longer Latin poems, was to have it granted to him for that which he claimed to value least, the poetic recollections of his love for Laura.

Petrarch nevertheless made the sonnet form essentially his own, even if he did not create it. It was to find popularity awaiting it, not only in Italy, but in France, Spain, Portugal and England as well. Perhaps its rigid form and construction, as much as the spirit it breathed, appealed to the classical tendencies of the period. The long, rambling poems of the Middle Ages were no longer in favor after the literature of antiquity had become familiar to every one. Remnants of the old mediæval spirit still remained in many different ways, as, for instance, in the expression of the lover's absolute devotion to his lady. The outward form, however, had been entirely recast; the style and metre especially became more polished. The rude language of former times no longer sufficed to express the subtler shades of meaning, the abundant conceits and imagery, and the ingenuity, considered necessary. Petrarch furnished the great model and example for the new poetry. On the one hand the novelty and technical perfection of his art, on the other the supposed depth of his passion, along with its Platonic ideas, made him the model for the court poets of Western Europe, who, trained in both the new humanism and the ancient spirit of chivalry, were eager to reform and refine the poetry of their native land.

Such poetry represented an ingenious effort to write of love without any true emotion of the soul, to pretend an ardent passion for an imaginary mistress, and relate in verse the story of a fictitious intrigue conducted along certain lines established by immovable tradition.[1] It was only necessary for an abstract idea of love to be embodied in a sensible image; to do this successfully, ingenuity and skill were far more essential than either learning or imagination. The usual

- Vide M. Piéri, *Pétrarque et Ronsard*, p. 88.

process was to take the ideas of Petrarch, and, imitating the sources of his inspiration and poetic phraseology, to reproduce the mannerisms. Petrarch's original selection of the sonnet form had kept him within a narrow range of ideas and feelings. It had obliged him to repeat himself and make the most of his talents, in dwelling at length and without too great monotony on the relentless heart-burnings he experienced. The narrow range prescribed for the emotions required variety in the metaphors by which they were presented, and this brought with it necessary exaggeration. The imitators of his school could easily discern through it all the method of his composition, with its affectation of ideas, its refinement of feeling and exaggeration of style. They could borrow this with the acquired ease of skilful rhetoricians. The main themes could thus be preserved, and at the same time new details added, while the methods of expression could be varied either in the direction of over refinement or exaggeration, thus escaping reproaches of plagiarism. Still another way for imitators was to take selected phrases from the sonnets, and, adding to them from their store, develop them in their own way.

Petrarchism included within itself certain quite different sides. Its idea of love, for instance, with its expression of austerity and sensuality in one, was little else than the literary survival of the past chivalric age, which found its noblest ideal in the Platonic affection for woman, regarding love as purifying the heart, uplifting the soul, and the fountain-

Thomas Earl of Surrey.

The Earl of Surrey by Holbein.

head, in a word, of all virtue. It was a revival which proved all the more popular, since, in its outward form at least, chivalry had become an amusement of the court, while it was aided by the reaction which had set in against Aristotle and the codified system of courtly love, and favored the Petrarchan expression of Platonic ideas.

The suffering of love, the timidity of the lover and the permanence of his passion were always expressed. In addition, there were certain tricks of phraseology and style which were later exaggerated by the followers of Petrarch. A straining after effect, an abuse of conceits and ingenuities, of antitheses and puns, were characteristic of this style. Its better side, however, could be found in the refinement, conciseness, polish and dignity which, especially beyond the Alps, distinguished it from previous poetry. Last of all, it offered endless opportunities for skill in versification and the technical development of the poet's art.

Wyatt and Surrey were "the two chief lanterns of light" to all who in that century wrote poetry in England. In the words of Puttenham, "their conceits were lofty, their styles stately, . . . their terms proper, their metre sweet and well proportioned, in all imitating very naturally and studiously this Master Francis Petrarch."[1] Yet the verse of neither was a slavish imitation of Petrarch. Wyatt's fresher English mind rebelled at the repetition of meaningless conceits, and at the same time the language he made use of was

[1] Puttenham, *op. cit.*, p. 76.

too imperfect a medium to convey with accuracy the subtler shades of meaning. The form he took from Petrarch, and he translated, either entirely or in part,[1] many of his sonnets, though rarely literally. His attempts to render adequately the master's conceits usually ended in failure; recognizing this, he often began his verse with a translation, and, realizing his inability to go on, developed fresh thoughts of his own.[2] In other sonnets he borrowed only a few lines from the Italian. It cannot be said that he felt at home in the rigid form he had selected; the self-imposed restraints were too many for his technical skill and proficiency; nor could he reproduce the construction of the successive steps which built up the Petrarchan sonnet. The busy life he led afforded him, perhaps, but little leisure to polish his verses. They are rarely smooth, and are in striking contrast to the polished lines of his master. Wyatt's imagery, moreover, was generally simpler and less involved than that of Petrarch. He could not compare with him in skill, and the conceits he attempted were clumsy and ill-fitting as a rule. Even the sonnet form he reproduced but feebly, the rhymes being often bad and the metrical effects by no means easy. He was unable to handle it properly, while his translation was inexact and his technique poor. He differed further from his model in closing the sonnet with a

---

[1] Cf. Wyatt, Sonnets 1, 2, 4, 5, 9, 11, 13, 14, 18, 19, 20, 22, 24, 31, with Petrarch, Sonnets 109, 61, 220, 136, 81, 12, 104, 156, 44, 99, 19, 188, 229, 120.

[2] Cf. Wyatt, Sonnet 4, with Petrarch, 220.

couplet as nearly as possible epigrammatic in form, instead of employing the usual Petrarchan ending.[1] In all likelihood both Wyatt and Surrey were quite unaware of the almost sacred spirit in which the Italian poets approached the sonnet form. They probably confused it with the popular *strambotto*[2]; the mistake they made resulted, however, in setting a new English example which was followed by the Elizabethans.

In spite of Wyatt's deficiencies and lack of originality, his position in the history of English poetry is of the greatest importance. Many have surpassed him in genius, few in influence. Although Wyatt's native strength and lofty ideal of patriotism will always endear him to lovers of English poetry, his historical significance came rather from his having been the first English Petrarchist. His study of the Italians had taught him that they alone offered new hope for poetry, and their forms and style he tried to reproduce in his own language. To use Leland's words, the English tongue, rude and rhythmless before, had been forced by him to acknowledge the master's file. He was the real teacher of the " courtly makers," who learned the new forms from his example.[3] Such men

[1] Mellin de Saint Gelays makes occasional use of the couplet ending.

[2] *Nuova Antologia*, July 1, 1895, article by De Marchi.

[3] " *Anglica lingua fuit rudis et sine nomine rhythmus*
Nunc limam agnoscit, docte Viati tuam . . .
Nobilitas dedicit te præceptore Britanna
Carmina pro varios scribere posse modos." — *Nænia.*

as Sir Francis Bryan and Lords Rochford, Vaux, Morley, and especially the Earl of Surrey, were to carry on to triumph the work he had begun.

Little is known of Surrey's literary surroundings. The legend which inspired Nash and Drayton, of his travels in Italy and his knightly challenge while in Florence to all who dared dispute the beauty of the fair Geraldine, has been proved without foundation. Almost the only certainty is that he himself was never in Italy. His acquaintance with Petrarch and his school came, therefore, from such men as Wyatt and Leland, who had returned from foreign travels, and perhaps also from some of the numerous Italians at the court. The romantic interest which attaches itself to his life is due in large measure to his surroundings, youth and his untimely death.

As a poet, however, he showed far greater readiness and ease in technique than did Wyatt ; he was not burdened by the form, nor did the language present such irksome restraints to him. The medium lay there before him ; it was his task to give beauty where previously there had been none, and lend to it style, distinction and polish. It is only necessary to compare his sonnet translations from Petrarch with corresponding ones by Wyatt to see the difference between the two and Surrey's artistic superiority. The latter fell in better with the Petrarchan tradition. Geraldine was his Laura, while Wyatt cannot be said to have had any ideal mistress. In form of thought, as well as in matter, Surrey was more akin to Petrarch, although in metrical structure he does not follow him so closely. Generally a single dominant idea runs through his poems, and around it are grouped kindred thoughts and images, often ending in an epigram, the same motive being repeated in different forms. The various moods and inconsistencies of love were among his favorite subjects, and these he expressed with a beauty and distinction gathered from the Italian. Just as Wyatt, by introducing the Italian verse forms into England, brought new vigor and life to its decaying poetry, so Surrey brought in the Italian artistic conscience, the love of polish and style and the aim toward perfection. Wyatt had striven in the right direction, but had misunderstood the nature of the Italian sonnet. Surrey likewise ignored the Italian structure, and made use of a model which was to be followed by Watson and Shakespeare. Surrey's innovations were generally in the direction of new forms. In one poem he employed the *terza rima*, a form which never took kindly root on English soil. In translating the *Æneid*, he also first made use in English of a decasyllabic blank verse, the *versi sciolti*, which Cardinal Ippolito de' Medici and Molza had employed in similar renderings only a few years before. Of his other innovations in syntax and metre little need here be said; he and Wyatt stand together as the exponents and advocates of the Petrarchan influence in the new English school of poetry they had founded.

The Petrarchan movement was slow at the start to

take root in England; neither its language nor its ideas proved congenial at first. Its very conceits were misinterpreted in the beginning by the slow-witted English, who took its stock of lovers' pangs and sufferings quite literally. Gascoigne complained bitterly of this lack of appreciation and of readers who construed " the contentions passed in verse long since between Mr. Churchyard and Camel to have been, in truth, a quarrel between two neighbors . . . of whom one having a camel in keeping, and that other having charge of the churchyard, it was supposed they had grown to debate because the camel came into the churchyard. Laugh not at this, lusty yunkers, since the pleasant ditty of the noble Earl of Surrey beginning thus, *In Winter's just return*, was also construed to be made indeed by a shepherd. . . . Of a truth my good gallants, there are such as having only learned to read English, interpret Latin, Greek, French, and Italian phrases or metaphors, even according to their own motherly conception and childish skill." [1] When, however, numerous Englishmen returning from Italian travels brought back with them a knowledge of the Tuscan revival which had swept over Italy, and reports of Bembo and his school holding their country's poets in no less esteem than the ancients, the vogue for the Petrarchan sonnet set in also in England.

Following an example often practised in Italy, *Tottel's Miscellany*, the first English collection of verse, was brought out in 1557. While many of the new forms

[1] Gascoigne's *Posies*, 1575, preface.

of poetry were here published for the first time in England, several of the poets who contributed to it were practically unaffected by the Italian lyric. Nicholas Grimald, for instance, in spite of his Italian origin, belonged rather to the classical school. An occasional use of conceits can be discovered in the verse of Barnabe Googe,[1] but he had no real conception of the rigid form and structure of the Petrarchan sonnet, although nearly all his lyrics, regardless of length, were called "sonnets" in accordance with the loose mediæval use of the word. Turbervile, likewise, although possessing a good knowledge of Italian,[2] made no real use of the sonnet; and George Gascoigne, whom an Italian friend called "an imitator of Petrarch,"[3] in spite of a few sonnets of the conventional type, preferred the less rigid structure of the *canzone*, and copied the Tuscan lyric in spirit rather than in form. Petrarch, however, was to become more and more the recognized leader of the school, the "head and prince of poets all."[4] No one, it was thought, could compare to him as a poet, nor had any one attained so lofty a style.[5] Several of the sonnets in the *Miscellany* were modelled on those of Petrarch, although they had already been translated by Wyatt.[6] The original

[1] *Poems*, p. 94 *et seq.*

[2] Vide *Anglia*, XIII, article by Koeppel.

[3] Gascoigne's *Posies*, 1575, commendatory letter in the preface.

[4] *Tottel's Miscellany*, p. 178.

[5] *Ibid.*, p. 178, second sonnet.

[6] *Ibid.*, p. 260; cf. Petrarch, Sonnet 156, and Wyatt, Sonnet 14.

type was by this time firmly established in the courtier's mind, and many people of note were writing imitations of the Petrarchan sonnet. For a time, however, the use of the sonnet form remained stationary in England. At first it had been known only at the court. A certain time was to elapse before it was generally adopted.

Thomas Watson, in his *Passionate Century of Love*, began afresh the later revival of the sonnet. His admirers had discovered that he could write verse in the Petrarchan manner.

> The stars which did at Petrarch's birthday reign
> Were fixed again at thy nativity,
> Destining thee the Tuscan's poesy,
> Who scaled the skies in lofty quatorzain.[1]

In his effort to improve the form, he added to it a four-lined stanza; at the same time he regarded himself as a successor to Petrarch, by translating whose sonnets into Latin [2] he had begun his poetical career.

Watson became the most popular poet of his time, and probably to him more than any one else was due the fashion of the sonnet in England. It is difficult to-day to explain the great vogue his verse enjoyed by any other reason than its reintroducing the Petrarchan fashion. His so-called "passions" had not even the pretence of true emotion or feeling in them, and were, in fact, little else than verses pieced together from the poetry of foreign Petrarchists. The sources in every case were openly acknowledged, as

[1] Commendatory Sonnet to Watson, by G. Burke.
[2] Watson, *Passion*, VI.

they tended to show the author's erudition. Petrarch, Serafino, Strozza, Firenzuola, and others, were alike brought under contribution to illustrate his wit. He imitated especially the conceits which formed so largely the stock of the Petrarchan school. The inward feeling of love which was the main theme of this kind of poetry offered but little variety of expression. The successors of Petrarch, therefore, in order to escape monotony, made use of extravagant metaphors and exaggeration. Watson took from the Italians chiefly their conceits and affectations — such, for instance, as Cupid shooting an arrow from his mistress's fair eyes, and so wounding the poet with love and desire that he was beyond all remedy.[1] Occasionally the affectation took an outward metrical form as well, and verse was written in the eccentric shape of " A Pasquin Pillar." Nowhere was any real attempt made at originality or freshness of expression, while at all times a display of erudition was aimed at: in a single poem[2] he cited no less than twelve sources. The form and spirit were alike handed down to him by the tradition of the Petrarchan school. His only task was to remodel in English the mosaic of Italian phrases.

The Elizabethan sonnets seem at first glance to yield a rich harvest of intimate thoughts and emotions, to take the reader into the poet's confidence and lay bare his soul for him.[3] It is only after comparing together, the English with the French,

---

[1] *Passion*, XXIV, from Serafino.   [2] *Passion*, LXXXIX.
[3] Cf. Lee, *Shakespeare*, p. 427.

Spanish and Italian, and tracing them back to their source in Petrarch and his imitators, that a common stock of expressions and conceits appears throughout. No matter how much the individual genius of the poet may have added new beauties of his own, underneath it all certain forms and modes of thought remain unaltered. The high artistic seriousness of the Italians may perhaps have been lessened when the sonnet was transplanted to English soil. A greater sensuality, and possibly a nearer approach to nature, made itself felt, but the groundwork of the whole remained identical. The same relations still existed between the lady and her lover. In the poetic jargon of the time, she was cold, cruel, insensible to him, while he was timid and unworthy of her. Petrarch had established a series of states necessary for every lover to pass through ; his Laura became a pattern for all poets.[1] To show the true spirit of devotion there were definite sufferings they had to endure : alternately to burn and freeze, to sorrow when removed from the beloved one's presence, to live only in her sight, and feel that all inspiration proceeded from her alone. Convention demanded certain things ; the Petrarchan lady was to be as beautiful and virtuous as she was cold and indifferent to her lover. The type never varied ; she possessed no individuality, no life nor movement ; she was, in fact, a stationary sun, radiating all happiness yet insensible of her own attraction.

A common poetic language was employed by the

[1] Cf. Daniel, *Delia*, Sonnet XLIII.

Petrarchists of the sixteenth century. There was a similarity, not only in spirit, but in expression as well. The same literary artifices can be traced throughout in the frequent use of antitheses, puns, conceits and even occasional grotesqueness. Tricks of enumeration, a constant display of erudition, a use of metaphysical ideas and abstractions, were all characteristic of this school. There had been a constant use, or rather abuse, in Petrarch, of eyes and hair, of tears and sorrow, of fire and cold. All this was greatly exaggerated by his successors; the happiness of nature was contrasted with the misery of the lover, and the same tricks of style were repeated again and again.[1]

The great faults in Petrarch had been excess of refinement, with its necessary removal from real life, and exaggeration of feeling. His followers, especially in Italy, developed his affectation in ideas and expression. To escape direct imitation or translation, foreign Petrarchists would fall into errors of taste and abuse of metaphor, which led to the over-employment of mythology to illustrate what they had in mind. Their poetic efforts were directed, therefore, toward form rather than to originality of expression. The Petrarchan tricks of style were easily mastered; its expressions, ideas and feelings were alike at the disposal of the poet-mechanic, while the form of allegory presented an easy method of expressing imaginary passion; the use of superlatives and a redundant phraseology could swell out any conceit to the re-

[1] Vide Piéri, *op. cit.*, pp. 88, 137.

quired fourteen lines. A poet had only to select some lady and celebrate her charms; in this fashion Sidney chose his Stella, Lodge his Phillis, Giles Fletcher his Licia, Constable his Diana. To imitate Petrarch became the greatest ambition of every poet. Churchyard spoke of "One Barnes that Petrarch's scholar is"; and Gabriel Harvey had already called Spenser "An English Petrarch," as the highest praise he could give, further justifying his imitation of him, since "all the noblest Italian, French and Spanish poets have in their several veins Petrarchized; and it is no dishonor for the daintiest or divinest Muse to be his scholar, whom the amiablest invention and beautifullest elocution acknowledged their master."[1] It was in vain that Sidney protested against this imitation; that he derided those who searched "every purling spring which from the ribs of old Parnasus flows," brought "dictionary's method" into their rhymes, and

> Poor Petrarch's long deceasèd woes
> With new-born sighs and denisened wit do sing.[2]

In spite, too, of his asserting that he was no "pick-purse of another's wit,"[3] he himself conformed to all the rules of the Petrarchan poetry. The spirit of his conceits was often very similar, and there was more than one resemblance between his sonnets and

---

[1] G. Harvey, *Pierce's Supererogation. Works*, II, 93.
[2] Sidney, *Astrophel and Stella*, Sonnet XV.
[3] *Ibid.*, LXXIV.

those of the Italian Petrarchists.[1] Stella represented the conventional type of lady, " cold and cruel," who found pleasure in her lover's pain ; he too felt heart burnings [2] and the power of love ; for his heartstrings had been stretched on Cupid's bow.[3] Many of his tricks of style were likewise thoroughly Petrarchan. In spite of calling those who flaunted their thoughts in fine phrases " Pindar's Apes," [4] he also made frequent use of conceits, employing at different times the various tricks of style of this school : enumeration, repetition, punning, antithesis and elaborate metaphors sustained to the end of the sonnet. His interspersing of songs with sonnets, moreover, was in strict accordance with the Petrarchan model. Sidney's poetry, however, in spite of the elements of imitation, differed from Petrarch's ; there was in it more life and vigor, and also less art. He was far younger and fresher, more natural and less restrained ; more sensual, too, as were indeed all the English Petrarchists, who, not satisfied with the distant adoration of their ladies, longed for their kisses as well.[5]

The numerous Elizabethan collections of sonnets betray alike in one form or another their Italian sources and ideas. The *Visions of Petrarch*, published in 1569 in Van der Noodt's *Theatre*, have now been assigned to Spenser.[6] This collection, which showed

---

[1] *Romanische Forschungen*, V, 90.   Article by E. Koeppel.
[2] Sidney, Sonnet LXXVI.   [3] *Ibid.*, XIX.
[4] *Ibid.*, III.   [5] *Ibid.*, LXXIX, LXXXI-II.
[6] *Englische Studien*, 1891.   Article by E. Koeppel.

traces of Ariosto, Sannazaro and Tasso as well as
Petrarch, he called by the Italian name of *Amoretti*.
Conceits which had been adapted or imitated can
be found even in Shakespeare's sonnets, for he assimi-
lated the thoughts and words of the Elizabethan Petrarchists with as little compunction as the plays and
novels of his contemporaries ;[1] his views of ideal beauty
as independent of time, of the power of love as superior
to its accidents, his very boasting that he would confer
immortality on the person he addressed, were merely
repetitions of what had become the commonplaces of
European poetry.[2]

The expressions of the English Petrarchists were
all variations of a single principle. The differences
between them were only of degree, some more than
others attaining the ingenuity and polish sought for.
All alike reveal a common fund of ideas and conditions, out of which their poetry developed. Sometimes indeed the Italianization proceeded a little
farther than at others ; thus Italian mottoes begin
and end the *Zepheria*, which also contained verses addressed *Alli veri figliuoli delle Muse;* in certain of the
" Canzons "[3] in this collection there was even a curious combination of the pastoral of Sannazaro and the
Petrarchan sonnet ; the English imitators of Petrarch,
however, often differed from their master in trying to
wind up their sonnets with a couplet in epigram.

[1] S. Lee, *Shakespeare,* p. 109 *et seq.*
[2] *Ibid.,* p. 114.   Vide also G. Wyndham, *Poems of Shakspeare,*
p. cxiii *et seq.*   [3] Canzon 11.

Henry Constable was, perhaps, after Watson, the most conspicuous of the Petrarchistic poets. His sonnets are full of *concetti* and exaggerated expressions of all kinds. His mistress's eye, he declared, was the glass through which he saw his heart, his own eye the window through which she might see his;[1] his only idea in writing was to sacrifice his sighs to verse.[2] The entire expression of his thought was of the conventional type ; he was the lover languishing, she the cruel mistress. The other sonnetteers of the age, Barnfield, Daniel, Griffin, Drayton, Lodge and the rest, betray the same tendencies.[3] Giles Fletcher openly acknowledged his sonnets to be imitations. Robert Tofte wrote most of the stanzas of his *Laura* in Italy.[4] Nearly all the English poets had then travelled abroad, and Dallington even gave advice to such of his travellers in Italy as were anxious to follow the muse.[5]

A reaction, however, set in against the domination of Petrarch. The very poets who felt most his influence were to revolt against it. Giles Fletcher, in the preface to *Licia*, protested against " those who think so basely of our bare English that they deem themselves barbarous . . . unless they have borrowed from Italy,

---

[1] Sonnet 5.   [2] *Ibid.*, 1.

[3] Cf. Lodge, Sonnet 11, with Petrarch, 156, and Wyatt, 14. Lodge was indebted as well to Dolce, Martelli, and Lodovico Pascale, etc. (*Edinburgh Review*, January, 1896, p. 51).

[4] *Laura, the Toys of a Traveler*, dedicated " Alla Bellissima Sua Signora," and signed " Affetionatissimo servitore della divina bellezza sua, R. T."   [5] *Method for Travel.*

Spain, and France, their best and choicest conceits."
Shakespeare likewise made fun of what he once had
practised himself,[1] and even Sir John Davies parodied
the craze in a series of " gulling sonnets."

III

A feeling of native excellence was springing up in
England.   Francis Meres echoed it, when he com-
pared his own countrymen, poets and artists to the
Greeks, the Romans and the Italians.   William Clarke
wrote in similar vein : " Let other countries sweet
Cambridge envy yet admire . . . thy Petrarch, sweet
Spenser."   He urged Englishmen to write as if " Italian
Ariosto did but shadow the meanest part of thy muse,
that Tassa's Godfrey is not worthy to make compare
with your truly eternizing Eliza's style." [2]   Samuel
Daniel, likewise, who had been in Italy and had met
Guarini,[3] looked forward to seeing " Great Sidney
and our Spenser " ranked as the equals of the Italian
poets —

> That the melody of our sweet isle,
> Might now be heard to Tyber, Arne, and Po;
> That they might know how far Thames doth outgo
> The music of declined Italy.[4]

---

[1] *Two Gentlemen of Verona*, III, ii, 68; *Henry Fifth*, III,
VII, 33 *et seq.*   Vide also Lee, *op. cit.*, p. 107 *et seq.*

[2] *Polimanteia*, 1595.

[3] Commendatory sonnet to Dymock's translation of the *Pastor
Fido*.

[4] Epistle to the Countess of Pembroke, in the preface to his
Cleopatra.

Spenser himself was fully aware of the magnitude of the task he had set out to accomplish, and considered himself in the direct line of epic inheritance from Homer and Virgil, Ariosto and Tasso. Not only did he model his own verse form on the *ottava rima* of the Italians, but in the entire structure of the *Faerie Queene* he kept the example of the Italian romantic epic constantly in mind. In a letter to Harvey, he wrote that he looked forward to " overgoing Ariosto." To Spenser, however, the aims of the Italian poets seemed lofty and moral. He read the *Orlando* from his own ideal point of view;[1] the bare facts of Ariosto he made use of just as he took his satire, quite seriously, entirely ignoring the irony; his imitation, however, was in many cases deliberate, and there are numerous passages both in the *Orlando* and in Tasso's *Gerusalemme Liberata* which he either adapted or translated from the Italian.[2] Frequently, too, he took only the external facts from Ariosto, but remodelled them in such a way as to remove all humorous suggestions; thus, for instance, the scene where Zerbino jousts with Marfisa over the old hag Gabrina was re-

---

[1] Vide Spenser's *Imitations from Ariosto*, Proceedings Modern Language Association, 1897, p. 70 *et seq.* Also Warton, *Observations on the Faerie Queene*, I, 272 *et seq.;* J. Schrömbs, *Ariosto und Englische Literatur.*

[2] Vide *Anglia*, XI. Article by E. Koeppel. Cf.:

Faerie Queene,	I, II, 30–31,	Gerusalemme Liberata,	XIII, 41–42.
"	" III, 31,	"	" III, 4.
"	" VII, 31,	"	" IX, 25.
"	" XI, 44,	"	" VI, 8.
"	" XII, 21,	"	" XV, 60, etc.

produced by Spenser in all seriousness.[1] Again, he occasionally reversed the situation as when he made a triumph of chastity out of an amorous scene,[2] treating with perfect decorum the most daring passages in Ariosto.

The importance of the Italian influence on Spenser has often been exaggerated, especially by continental critics, who, looking at the surface rather than the spirit, have seen reflected in the poem the art and beauty of the Italian Renaissance. Even where Spenser made use of characters and situations suggested by Ariosto, and of descriptions by Tasso, the *Faerie Queene* was yet written in a spirit far different from that which inspired the Italian romantic epic. Its austerity inclined rather to the Platonism of Petrarch than the easy self-indulgence of Ariosto, or the high-colored seriousness of Tasso. The Italian literary influence can be traced in Spenser in outward form rather than in inward spirit. It was well for Watson or Constable, devoid of originality, to borrow feelings and thoughts where they themselves possessed none. Minor poets who wrote sonnets because others did likewise could steal outright from their Italian sources. The greater ones, however, like Shakespeare, would seek in Italy only those elements which England did not offer; the outer shell, the framework and structure,

---

[1] *Orlando Furioso*, XX, 113 *et seq.;* cf. *Faerie Queene*, IV, IV, 9.

[2] *Orlando Furioso*, VII, 21 *et seq.;* cf. *Faerie Queene*, II, III, 21 *et seq.*

could be obtained there better than at home. A learned poet like Spenser would find there as well a more serious conception of the dignity of poetry, an artistic conscience, and a love of beauty for its own sake, which he could well emulate. But beyond it all went something deeper, and any appreciation of the *Faerie Queene*, other than as a gallery of splendid pictures and a stringing together of beautiful lines, must find behind it the genius of Spenser, almost untouched in spirit by foreign influence. As an artist he obeyed willingly the canons of the romantic epic; he made use in introductory stanzas of certain of Ariosto's mechanical details. His imitation extended even to the characters of the plot; Arthur, like Orlando, was merely the ostensible hero; Braggadocchio was suggested by Rodomonte and Mandricardo, Archimago by Atlante; Arthegall and Britomart, likewise, were based to a certain extent on Ruggiero and Bradamante; their various actions had all their counterparts in the *Orlando*.[1] The structure of the poem showed that at every stage of the composition he was influenced by the manner and methods of Ariosto, just as Tasso appealed to him in descriptions.[2] Spenser felt, however, no deep interest either in the story or in his characters; the *Faerie Queene* was both reflective and picturesque, differing altogether from its model. The resemblances between the two poems were thus on the surface, the differences in

[1] Proc. Mod. Lang. Assoc., 1897, p. 128.
[2] Courthope, *English Poetry*, II, 259.

the spirit. The one poet was the Puritan Platonist of the English Renaissance inheriting the traditions of mediæval allegory; the other was the child of sixteenth century Italy, the contemporary of Machiavelli and Aretino. The one was anxious to present the perfect gentleman "in virtuous and gentle discipline," concerned alone with his moral qualities; the other wished merely to amuse, serious only in his artistic conscience. Art was thus the common bond uniting them; it drew Spenser toward Italy, and made his greatness as a poet shine in the austerity and purity of his spirit, presented with the beauty of his art.

Art was the great lesson Italy had to teach England. Energy, freshness, imagination, purity and sweetness belonged alike to the English of the sixteenth century. They were deficient, however, in form and measure, and the artistic qualities of style. It was precisely in these qualities that the Italians were supreme. In Italy the development of two centuries had brought with it a technical perfection in art; hardly would one literary form be exhausted before another would spring up. When the lyric had nothing further to offer, the romantic epic and pastoral took its place, each in turn finding its perfect expression. The constant presence, moreover, of classical models strengthened the artistic conscience of Italian poetry, while the lack of all other restraints in life served to concentrate on art the same qualities which in northern Europe found their outlet in moral conduct. It was only in Platonism that the spirit of Spenser can be said to have been affected by Italy. The intellectual atmosphere of Cambridge was then Platonic, which meant not only the influence of the master, but even more of the fifteenth-century neo-Platonists whose aims had been directed toward reconciling the doctrines of Plato with Christianity. Spenser himself was perfectly familiar with Italian Platonism, and repeated its current thoughts in his hymns on heavenly love and beauty.

The Platonic writings of Ficino and Pico della Mirandola had been known in England since the time of Colet. Later, Sir John Cheke, who had lived at Padua, and Roger Ascham both taught Platonism at Cambridge. Other Italian books on philosophical subjects were translated into English.[1] The influence of Italian philosophy was likewise felt when Giordano Bruno, whose doctrines of love were neo-Platonic, came to England, where he lived for two years, lecturing at Oxford on the immortality of the soul and holding there a public disputation. Bruno, while disgusted by the ignorance and conceit of the doctors of the university with whom he disputed,[2] was more than pleased at his reception by the cultivated circle of which Sidney and Fulke Greville were the chief luminaries. In their pres-

---

[1] *Circes of John Baptiste Gello, Florentine,* translated out of Italian into English by Henry Iden, 1557. *The Fearful Fancies of the Florentine Cooper written in Tuscan by John Baptiste Gelli, one of the free study of Florence,* translated into English by W. Barker, *Pensoso d' Altrui,* London, 1568.

[2] *La Cena dei Ceneri,* ed. Wagner, p. 179.

ence he expounded the new Copernican philosophy, while he dedicated two of his books to Sidney.[1]

IV

Italy, where the influence of rediscovered classic form arrested, for a century, the course of native literature, led the way in reviving the writing of Latin verse. Petrarch, whose Latin *Africa* gave an example, found worthy successors in Vida, Fracastoro and Sannazaro. Several of the Italian classical poets, it will be remembered, came to England. Peter Carmeliano of Brescia wrote a poetical epistle on the birth of Prince Arthur ; Johannes Opicius, who was probably an Italian, composed royal panegyrics in the classical style and Giovanni Gigli, Bishop of Worcester, wrote a Latin epithalamium on an English subject. Later, Ammonio and Adrian de Castello were both to be celebrated for their classical verse. Marcellus Palingenius, however, was the Italian whose works proved most popular beyond the Alps. His *Zodiac of Life*,[2] translated by Barnabe Googe, went through half a dozen English editions. Its supposed Protestantism and violent denunciation of the loose living of the clergy made it

[1] G. Bruno's most important Italian works were also printed in London: *Spaccio De La Bestia Trionfante* . . . Parigi (London), 1584; *Giordano Bruno Nolano, Del gl' Heroici Furori Al molto Illustre et eccellente Cavalliero, Signor Phillippo Sidneo*, Parigi (London?), 1585.

[2] *The First Six Books of Marcellus Palingenius*, translated by Barnabe Googe, 1561.

rank almost as a classic in England and other Protestant countries.[1]

Sir Thomas More, George Buchanan and Alexander Barclay were conspicuous among those who distinguished themselves by their Latin poetry, More by his epigrams, and Buchanan by his classical tragedies, though he excelled no less in other forms of verse. The fashion for writing Latin verse, however, was in no sense an original movement, but merely continued what had long since begun in Italy. It seemed in many cases as if antiquity interpreted by Italians was more congenial to the English than the ancient works themselves. This perhaps accounted for the extraordinary vogue enjoyed by the eclogues of Baptista Mantuanus,[2] which in Shakespeare's boyhood were even read in the grammar schools.[3] Alexander Barclay, in his own eclogues,[4] imitated openly both Mantuanus and Æneas Sylvius, calling the former "the best of that sort, since poets first began."

The literary forms of antiquity, after remaining sterile for many centuries, came into use once more with the Renaissance. The influence of classical models was to breathe new life into poetry. The pastoral was only one of the many forms which, first imitated in Italy, were later to flourish in other European

[1] Warton, *English Poetry*, IV, 282.

[2] *The Eclogues of the Poet B. Mantuan*, translated by George Turbervile, 1567.

[3] Lee, *op. cit.*, p. 13. Vide also *Love's Labour's Lost*, IV, 2, 100.

[4] Alexander Barclay, prologue to the *Eclogues*, 1570.

countries. Barnabe Googe, for instance, showed the
influence of Sannazaro through the medium of the
Spaniard Garcilaso de la Vega.[1] At other times France
was to be the intermediary between Italy and England. With Spenser, however, the influence was direct
and the *October* in his *Shepheard's Calendar* was openly
imitated from Mantuanus.[2] From E. K.'s introductory epistle it is apparent that Mantuanus, Petrarch,
Boccaccio and Sannazaro were regarded in the direct
line of tradition from Theocritus and Vergil. Spenser,
whom Drayton called the "great reformer,"[3] was in fact
introducing in England the pastoral which had first
been revived in Italy.

The subsequent development of the English pastoral was largely influenced by the *Aminta* of Tasso
and Guarini's *Pastor Fido*. The first was translated into Latin hexameters by Thomas Watson in
1587. An unauthorized English rendering was made
from this by Abraham Fraunce, which proved far more
popular than the Latin version of Watson. The *Pastor
Fido* was not translated till some years later;[4] it was
first printed in London, in the original Italian, as was
also the *Aminta*. The influence of Tasso and Guarini
can further be traced, not only in the pastorals proper
of Thomas Lodge and Giles Fletcher, but in the drama

---

[1] Underhill, *op. cit.*, p. 242.

[2] For Mantuanus' influence on Spenser, vide *Anglia* III, 266,
and IX, 205, articles by F. Kluge.

[3] *The Barons' Wars*, preface.

[4] The *Pastor Fido*, translated by Sir Edward Dymock, 1602.

as well; in Lyly's, Greene's and Peele's pastoral plays, as also much later, in the *Faithful Shepherdess* and the *Sad Shepherd*.

Several of Sidney's songs in the *Arcadia* were intended to be sung to the time of Neapolitan " Villanells." Sir Thomas Wyatt's most successful ventures had been his songs, often imitated from the Italian. The musical accompaniment to which such songs were sung came in many instances from across the Alps. Madrigals also which were especially popular in England had most of them originated in Italy.[1] The first collection of Italian madrigals printed in England was by Nicholas Yonge.[2] It was followed by Thomas Watson's collection after Marenzio, Nannio and Converso.[3] Morley and Dowland continued the work,[4] while Yonge later brought out a second series.[5] John Dowland, who when in Italy had made friends with Giovanni Croce, Luca Marenzio and the other great composers, was the

---

[1] Vide T. Oliphant, *Madrigals*, 1836.

[2] *Musica Transalpina . . . with the first and second part of ' La Verginella' made by Master Byrd upon the two stanzas of Ariosto, and brought to speak English with the rest*, N. Yonge, 1588.

[3] *The First Set of Italian Madrigals Englished* . . . by T. Watson, 1590.

[4] *Alto di Thomaso Morlei. Il primo libro della Ballatte a cinque voci, in Londra appresso Tomaso Este*, 1595 (dedicated to Sir Robert Cecil; both the dedication and the letterpress were in Italian). *The First Book of Songs or Airs*, by John Dowland, 1596.

[5] N. Yonge, *Musica Transalpina*, translated out of sundry Italian authors, 1597.

most celebrated, perhaps, of the English musicians of the day. These English musicians formed the last link in the chain of those who brought back new lessons from across the Alps. They also found a new art to learn in Italy, where some of them became thoroughly Italianated. John Cooper, for instance, called himself *Giovanni Coperario* after having been in Italy. He was among the first to bring back a knowledge of the new homophonic school which had arisen there, and which was later to be developed in England by his two pupils, William and Henry Lawes. At a time when the musical drama originated, Cooper forms, with Laniere and Ferrabosco, the binding tie between Italy and England. Ferrabosco himself was the son of an Italian musician, and had studied music at Bologna, where he attached himself to the new school then growing up.

In examining the different English books of madrigals of this time, one cannot but be impressed by their almost exclusively Italian origin. Nicholas Yonge wrote that he had "carefully culled out of the compositions of the best authors in Italy," alluding to the musical books yearly sent him thence. Morley, Dowland, Byrd and Watson alike frankly acknowledged the sources of their collections, and mentioned the Italian composers whose songs they reproduced. In Italy, during this time, music, the last product of the Renaissance, was at its height, and Dowland spoke of its flourishing in all the cities he visited. In England, too, Italian musicians such as the Bassani, the Lupos and the elder Ferrabosco were to be found at court, while they were also in the service of great noblemen.[1] In music, as in the sciences and arts, Italy led the way for the rest of Europe to follow.

V

The Italian influence on English satire began already with Sir Thomas Wyatt, who imitated Alamanni both in the form of epistolary satire and in his use of the *terza rima*.[2] Wyatt was the first English poet to imitate the original model of classic satire revived in Italy, and adapt the ancient style to the conditions of his own time and place. English satire, however, in the sixteenth century was to follow a course similar to that taken by lyric poetry, especially the sonnet. The classical model introduced by Wyatt was not to flourish in England until toward the end of the century, when Hall and Marston took it up. In the meantime, satires continued to be written in accordance with earlier models; Edward Hake, for instance, belonged almost to the mediæval satirists and followed no classical examples, while Gascoigne's *Steel Glass* betrayed few evidences of the new style.

The influence of Italy on English satire was twofold. On the one hand was felt the revival of the classical traditions in Alamanni and Ariosto; on the other, was the prose satire, of which Aretino's writings offered the great example. Aretino himself was one

[1] Cot. Mss. Brit. Mus., Titus B. VII, 155.
[2] Cf. Wyatt, *Satire* II with Alamanni, *Satire* XII.

of the Italians whose name was in every Englishman's mouth, where it became a byword for sensuality. He had even dedicated a volume of letters to Henry the Eighth,[1] who finally granted him a pension after years of delay.[1] William Thomas in turn dedicated his *Pilgrim* to Aretino whom he called a "right natural poet . . . whose virtue consisteth in nature without any art."[2] His influence was chiefly noticeable, however, in the closing years of the sixteenth century, with the Bohemian group of pamphleteers, which included Robert Greene, and especially Thomas Nash, known as the "English Aretine." The latter described his master as "one of the wittiest knaves that ever God made," one whose pen was sharp like a poniard, and who wrote never a line that failed to make a man drunk with admiration.[3] Nash relied, like Aretino, on a free use of the vernacular to obtain his humorous effects, and would coin words from the Italian where the English was not to his taste. He copied him especially in his too frequent abuse and vituperation. Gabriel Harvey censured him for this licentiousness,[4] though trying himself to imitate the wit of him whom he called *Unico Aretino*.

The classical satire, first revived in Italy with Vinciguerra, did not really begin to flourish in England until the last decade of the sixteenth century. Like so many

[1] Vide Letters, II *passim*, IV, 53.
[2] *The Pilgrim*, dedication.
[3] *Jack Wilton*, p. 107 *et seq*.
[4] *New Letter of Notable Contents, Works*, I, 272 *et seq*., 289.

other foreign literary forms, it failed to attain its popularity at first. The sonnet, the pastoral and the Senecan tragedy were all to enjoy their fashion before its turn came ; between Wyatt and Donne there extended an interval of half a century. Satire in Tudor England never became, in fact, thoroughly acclimated. The Elizabethan satirists followed, as a rule, the Latin traditions belonging rather to the school of Juvenal and Persius, even though the Horatian influence was very perceptible in Hall. The English satires, however, contained numerous Italian words and expressions. Guilpin, Marston, Lodge and the rest referred frequently to the "filthy Aretine," and alluded to the vices and crimes of Italy. Hall even prefaced his satire with an Italian motto[1], and on more than one occasion borrowed from Ariosto.[2]

Beginning with Wyatt and Surrey, the English often found models for their religious verse in Italian poetry ; Wyatt's penitential psalms, for instance, were, like his satires, adapted from Alamanni. The fashion for this kind of poetry came also very much later. George Chapman, for instance, translated Petrarch's hymns. On the other hand, Laurence Bodley, an Oxford fellow, translated into Italian a number of the psalms.[3] This religious influence in poetry became far more important, however, in the days of the Stuarts when Crashaw echoed Marini.

[1] Book IV, i.

[2] Alden, *Rise of Satire in England*, p. 113. Vide also Hall, *Satires*, I, iv.   [3] Ms. Bodleian Library.

The Italian influence was, likewise, responsible in part for the narrative poems of the later Elizabethan Age. *Hero and Leander, Venus and Adonis, Pygmalion* and the *Hermaphrodite* were all conceived in the florid and sensuous Italian manner. At times this meant merely that the Elizabethans read the classical stories on which these tales were founded in the Italian, which was far more widely known than the ancient tongues. In Italian there existed usually both literal and poetic translations. Bernardo Tasso, for instance, paraphrased freely the *Hero and Leander* of Musæus, after Baldi had translated it literally. Tasso's rendering was certainly made use of by the Spaniard, Boscan,[1] and was perhaps not unknown to Marlowe himself, whose word painting was thoroughly Italian. Musæus, for instance, described in two lines Leander's first swimming of the Hellespont; Tasso and Boscan both required over twenty to do so, while Marlowe elaborated it to even greater length. Certain of the lines not in the original Greek bear likewise a decided resemblance to each other.

> *Le figlie di Nereo per l' onde salse*
> *Scherzando coi Tritoni,*

of Tasso, is not unlike the

> *Sweet singing mermaids sported with their loves.*
> *Hero and Leander*, II, 162.

True classical scholarship was a rare acquisition among the earlier Elizabethans, while the Italian

[1] Vide Flamini, *Studi di Storia italiana e straniera*, Livorno, 1895.

offered a means of approach easy to all.   The literary
influence of Italy had further means of filtering into
England through the hundreds of translations from the
Italian.[1]   Plagiarism was not considered a vice in the
sixteenth century, and, commencing with Wyatt, there
began a long list of debts acknowledged and un-
acknowledged to Italian literature.   Works of every
kind were translated, especially in the last quarter of
the century.   The charge once made by Sir Thomas
Hoby that Englishmen were selfish in their studies and
unmindful of the intellectual wants of their countrymen, in contrast to the Italians who translated books
in foreign languages for the benefit of their less fortunate compatriots, was no longer true ; translators were
highly regarded, and a perfect mania for translating set
in.   There were few books of importance which did not
speedily appear in English.   Some complained of these
renderings, urging against them all kinds of objec-
tions.   George Pettie satirized those who, through
ignorance, were unable to see the faults in the original
which they discerned in the translation, and thought
nothing was good unless written in a foreign language.[2]
The translators as well were to have their apologists
and defenders.   Hoby declared that a man skilled in
English translations was no less learned than he who
had read the same in the original Latin and Greek.[3]

---

[1] Vide *Bibliography of Elizabethan Translations from the
Italian*, M. A. Scott, Proc. Mod. Lang. Assoc., 1895–98.

[2] Guazzo's *Civil Conversations*, preface.

[3] "Epistle to the Reader," *Courtier*, p. 9.

Another writer quoted Giordano Bruno's saying that all sciences owed their offspring to translations,[1] in order to persuade Daniel not to be ashamed " to open another man's shop " and " sell Italian wares " as though being " a bankrupt in philosophy " he " could not afford any pretty conceit without borrowing or embezzling." Lodowick Bryskett, the friend of Sidney and Spenser, in the introduction to his translation of Giraldi Cinthio's *Discourse of Civil Life*, wrote that he envied the Italians who had popularized moral philosophy by explaining Plato and Aristotle in their own language, wishing that English writers would follow their example. Bryskett urged Spenser to set himself to such a task, but he was already occupied with the *Faerie Queene*.

The Italian epic poets were well known in England. Florio had already quoted from Ariosto.[2] To Sir John Harington, however, a court wit and humorist, was left the task of translating the *Orlando* into English verse, one of the few translations which has remained famous to this day. Drayton, in his *Barons' Wars*, was later to take the verse form from Ariosto on account of its being " of all other the most complete and and best proportioned." A portion of Boiardo was then translated into English.[3] Tasso also was popular in England from the very beginning, and Abraham

---

[1] *The Worthy Tract of Paulus Jovius*, by Samuel Daniel, 1585.

[2] *First Fruites*, ch. 25, 1578.

[3] *Orlando Innamorato ;* the first three books were translated by Robert Tofte in 1598.

* Primo Augusti anno Domini 1591 ætatis suæ 30
FIN CHE VEGNIA
Il tempo paßa.

Fo. Coxton sculp.

Sir John Harrington.

Fraunce quoted freely from him as early as 1579.[1] The first five cantos of the *Jerusalem Delivered* were translated by Richard Carew, who attempted to follow the original line for line. There are many passages of great beauty in this rendering,[2] although it is by no means accurate. The more famous version by Edward Fairfax appeared a few years later.[3] His poem has almost the ring of the original, and far surpassed Carew's translation, of which he made considerable use.

VI

The classical influence in English literature came largely from Italy. Classical metres, which Tolomei had long before attempted to revive in Italy, were tried by Sidney and Spenser, and found apologists in Drant and Gabriel Harvey. Roger Ascham was, however, the first to advocate the use of quantity in English poetry. From Gabriel Harvey's letters[4] one can realize the extent of this movement, as well as the attempt which was made then to introduce such metres into English verse.[5] Sidney, Spenser, Dyer and Greville formed a society bearing the name of the *Areopagus*, perhaps in imitation of the Florentine Academy

---

[1] *Arcadian Rhetorike.* Vide Koeppel, *Anglia*, XI, XII, XIII.

[2] *Godfrey of Bulloigne*, translated by R. C., 1594.

[3] *Godfrey of Bulloigne*, translated by Edward Fairfax, 1600.

[4] *Three proper and wittie familiar letters; Two other very commendable letters*, in Haslewood, *Arte of English Poesy.*

[5] Spingarn, *Literary Criticism in the Renaissance*, p. 299 *et seq.*

in the time of Lorenzo, which bore the same name,[1] although probably based on the one which Baïf had founded in Paris shortly before. The original model for all such learned societies was Italian, but the idea of academies had long been present to the English mind. William Thomas, so far back as 1549, described the Academy in Florence as among the most interesting things he saw in all Italy. Later, Edmund Bolton advocated an English Academy, and Richard Carew deplored the lack[2] of such an institution in his own country. The idea of an Academy in England was even present in the mind of Milton.[3]

The dominant influence in Elizabethan criticism was Italian, and the introduction of the poetic canons of Aristotle into England resulted from the influence of Italian critics. Sir Philip Sidney introduced Italian criticism just as Wyatt and Surrey had introduced the Italian lyric. His *Defense of Poesy* has been called an "epitome of the literary criticism of the Italian Renaissance," and its sources have been laid bare in the treatises of Minturno and Scaliger;[4] Dolce, Trissino and Daniello were all placed by Sidney under contribution. Puttenham, likewise, as he was careful to inform the reader, had lived at the Italian courts; his conception of the poet was based directly on that

---

[1] Cf. Pulci, *Morgante Maggiore*, XXV, 117.

[2] Richard Carew in a letter to Cotton (1605), cited by Ellis, *Original Letters of Eminent Literary Men*, Camden Society, p. 99.

[3] *Prose Works*, edited by St. John, 1848, II, pp. 477, 480.

[4] Spingarn, *op. cit.*, p. 268 *et seq.*

of Scaliger.[1] The Italianated Harington, in his defence of the *Orlando Furioso* against the attacks made
on it, gave for the first time in English the Aristotelian
theory of the epic as revived in Italy.[2] Italian poetic
criticism was also to have its influence in Elizabethan
literature. The dramatic unities of time and place,
formulated for the first time by Lodovico Castelvetro
in 1570, were copied by Sidney in his *Defense*,[3] and
utilized later in the classical plays of Daniel and
Fulke Greville. The Senecan tragedy also in part
through the Italian medium[4] influenced English attempts at classical tragedy; Gascoigne's translation
of *Jocasta*, for instance, was made, not from the
original Greek of Euripides, but from Dolce's Italian
rendering.

A set-back was, however, experienced in the attempt
to classicize English poetry; Hall satirized the movement,[5] and it received its death-blow in Daniel's
Defense of Rhyme.[6] It was a part of a similar reaction
felt no less in other directions. With the growth of
the Renaissance in Europe, Italian words and expressions had been introduced into other languages

---

[1] Spingarn, *op. cit.*, p. 264.

[2] *Ibid.*, p. 293. Jacopo Castelvetro, who had lectured on
poetics in Paris (where he may have met Sidney), published in
London, in 1585, Julius Cæsar Stella's Epic on Columbus, and
dedicated it to Raleigh in appreciation of his exploits.

[3] *Ibid.*, p. 290.

[4] Vide Cunliffe, *The Influence of Seneca on the Elizabethan
Drama*, London, 1893.

[5] *Satires*, I, 6.   [6] Spingarn, p. 298.

and this movement was now opposed in its turn ; thus, in France, Henri Estienne ridiculed such imitation in his celebrated *Dialogues du Françoys Italianizé*.

The feeling was undoubtedly growing that every nation should take pride in developing its language, without borrowing from classical or Italian sources. This movement, which was intended as a reaction against Italy, was really the counterpart of a similar one begun by Bembo[1] and the Purists. In England, however, the problem was somewhat different. Not only was the English language burdened by "ink-horn" terms as they were then known, but the different continental languages, especially the Italian, contributed to form its vocabulary. This tendency had begun already with Wyatt, who borrowed words here and there.[2] Thomas Wilson had complained of those who, returning from foreign travel, "powder their talk with oversea language; . . . some seek so far for outlandish English, that they forget altogether their mother's language; . . . another chops in with English Italianated and applieth the Italian phrase to our English speaking."[3] E. K. likewise, in his defence of the *Shepheard's Calendar*, spoke of the English language as a "hodge-podge of all other speeches," and alluded to those who desired to patch

[1] Harvey was familiar with the works of Bembo. The first lectures he gave at Cambridge were based on his ideas. Vide Morley, *English Writers*, 1892, IX, 17 *et seq.*

[2] Cf. Sonnet XV, "*Avising* the bright beams," from the Italian *avvisare*.

[3] *Art of Rhetoric*, f. 82 *b*.

up its holes " with pieces and rags of other languages."
There were Englishmen who proclaimed their tongue
to be "barren" and "barbarous."[1]   On the other
hand, John Kepers spoke of the necessity of making
new words, and thought this could best be effected
by those "conversant in foreign writers."[2]   Greene's
language was interlarded with Italian words and expressions. Nash, however, was the great example
of this tendency. He wrote of those who objected
to "the multitude of my boisterous compound words,
and the often coining of Italianate verbs, which end
all in *ize*, as mummianize, tympanize, tyrannize."
He had made use of such words because, more than
any other language, English swarmed with monosyl-
lables, which he likened to small currency in a shop-
keeper's box. His task had been to exchange these
small coins "four into one and others into more, according to the Greek, French, Spanish, and Italian."[3]
Harvey, however, accused Nash of quite renouncing his
natural English accent in his affectation of Tuscanism.
Others likewise wrote against the foreign danger in
the language. Sir John Cheke argued for English to
be written "clean and pure," and without borrowing
from other tongues.[4] Mulcaster and Ascham both advocated its use without foreign expressions. Even Gascoigne, who had taken much from the Italian, prided
himself on retaining old English words rather "than in

[1] Guazzo, preface.
[2] *The Courtier's Academy*, introduction.
[3] Nash, IV, 6 *et seq.*   [4] Castiglione, *op. cit.*, p. 12.

borrowing of other languages, such epithets and ad-
jectives as smell of the inkhorn."[1]

VII

The Italian influence in English fiction in the sixteenth century was on the one hand that of Boccaccio,
on the other that of Sannazaro. The first was to show itself especially in the tales of love, intrigue and adventure
of Robert Greene, who had himself travelled in Italy.
The scenes of many of his novels were laid there, while
his stories were drawn largely from Italian sources ;
Perimides and Philomela, for instance, was so closely
imitated from Boccaccio that it amounted almost to
a translation.[2] Greene proved himself thoroughly
familiar with the literature and ideas of the Peninsula.
He described the Italianate Englishmen returning
home with vices acquired abroad ; he himself confessed to have done this.[3] Although the origin of
the style he made use of still remains a disputed
point, the names of his love tales, *Mamillia*, *Arbasto*,
Alcida and *Pandosto* give a clew to the Italian sources
of his inspiration.

Greene, as a novelist, found his successors in Nicholas Breton and Emanuel Ford, who was also an imitator
of Boccaccio. If Boccaccio offered the model for all
stories of intrigue, the pastoral novel of Sannazaro,
which revived in Renaissance Italy the Arcadian tales

[1] *Works*, preface.
[2] M. A. Scott, *Proc. Mod. Lang. Assoc.*, 1898, p. 250.
[3] R. Greene, VI, 24; X, 6, 73; XI, 217, etc.

of late Greek literature, was to prove no less popular in England. Sannazaro's romance of the ideal love of shepherds and shepherdesses amid the scenes of an imaginary poetic landscape possessed little human interest and but slight action. These elements were later supplied by his Portuguese imitator, Jorge de Montemayor, who added to the conventional Arcadianism incidents from real life. Sidney, in his *Arcadia*, united the two models, combining certain elements of romantic adventure which he added to the pastoral simplicity. The lyrics he introduced likewise imitated the example of Sannazaro, who interspersed poetry with prose. Sidney's descriptions called up other Italian reminiscences; the one of the beautiful *Philoclea*, for instance, may well have been suggested by the paintings of Titian and Veronese he had seen in Venice.[1]

Robert Greene's *Menaphon* and *Pandosto*, both of which were Arcadian in style, breathed the spirit of the Italian pastoral novel; Thomas Lodge, also, who had imitated the Italian lyric poets in his *Margaret of America*, copied Sannazaro in *Rosalind*, from which, later, Shakespeare drew the plot of his own semipastoral drama.

Before the vogue of the pastoral novel had set in, however, numerous translations of Italian *novelle* and romances had been made. The tale of *Titus and Gisippus*, translated by Sir Thomas Elyot, was probably the earliest English rendering of Boccaccio in

[1] Jusserand, *English Novel in the Time of Shakespeare*, p. 244.

the sixteenth century. It only began the long list of such translations. Painter's *Palace of Pleasure* appearing in 1566, Fenton's *Tragical Discourses* a year later, and the collections which followed by Fortescue,[1] Pettie,[2] Smythe,[3] Turbervile,[4] and others, familiarized Englishmen with an entirely different class of literature. They could now read the tales of Ser Giovanni, Straparola, Bandello and the followers of Boccaccio.[5] Some stories were directly translated from the Italian, others from their French versions as in the case of Bandello. So great was the popularity of these tales that an English novel of the time in order to secure a larger sale, was falsely stated to be a translation from the Italian, foreign words being even introduced to mislead the reader.[6] George Gascoigne, likewise, in his English imitation of a *novella*, the adventures of *Don Ferdinando Geronimi*, pretended to be translating a story by " Bartello."

Ladies were said to " entertain Bandel or Ariosto in their closets,"[7] and Ascham spoke of such books being " sold in every shop in London." Their popu-

---

[1] T. Fortescue, *Forest or Collection of Histories*, 1571.

[2] George Pettie, *Pettie's Palace of Pettie his Pleasure*, 1576.

[3] Robert Smythe, *Strange and Tragical Histories*, 1577.

[4] *Tragical Tales translated by Turbervile*, 1587.

[5] Vide L. Fraenkel, *Zeitschrift für Vergleichende Litteratur*, III, IV.

[6] *The pitiful History of two loving Italians, Gaulfrido and Bernardo. . . .* Translated out of Italian into English metre by John Drout, 1570.

[7] Paulus Jovius, preface by N. W. to Daniel's translation.

larity and licentiousness resulted in the inevitable reaction. Stephen Gosson wrote of the devil sending
over "many wanton Italian books which, being translated into English, have poisoned the old manners of
our country with foreign delights."[1] Ascham's objec-
tions are too well known to need further repetition.
In 1599 many of these books were ordered to be
burned, and, to use Warton's own words, the Stationer's
Hall "underwent as great purgation as was carried on
in Don Quixote's library."

The translations of the Italian *novelle* were to
awaken further interest in Italy among the people at
large. Italy gave the subject-matter and incidents to
such a tale of adventure as *Jack Wilton*, although its
literary form was Spanish. Italy offered, so to speak,
the stage setting and scenery for the Elizabethan
dramatists. Its richer life, with its promise of adventure and bloodshed, gave free rein to their thoughts.
The crimes of Italy were destined to furnish the subject-matter for nearly half the tragedies writte: in
the reigns of Elizabeth and James.[2] The dramatists,
in addition, could borrow plots ready made from
Italian *novelle* at a time when plagiarism was thought
legitimate. The Italian drama in itself had but little
direct influence in England. A morality play called
Free Wyl had been translated both by Hoby and
Cheke, and Ochino's *Tragedy* was likewise rendered
into English by Bishop Ponet. Still another famous

---

[1] *Plays confuted in Five Actions.*
[2] Vernon Lee, *Euphorion*, p. 70.

morality, the *Conflict of Conscience*, had for its hero one Francis Spira, an Italian lawyer, who, for purely worldly reasons, abandoned his Protestant convictions. The popularity of such plays in England was due rather to their religious lessons than to intrinsic literary merit. The Italian influence on the English drama came chiefly through the translation of *novelle*, although the dumb show and the play within the play were both of Italian origin. Italian examples, however, aided greatly the transition from morality to comedy in England.[1] George Gascoigne's *Supposes*, a translation of Ariosto's *Suppositi*, which appeared in 1566, was the first English prose comedy, and with it began the refinement of dialogue.

It is interesting to note that an Italian company, under a certain Drusiano, acted in London in 1577,[2] their improvised dialogue being commented on by Hieronimo in Kyd's *Spanish Tragedy* : —

> The Italian tragedians were so sharp of wit,
> That in one hour's meditation
> They would perform anything in action.

Italian words and expressions were by no means unusual on the Elizabethan stage. Gascoigne introduced them in a masque.[3] Even Shakespeare made occasional use of them, while Marston and Ford both brought in Italian sentences.[4]

---

[1] Ward, *English Dramatic Literature*, I, 145.

[2] J. P. Collier, *History of English Dramatic Poetry*, III, 398.

[3] Gascoigne, edit. W. C. Hazlitt, I, 86 *et seq.*

[4] Vide I *Antonio and Mellida*, II, i, 212, III, i, 275. *'Tis Pity She's a Whore*, IV, iii, *passim*.

In addition to what they were able to learn from the *novelle*, Elizabethan dramatists obtained further insight into Italian manners and customs from the many manuals of courtesy which were translated into English. They found depicted in them a society far more cultivated and refined than anything which existed in England in that age. Such books taught them the existence of a new world and a new life. At the same time, the dialogue form, so popular among Italians, and in which these books were written, gave English dramatists the models for their prose conversations.

Tancred and Gismunda, produced in 1568, was the first English drama, the plot of which is known to have been based on an Italian tale. Not long afterward every Elizabethan playwright was borrowing from the *novelle*. In parallel movement the more learned poets, such as Sackville and Gascoigne, from reading Seneca and his Italian imitators, began themselves to write English plays.[1] The Italian influence in the English drama was thus twofold. On the one side it contributed to bring to life the ancient forms of tragedy, and teach the canons of Aristotle as interpreted in Italy. This conscious classical influence, first brought in through translations, imposed the unities on the later Elizabethan drama. Nevertheless, it was with few exceptions destined to barrenness, for Fulke Greville's plays are hardly more than literary curiosities. On the other hand, the Italian romantic side

[1] Ward, I, 117, 144.

influenced the spirit of the Elizabethan drama, by infusing it with its own ideals of *virtù*. The unconscious
influence of Italy proved a living breath to English
playwrights, who found their subject-matter in its tales
of passions and crimes.

Many signs of Italian influence are apparent in
the dramas of the period. Gosson alluded to the
"bawdy comedies" in Italian furnishing the playhouses
in London.[1] One play by the name of the *Orlando
Furioso* was presented on the stage, another called
Machiavelli was acted at the Rose Theatre. It must
be acknowledged, however, that many of the so-called
Machiavellian sayings of the dramatists were so only
in the popular Elizabethan sense of the name, and
appear to have been inspired rather by Gentillet's
polemic.[2] Nevertheless, it can scarcely be doubted
that Machiavelli's doctrine of *virtù* fitted in with the
ideas of the age. It animated Marlowe's heroes, who
first brought his spirit into the English drama. All
of them are governed by the craving for the infinite,
either in wealth, knowledge, or power, attainable through
force of will, regardless of the means employed. In
Tamburlaine he represented energy and strength, in
contrast to the weakness of Mycetes. So Faustus, to
obtain forbidden knowledge, was ready to sacrifice his
soul. Barabas likewise typified hatred and revenge,
while Mortimer represented personal ambition carried to extreme. All his plays were thus inspired by

[1] *Plays confuted in fine actions.*
[2] Meyer, *op. cit.*, p. 43 *et seq.*

the same desire — to bring to a dramatic climax the consequences produced by the determination of will power in its pursuit of selfish objects.[1] Machiavelli himself was brought on the stage as the impersonation of all villany.[2]

Shakespeare's knowledge of Italy, like his own life, remains a paradox. On the one hand, the remarkable amount of information he possessed about Italian cities does not seem as if it could have been acquired except from personal observation. On the other, certain of the errors he made were of such a nature as almost to preclude the possibility of his having been there. Thus, for instance, Valentine is supposed to travel by sea from Verona to Milan, while Prospero embarks on board a ship at the gates of Milan.[3]

His plays treating of Italian subjects were of three kinds. In such as *Othello* and the *Merchant of Venice* he showed undeniable knowledge of Italy. In a second class, comprising *Romeo and Juliet* and the *Taming of the Shrew*, a certain knowledge of Italy is seen, though not more than could be gathered from hearsay and books. Last of all were such dramas as *The Tempest* and the *Winter's Tale*, where the locality and names were alone Italian.[4] Thus only the first kind remains not easily explicable ; even granting that he obtained information from the tales of travellers, and

[1] Courthope, II, 405.   [2] *Jew of Malta*, prologue.

[3] *Two Gentlemen of Verona*, I, I, 71; *The Tempest*, I, II, 129–144.

[4] Vide Elze, *Shak. Jahrbuch*, XIII, XIV, XV.

from such books as Thomas's *History of Italy*, there seems no sufficient reason for his preferring Venice and Padua. Neither Florence nor Rome attracted him in the same way. His interest in the North can be accounted for in part by his fondness for Bandello and certain of the *novellieri;* but this does not tell all. Nor for that matter does his ridicule [1] of English-men returning home from foreign travel dissatisfied with their surroundings, prove, as some have thought, that he had not been abroad. He himself in after years made fun of the sonnet he had once been so fond of.

If Shakespeare was ever in Italy, it was not as an ordinary traveller. His exact knowledge was confined almost to Venice and Padua; other places he knew of only by hearsay. Nor does he mention the long journey across the Alps. He went there, if at all, on board ship, perhaps as a sailor or as an accountant or clerk in the employ of some commercial house in London, for direct trade between the two places was then of common occurrence. It is barely possible that his name may still be found among the papers of some London merchant; his visit in such a capacity would alone account for his partial knowledge of Italy, coupled with its gigantic blunders. It would explain both his fondness for Venetia as well as much of the mystery surrounding his early life.

In spite of the uncertainty and lack of direct proof which attends Shakespeare's travels, more certain ground

[1] Vide p. 164.

is reached in approaching the books he read. The sources of fourteen of his dramas are found in Italian fiction. Not only was he familiar with the Italian *novelle*, even such as the story of *The Merchant of Venice*, which was then inaccessible in English, but, as might be expected, he had read many of the books relating to Italian subjects then published in England. Touchstone's description of the various forms of a lie and Orlando's wrestling bout with Charles was probably suggested by Saviolo's *Practise*. Likewise the lines

> *Venetia, Venetia,*
> *Chi non ti vede, non ti pretia,*[1]

if not taken from Florio's *Second Fruites*, which he might well have seen in manuscript, could be found in James Sanford's collection of Italian proverbs. Shakespeare, however, undoubtedly knew Florio when he was a protégé of Southampton.[2]

In spite of the books he read and his acquaintance with Italy and Italians, perhaps even his knowledge of Bruno's philosophy[3] and his allusions to Machiavellian ideas,[4] Shakespeare's individual genius was far too great to be deeply touched by outward influences. His spirit, like Spenser's, remained English, unaffected by foreign imitation. At the same time the Italian

---

[1] *Love's Labour's Lost*, IV, II, 100.

[2] S. Lee, *op. cit.*, p. 85.

[3] Vide R. König, *Shak. Jahrbuch*, XI; R. Beyersdorff, *Shak. Jahrbuch*, XXVI.

[4] *III Henry VI*, III, II, 182; *Titus Andronicus*, V, I, 125; *Merry Wives of Windsor*, III, I, 102, etc.

atmosphere with which he invested his dramas aided to bring out their beauty, while the *novelle* on which he based his plots set free his imagination.

The Italian influence in English literature was thus twofold. On the one hand, it taught the value and beauty of artistic form in poetry, and introduced new poetic models; on the other, it gave, so to speak, the raw material from which the Elizabethan dramatists drew the subject-matter of their inspiration. At the same time it offered a model for the novel and the epic, and the critical criteria for the judgment of literature. The first two influences were romantic; the influence of the Italian humanists, on the other hand, was classical. While this influence was paramount in criticism, it yet failed to attain any results in poetry and the drama, the desultory attempts made to introduce it in England proving sterile. The romantic influences, however, did not fetter the originality of English poetry; the models of Petrarch and Ariosto breathed new life into it, while the tales of Boccaccio and his followers stirred the imagination of Elizabethan dramatists.

APPENDIX A

ENGLISH CATHOLICS IN ROME

Perhaps the most permanent and binding chain, which from the earliest times familiarized Italy with England, was the constant stream of pilgrims journeying to and from Rome. These pilgrimages had already begun long before the Conquest and had continued through the Middle Ages. In the fourteenth century one John Shepherd, a London merchant, established a hospital in Rome for English pilgrims and travellers. So early as 727, King Ina had founded a hospice for Saxon pilgrims beyond the Tiber. The English records of these early days are either lacking or scanty. Some information can be obtained, however, from a partial register of the pilgrims written in the first years of the sixteenth century.[1] The guests then received were of two kinds, — noblemen (*nobiles*) so called, who paid for their board, and poor people (*pauperes*) who were lodged free. The names and occupations of the guests were in each case given; thus John Vaughan, priest, John Williams, knight, Thomas Halsey, student at Bologna, shows the general nature of the lodgers. Most of them were designated either as scholars or priests; but others lodged there as well, even the ambassadors sent by Henry the Seventh

[1] *Liber Primus Instrumentorum*, English College, Rome.

373

to the Vatican, Edward Scot and John Alen, the first of whom died of fever in the hospital. In one year, 1505, fifty-five persons were registered as "nobles." Among the poor were the names of an occasional Oxford student, of sailors, and again of a dozen Welshmen, together with a pilgrimage of priests from Norfolk and Suffolk. In all over two hundred pilgrims went there in a single year. Women, also, were among the pilgrims, such names occurring as Juliana Lutt of London, and Elizabeth Welles, a widow, of Norwich. This constant intercourse with Rome which had always existed must have spread a knowledge of Italy among Englishmen; the first English accounts of travel in Italy were certainly written by just such pilgrims.

Although it would be outside the province of this study to sketch even hastily the development of the English Reformation, at the same time certain of its effects must be alluded to among the connecting links between England and Italy. With the growth of Protestantism pious English Catholics began more and more to take refuge in the latter country. While this was not so much the case in the first half of the sixteenth century, when strong hopes were entertained that there might be a return to Rome, after these had vanished with the death of Mary, the movement became an important one, and numbers of Englishmen found new homes on the banks of the Tiber and elsewhere in Italy. At the same time the beginnings of the movement may be found in the period now treated. It will only be necessary to mention very briefly certain of the English Catholics of this time who resided in Italy, chiefly on account of their religious convictions. They form, as it were, the nucleus around which the Italian influences surrounding them could take action. Without ever ceasing to be Englishmen, many of them yet show to a marked degree the effect of their environment. John Clerke was an example of this; after graduating at Oxford, he travelled in Italy and lived there for many years, writing books on theology, several of which were in Italian; he openly professed his preference for its literature to the Greek and Roman. George Lily, the son of the grammarian, was another one who lived in Rome, where he became noted for his erudition, and was protected by Cardinal Pole. Still a third was Ellis Heywood, brother of the poet, who, after graduating at All Souls, travelled in Italy, where he was received in the household of Reginald Pole, and was appointed by him one of his secretaries; later in life he became a Jesuit. He also wrote in very good Italian two dialogues[1] purporting to be Sir Thomas More's conversations with certain learned men of his time on virtue and love, the great Renaissance topics of discussion. The locality selected was the garden of More's country-house near London, in accordance with the Italian fashion of laying the scenes of conversation in the open air. Apart from this, however, there was little truly English about the book which might as well have been written by some Italian.

[1] *Il Moro d' Heliseo Hevodo Inglese*, Florence, 1556.

Both Lily and Heywood centre around the greater commanding figure of Cardinal Reginald Pole. It was he who, during the period when England was drifting away from Rome, stood for the highest type of English Catholic churchman, and, more than any one else, maintained in Italy the dignity of England. In himself he formed one of the great links between the two countries. A connection of the royal family, he had first studied at Oxford under Linacre and Latimer, and had graduated at Magdalen. In 1521 he was sent by the king to Padua, then known as *Helladis Hellas*, to continue his studies; while there he made friends with some of the great scholars of the time, Leonicus and Longolius, through whom he became acquainted with Bembo. He met there, as well, Thomas Lupset, who had gone to study in Italy by the advice of Vives, the Spanish humanist, and two men who were to be his lifelong friends, Ludovico Priuli, a young Venetian nobleman, and Gaspar Contarini, who later became cardinal. At Padua, Pole entertained considerably, and on account of his royal kinship much attention was paid him by the authorities. His interest in learning he maintained through life; the scholar Longolius, who died in his house, left him his library. When Pole returned to Padua ten years later, he took into his household Lazzaro Buonamici, a well-known classical scholar, to study once more Greek and Latin. But Pole, in spite of his interest in humanism and learning, unlike his Italian friends, cared nothing for literary fame. His one aim and object in life, to which he

devoted himself with unswerving purpose, was to restore in England the supremacy of Rome; and though
he failed in this, he yet stands out in bold relief as
one of the commanding figures of the age, and as
the highest type of learned churchman. He gave
a personal example (for the alleged scandals of his
private life have been proved untrue) that it was
possible to live in Italy and be unaffected by its
vices. He himself had refused from Henry the
Eighth the highest inducements to approve of his
divorce; he had been steadfast through thick and thin
to what he believed to be right, and though he saw
gleams of triumph when Mary came to the throne, his
own death fortunately prevented him from realizing
that his life's work had been in vain. As one of the
great links between Italy and England, his influence,
however, was considerable. To each country he held
up the mirror of the other's virtues. And while
Englishmen saw in his presence the authority and
grandeur of Rome, to Italians he reflected the piety
and austerity of England.

There is little use in going through the catalogue of
churchmen who contributed to familiarizing the one
land with the other. Italians, just as before, came to
England; Giberti, Bishop of Verona, who posed as
the special protector of England; Ghinucci, Bishop of
Worcester and of Salisbury; and Cardinal Campeggio,
who had first been sent to England to urge Henry
the Eighth to unite with the other princes of Christendom in a campaign against the Turk, and returned

as judge to listen to the divorce suit of Henry against Catherine of Aragon. In Italy, on the other hand, lived such men as Sir Edward Carne, sent to Rome as *excusator* of Henry the Eighth, who had been cited to appear there in person. Carne remained there until his death, the Pope ostensibly keeping him as hostage and refusing to allow him to depart, although he gave him the government of the English hospital at Rome. The detention, it is now known, was entirely voluntary on his part, and the Pope's seeming refusal was merely that Carne's property in England should not be confiscated.

It will be seen, from the few facts mentioned, how great were the possibilities of an interchange of ideas between the two countries. Interchange, however, is a misnomer. It cannot be said that the ideas and culture of England had the slightest influence in Italy. The Italians were only shocked at the audacity of the monarch who dared break loose from that most national of institutions, the Papacy. How deep was their interest in England was apparent when the news arrived of Mary's accession to the throne, and it was supposed that England would again become Catholic. There were rejoicings all over Italy, and in Florence alone a solemn mass was held, followed by a procession and display of fireworks, to celebrate England's return to papal obedience.[1]

[1] Settimanni, *Diario Fiorentino*, II, Pt. I, 737, Archives Florence.

In England, during the reign of Elizabeth, the Papacy was looked upon by Protestants as the arch enemy. It was true that every influence, every action, every attempt, to win back what had been lost to the Catholic Church, radiated from Rome. It was there that English Catholics found a new home and sanctuary where they could be safe and secure from insults and injury. Between Catholics in England and English Catholics in Italy there was a constant intercourse, a going and coming, a series of movements and ties, all the closer for being below the surface ; and when gradually the hope for the reconversion of England disappeared, numbers of Englishmen forsook their native land and passed the remainder of their lives in the country of their adoption.

The most prominent among English Catholics of this later time was Cardinal Allen, who, in 1575, had been summoned to Rome by Gregory the Thirteenth, to give advice regarding a college for Englishmen which the Pope proposed to found. A few years later the old English hospital, with all its revenues, was annexed to it. The seminary, as a result of internal dissensions and the jealousy between the English and Welsh students, was placed, in 1579, in charge of the English province of the Society of Jesus,[1] and under the protection of a cardinal. It was presided over by a

---

[1] H. Foley, *Records of the English Province of the Society of Jesus*, VI, 541. Vide Cardinal Sega, *Relazione del Collegio Inglese*, 1596, Fondo Ottoboni, 2473 ff., 185–226, Vatican Library, Rome (cited also by Foley *op. cit.*).

rector, not necessarily an Englishman. A year later it received its first stable endowment and was chartered by an apostolic brief.[1]

On entering the college an oath was administered to the student. He was obliged to swear always to be ready at the order of the Pope or other lawful superior, to take Holy Orders, and to proceed to England for the aid (*i.e.* conversion) of souls. The form of interrogation used is an interesting one.[2] The novice was questioned, among other things, regarding his relatives, and especially of their religious beliefs ; of his own studies, and also of the health of his body and mind. He was asked whether he had been a heretic or schismatic ; how, and by what means he had become a Catholic ; what things had happened to him on account of this, and if he had suffered anything ; last of all, what were the reasons which prompted him to follow an ecclesiastical life.

Between 1579, the year in which the college was founded, and 1603, that of the death of Elizabeth, over three hundred and fifty Englishmen studied there and were admitted to the priesthood. Each year the college sent out its missionaries to England " for the help of perishing souls." Before leaving, they went to kiss the feet of the Pope, who supplied them with funds for their journey. In the records which have been preserved, after each one's name there followed a

[1] Foley, VI, 70.

[2] Vide Stevenson, *Roman Transcripts*, English College Series, Vol. 9, Record Office, London.

brief account of his fate; sometimes it was only imprisonment; but often the *factus est martyr* and the
accounts of those hanged, quartered, and disembow-
elled showed the perils and dangers which awaited
such missionaries in the task they had taken on themselves.[1] To the stanch English Protestant, however,
the college of Rome seemed a centre of popish
abominations and conspiracies, and Anthony Munday, in his *English Roman Life*, described what he
called the treasonable practices and plans concocted
there.

Any account of the graduates of the college, who,
sent back to England, did their best to make converts
and stir up disaffection against Elizabeth, would par-
take too much of both political and religious history
to have any place in the present study. The lives and
martyrdoms of such enthusiasts as Parsons, Campion
and Southwell prove interesting reading, however.[2]
Robert Parsons was perhaps the ablest of them all.
At one time a fellow at Balliol, he had studied medicine at Padua and then became a Jesuit. With Campion, he led the first Jesuit mission to England, which
brought many back to the old faith. When his companion was executed after prolonged tortures, he himself escaped discovery and fled to the Continent to
plot with Philip of Spain to attack England. His life
was spent in one single devotion to restore Catholicism
in England, even at the cost of foreign subjugation,

[1] Vide Cardinal Sega, Ms. cit.
[2] Vide E. L. Taunton, *Jesuits in England*. London, 1901.

and he hoped finally to attain it through the conversion of James the Sixth of Scotland, who he recognized would succeed to the English throne. " I would give up my very life blood," he wrote,[1] " to see him converted and king of England."

England through the long reign of Elizabeth became the seat of many Catholic conspiracies which were hatched for the most part in Italy. In the foremost rank among the conspirators in England was Ruberto Ridolfi, against whom nothing could ever be proved, in spite of the fact that he was implicated in nearly all. His career was a remarkable one ; he had been brought up as a banker, and, going to London, acquired an influential position in social and mercantile circles. In addition he aided the different Catholic conspiracies, but escaped all punishment. The rôle he played can best be seen from a letter to the Pope.[2] He had been the secret agent of Pius the Fifth, at a time when the Vatican was unable to send its nuncios to England, and had been in touch with all the Catholic noblemen who were anxious to serve the Church. In order to prevent Elizabeth from assisting the Protestants in France and Flanders, the Duke of Northumberland with other noblemen had begun an insurrection in the border counties intended to keep the queen in check; but the conspiracy fell through and its leaders were imprisoned or executed.

[1] Letter written in December, 1602 (indexed wrongly, as being by Possevino), *Arch. Med.*, 4185, Florence.

[2] *Arch. Med.*, 4185.

Ridolfi, however, escaped, and begged the Pope to reimburse him for his outlays and property, all of which had been confiscated.

The annals of this period were full of accounts of Catholic conspiracies. But the intrigues of Italian churchmen and English Jesuits came to an untimely end with the destruction of the Armada, and, though their efforts did not cease, the issue was never thereafter in doubt.

In addition to the students of the English College at Rome, many other Englishmen lived in Italy toward the end of the sixteenth century. In a report made to the Pope in 1596 by Cardinal Sega, on the condition of the English College, he ascribed its disturbances to the Englishmen residing outside the college, and recommended in consequence that all communications between students and outsiders should come to an end. Italy was then full of English Catholics. Anthony Munday spoke of Cardinal Borromeo's confessor in Milan as one Robert Griffin, a Welshman, who sent him to the house of an English priest there, named Harris. Another English Catholic of prominence was Thomas Goldwell Bishop of St. Asaph, who studied at Padua in his youth and had been a friend of Cardinal Pole. Many of these Catholics proved themselves stanch Englishmen, however, and Sir Richard Shelley, known in Italy as *Signor Conchilio*, sent valuable information from Venice about the Spanish Armada. It is scarcely necessary to mention more names; enough has already been said here and elsewhere to indicate the extent and permanence of one of the great chains which linked Italy to England.

Occasionally the rôles were reversed and an ardent English Protestant would penetrate Italy filled with desire for proselytizing. Such a one was Richard Atkins, fanatic and martyr, who went to Rome with the intention of converting the Pope. After he had committed several excesses against the Roman Church, and had insulted the host, he was denounced, tortured, and finally executed. Chamberlain spoke in his letters[1] of Englishmen " clapt up in the Inquisition at Rome." Oftener it was Italy that had for its effect the Catholic conversion of Protestants. So it turned out with Sir Tobie Matthew, who was to be known as " the most Italianate Englishman of his day." His parents, who had puritanical leanings, refused their consent when he first expressed a wish to see the antiquities and sights of the country of which he had heard so much ; but he went in spite of them. In Florence he met some of the English Catholics who lived there, among others Sir George Petre, Robert Canfield and one Partridge, a nephew of Sir Henry Western. He then moved on to Siena, that he might be " with Italians only in order to learn their language." In Rome he met Robert Parsons, was received by Cardinal Pinelli, and while there became converted to Catholicism. In after years he was ordained a priest ; he also translated Bacon into Italian. Sir Tobie Matthew is interesting as showing one of the reasons

[1] Chamberlain's Letters, March 5, 1600.

for the distrust with which English Protestants regarded Italy. Its influence had made him become
a Catholic, even a priest; his tastes, his habits all
became Italian: he had lost in their opinion his
English manhood.

APPENDIX B

ENGLISH ACCOUNTS OF ITALY IN THE SIXTEENTH CENTURY [1]

1506. The Pilgrimage of Richard Guylforde to the Holy Land.

1517. Sir Richard Torkington's Diary of his Pilgrimage.

1547–1549. The Travaile and Life of Sir Thomas Hoby (Eg. Ms., 2148, Brit. Mus.).

1549. The History of Italy, by William Thomas.

1563. Unton's Journey to Italy, written by Richard Smith (Sloan Ms., 1813, Brit. Mus.).

1573. Sidney's letters to Hubert Languet.

1575. Jerome Turler — The Traveller : Description of Naples.

1582. Anthony Munday — English Roman Life.

1584–1600. Description of Italy — (Harleian Miscellany, XII).

1585. J[ohn] F[lorio], translator — A Letter written from Rome, by an Italian gentleman.

1588. Edward Webbe's Travels — Account of Rome.

1592. Description of Italy — (Lansdowne Ms., Brit. Mus., 775).

[1] Such incidental descriptions as are given by Nash in *Jack Wilton*, etc., Greene and the dramatists have not been included in this list.

1593. Fynes Moryson — Account of his Visit to Italy.

1596. Robert Dallington — Survey of Tuscany (published 1605).

1599. G. Contarini — Government of Venice — translated by L. Lewkenor.

1599. Edwin Sandys — Europæ Speculum (published 1605).

1600. J. B. Marlianus — Topography of Rome.

1600. Samuel Lewkenor — Description of Italian Universities.

APPENDIX C

ITALIAN ACCOUNTS OF ENGLAND IN THE SIXTEENTH CENTURY [1]

1500 (*circa*). A Relation of the Islands of England.

1516. Travels of a Milanese in England — (Brit. Mus. Add. Mss., 24180).

1515–1519. Sebastiano Giustiniani — Four Years at the Court of Henry the Eighth.

1531. Relazione di Lodovico Falier.

1551. Relazione di Daniele Barbaro.

1552. Relazione d' Inghilterra, Petruccio Ubaldini (Add. Ms., 10169, Brit. Mus.).

1554. Relazione del Giacomo Soranzo.

1554–1558. Relazione di Anonimo del tempo della Regina Maria.

1555. Ritratti d' Inghilterra di Giulio Raviglio. (Lib. Com. Siena, K. X. 29.)

1557. Relazione di Giovanni Michele.

1580 (*circa*). Relazione del Giovanni Sovico Milanees (Arch. Med. Flor., 4185).

---

[1] Only the more important descriptions have here been mentioned. Accounts will also be found in looking through the *Calendars of State Papers, Venetian*, the *Cena dei Ceneri* of Giordano Bruno, Cardan's *Diary*, the *Description* of Paulo Giovio, and Botero's *Geography*, etc.

1573–1588. Relazione di Inghilterra, attributed to
Nicolo Millino (Molino?), (cited by Sneyd,
as being in the Earl of Leicester's Library
at Holkham, Rel. of Eng., Camden Soc.,
1847).

BIBLIOGRAPHY[1]

I. MANUSCRIPT SOURCES

FLORENCE.   Archivio di Firenze.

> Atti Publici, 1498.   Miscellaneous letters from Henry the Seventh, etc.
>
> Atti Publici, 1502.   Miscellaneous letters.
>
> Carteggio Mediceo Avanti il Principato, filza 94.
>
> Carteggio Mediceo Avanti il Principato, filza 99.
>
> Carteggio Universale Mediceo, 371, 372.
>
> Carteggio Mediceo, N. 5.
>
> Guardaroba Medicea, T. 34.   Miscellaneous.
>
> Guardaroba Medicea, 293.   Miscellaneous.

Archivio Mediceo.   Firenze, No. 4183.

> Lettere della Regina d' Inghilterra e del Re dall' anno 1524 fino 1621.

Archivio Mediceo, No. 4185.

> Varie Scritture, contenuti, notizie el Avvisi d' Inghilterra dall' anno 1526 a 1625.

Archivio di Firenze.

> Minute del 1545, filza N. 6.
>
> Carte Strozziane, 1448–1588.   Scritture che si riferiscono all' Inghilterra del 1488 al 1588.
>
> Filza Strozziana, 294.

Settimanni.

> Diario Fiorentino.   Archivio Mediceo, Firenze.

---

[1] This bibliography is intended merely as a convenient enumeration of the principal manuscripts and books used in the preparation of this study.   A far more complete list of the numerous articles on the literary relations between England and Italy may be found in Betz's *La Littérature Comparée*.   Further bibliographies can likewise be obtained from the invaluable *Dictionary of National Biography*.

Biblioteca Magliabecchiana.

Duodo, Pietro.

Relazione d' Inghilterra e Scozia. Scritto da un Segretario
dell' Illmo Sig^e Pietro Duodo, stato ambasciatore per la
Signoria di Venezia appresso al Re Giacomo, 1606.
Magliabecchiana. Ce. XXIV, Cod. 49.

Biblioteca Capponi. Magliabecchiana Cassetta 10^a No. XVII.

LONDON. Brit. Mus. Addit. Mss., 24180.

Travels of a Milanese Merchant in 1516.

Brit. Mus. Addit. Mss., 4121, f. 265; addit. Mss., 4122, ff. 43,
111, 139.

[Cited by Harris Nicolas in his Edition of Davison's Poetical Rhapsody.]

Brit. Mus. Cot. Mss.

Nero, B. VI, f. 1; Nero, B. VII, *passim;* Titus, B. II, f. 210;
B. VII, f. 155; Vitellius, B. XIV, ff. 173, 241, 285.

Brit. Mus. Mss., 4827.

New Year's gifts of Queen Elizabeth.

Brit. Mus. Harl. Ms., 284.

Fragment of some noblemen's letters from Italy, 1603.

Brit. Mus. Harl. Ms., 1878.

Brit. Mus. Mss., 2481.

Household Book of Henry VIII.

Brit. Mus. Egert. Mss., 2148.

Hoby, Sir Thomas. The Travails and Life of Sir Thomas
Hoby; ff. 186–202, A Description of the State of Italy.

Brit. Mus. Lansd. Mss., 775, ff. 105–128.

A Description of the Estate of Italy in the year 1592.

Brit. Mus. Addit. Mss., 10169.

Michele, Giovanni. Relazione d' Inghilterra, 1557.
[Contained also in Alberi, Ambasciatori Veneti.]

Brit. Mus. Addit. Mss., 10169.

Ubaldini, Petruccio. Relazione d' Inghilterra, circa 1555.

Brit. Mus. Sloane Mss., 1813.

Unton, Sir Edward. Unton's journey to Italy, written by
Richard Smith, gentleman, some time servant to S^r
Edward Unton [1563].

Public Record Office.

    Acontio, J. Study of History. (Dom. Series, Vol. XXXIV, August, 1564.)

    Foreign Papers: Italy. Bundles 1-2.

    Roman Transcripts by J. Stevenson. (English College Series, 9 vols.)

    Venetian Bundle, No. 1.

MUNICH. Königlichen Bibliothek Mss., Latin, 222.

    Letters of Pier Candido Decembrio and Duke Humphrey of Gloucester.

OXFORD. Bodleian Library. Ms. 587.

    Free, John. Letters.

All Souls' Library. Ms. CLV.

ROME. Vatican Library.

    Relazione del Collegio Inglese, 1596. Fondo Ottoboni, 2473, ff. 185-226.

    [Cited by H. Foley in Records of English Jesuits.]
English College.

    Liber Primus Instrumentorum.

    [Cited by H. Foley in Records of English Jesuits.]

SIENA. Libreria Communale K. X. 29.

    Raviglio, Giulio. Ritratti d' Inghilterra, 1555.

II. PRINTED SOURCES

ACONTIO, JACOPO. The true order and method of writing and reading Histories according to the precepts of Francisco Patrizio and Accontio Tridentino. . . . By Thomas Blundeville. London, 1574.

Una Essortazione al Timor di Dio con Alcune rime Italiane novamente messe in luce. Londra circa 1580.

AGNELLO, G. Esposizione di Giovanbattista Agnello Venetiano sopra un libro intitolato Apocalypsis spiritus secreti. Londra, 1566.

ALBERI, E. Relazioni dello Impero Brittanico nel Secolo XVI Scritto da Veneti Ambasciatori e pubblicate dal Prof. Eugenio Alberi. Firenze, 1852. [Containing the relations of Daniele Barbaro, Giovanni Michele, Lodovico Falier, Giacomo Soranzo, and an anonymous relation.]

ALBERTI, L. B. Hecatonphila, The Art of Love or Love discovered in an hundred several kinds. London, 1598.

ANGLERIUS, PIETRO MARTIRE. The Decades of the New World or West India. Translated by Richard Eden. London, 1555.

The History of Travel in the West and East Indies. Gathered in part by Richard Eden, and augmented by Richard Willes. London, 1577.

ARETINO, PIETRO. Epistole. 6 vols. Paris, 1609.

ARIOSTO, L. Orlando Furioso. In English Heroical Verse by John Harington. 1591.

ASCHAM, ROGER. The Scholemaster. 1570. Edited by E. Arber. London, 1897.

BALE, JOHN. Summarium Scriptorum Illustrium. Bâle, 1557.

BANDELLO, M. Certain Tragical Discourses of Bandello. Translated by Geoffrey Fenton. 2 vols. London, 1898.

BARBARO, J., and CONTARINI, A. Travels to Tana and Persia. Translated by Wm. Thomas. Hakluyt Society, London, 1873.

BARCLAY, ALEXANDER. The Ship of Fools. London, 1570.

BARKER, WILLIAM. Epitaphia et Inscriptiones Lugubres a Gulielmo Berchero cum in Italia causa, peregrinaretur collecta. London, 1566.

BARTOLUS. Tractatus de Insignis et Armis. Altdorf, 1727.

BECKYNTON, THOMAS. Correspondence. 2 vols. Rolls Series. 1872.

BIZARI, PIETRO. Historia. Lyons, 1568.

BOCCACCIO, GIOVANNI. The Tragedies ... of all such Princes as fell from their Estates through the Mutability of Fortune ... Translated by John Lydgate. 1558. [First Edition, 1494.]

BOIARDO, M. Orlando Innamorato. The first three Books ... done into English Historical Verse by R[obert] T[ofte]. London, 1598.

BOTERO, G. The Traveller's Breviat. Translated by Robert Johnson. London, 1601.

BOURNE, WILLIAM. A book called the Treasure for travellers. London, 1578.

BRUNO, GIORDANO. Spaccio De La Bestia Trionfanto . . . al eccellente Cavalliero Sig. Philippo Sidneo. London, 1584.

Giordano Bruno Nolano, De Gl' Heroici Furori al Molto illustre el eccellente Cavalliero Signor Philippo Sidneo. London (?), 1585.

Le Opere Italiane di Giordano Bruno. Edited by A. Wagner. 2 vols. Leipsic, 1830.

BRYSKETT, LODOWICK. A Discourse of Civil Life Containing the Ethike part of Morall Philosophie. London, 1606.

BUCHANAN, G. Opera Omnia. 2 vols. Leyden, 1725.

CAIUS, JOHN. De Antiquitate Cantabrigiensis Academiæ. London, 1574.

CARDANO, GIROLAMO. Cardanus Comfort translated into English . . . by T. Bedingfield. 1573.

Vita. Milan, 1821.

CASA, GIOVANNI DELLA. Galateo of Master John Della Casa, archbishop of Benevento . . . Translated by Robert Peterson. 1576.

CASTIGLIONE, B. Lettere del Conte Baldessar Castiglione. Edited by P. A. Serassi. 2 vols. Padua, 1769–1771.

The Courtier. Translated by Sir Thomas Hoby. Edited by W. Raleigh. London, 1900.

CATANEO, GIROLAMO. Most Briefe Tables to know readily how many ranks of footmen armed with corselets, as unarmed, go to the making of a just battle. Translated by H[enry ?] G[rantham ?]. London, 1574.

CHAMBERLAIN, JOHN. Letters. Edited by S. Williams. Camden Society, 1861.

CHEKE, HENRY. A Certain Tragedy written first in Italian by F. N. B. entitled Free Will and translated into English by Henry Cheeke. N.D.

CLARKE, W. Polimanteia. 1595.

CLERK, JOHN. Opusculum Plane Divinum de Mortuorum resurrectione et extremo juditio, in quatuor linguis, . . . Latyne, Englyshe, Italian, French. London, 1545.

CONESTAGGIO, G. The History of the Uniting of the Kingdom of Portugal to the Crown of Castile . . . Translated by Edward Blount. London, 1600.

CONSTABLE, H. Diana. Edited by W. C. Hazlitt. London, 1859.

CONTARINI, G. The Commonwealth and Government of Venice, written by the Cardinal Gaspar Contarini . . . Translated by Lewis Lewkenor. London, 1599.

COPLEY, Sir THOMAS. Correspondence. Roxburghe Club, 1897.

CORTE, CLAUDIO. The Art of Riding . . . in the Italian toong by Maister Claudio Corte . . . Translated by Thomas Bedingfield. London, 1584.

DALLINGTON, Sir ROBERT. A Survey of the Great Duke's State of Tuscany in the year of our Lord 1596. London, 1605.

A Method for Travel shewed by taking the view of France as it stood in the year of our Lord 1598. London (1606 ?).

DANIEL, S. Works. Ed. A. Grosart. 5 vols. London, 1885.

DAVISON, FRANCIS. The Poetical Rhapsody. Edited by N. Harris Nicolas. London, 1826.

DOWLAND, JOHN. The First Book of Songs or Airs. London, 1597.

DRAYTON, M. Poems. London, 1613.

DROUT, JOHN. The pitiful History of two loving Italians: Gaulfrido and Bernardo . . . Translated out of Italian into English metre by John Drout. London, 1570.

ELLIS, Sir HENRY. Letters of Eminent Literary Men. Camden Society, 1843.

ELYOT, Sir THOMAS. The Governour. Edited by H. H. S. Croft. 2 vols. London, 1880.

Epistolæ Academicæ Oxonienses. Edited by Rev. Henry Anstey. 2 vols. Oxford, 1898.

EPULARIO. Epulario or the Italian Banquet. London, 1598.

ERASMUS, D. Epistolæ. Edited by Le Clerc. 2 vols. Leyden, 1706.

FEDERICI, M. CESARE. The Voyage and Travel of M. Cæsar Frederick, Merchant of Venice, into the East India, the Indies, and beyond the Indies. Translated by T[homas] H[ickock]. London, 1588.

FENTON, G. Golden Epistles . . . gathered as well out of the remainder of Guevara's works as other authors, Latin, French, and Italian. London, 1595.

FLORIO, JOHN. First Fruites. London, 1578.

Florio's Second Fruites . . . of divers but delightsome tastes to the tongues of Italians and Englishmen. To which is annexed his Gardine of Recreation yielding six thousand Italian proverbs. London, 1591.

Giardino di Ricreatione nel quale crescono fronde, fiori e frutti . . . Sotto nome di sei milla Proverbii e piacevoli riboboli Italiani, colti e Scelti da Giovanni Florio. Londra, 1591.

A Worlde of Wordes or most copious and exact Dictionary in Italian and English, collected by John Florio. London, 1598.

FRAUNCE, ABRAHAM. The Arcadian Rhetorike. Or the Precepts of Rhetoric made plain by example, Greek, Latin, English, Italian, French, Spanish, and Homer, Virgil, Tasso, etc. *circa* 1579.

FULWOOD, WILLIAM. The Enemy of Idleness. Teaching a perfect platform how to indite Epistles and Letters of all sorts, as well by answer as otherwise: no less profitable than pleasant. London, 1568.

GASCOIGNE, GEORGE. A Hundred Sundry Flowers, bound up in one Small Posy . . . Gathered in the fine outlandish Gardens of Euripides, Ovid, Petrarch, Ariosto . . . London, 1565.

The Whole Works of George Gascoigne, Esquire. London, 1587.

GELLI, GIOVANNI BATTISTA. Circes of John Baptista Gello, Florentine. Translated out of Italian into English by Henry Iden. 1557.

The Fearful Fancies of the Florentine Cooper . . . Translated by W. Barker. London, 1568.

GENTILE, ALBERICO. Regales Disputationes tres de Potestate Regis Absolutis. (1606 ?)

England's Monarch, or a Conviction and Refutation by the Common Law of those false principles and insinuating flatteries of Albericus. London, 1644.

GENTILLET, I. A Discourse . . . against Nicholas Machiavell. Translated from the French by Simon Patericke. London, 1602.

GIOVIO, PAOLO. Descriptio Britanniæ, Scotiæ. Ex Libro Pauli Jovii. N.D.

The worthy tract of Paulus Jovius, Containing a Discourse of rare inventions both military and amorous called Imprese. Translated by Samuel Daniel. 1585.

GIUSTINIAN, S. Four Years at the Court of Henry VIII. Edited by Rawdon Brown. 2 vols. London, 1854.

GOOGE, BARNABE. Eglogs, Epitaphes and Sonettes. Edited by E. Arber. London, 1871.

GOSSON, STEPHEN. Plays Confuted in Fine Actions. London. School of Abuse. Shakespeare Society, London, 1841.

GRATAROLUS. The Castel of Memorie. Translated by William Fulwood. London, 1563.

GREENE, ROBERT. Works. Edited by A. Grosart. 15 vols. 1881–1886.

GRISONE. A new booke containing the art of riding and break-ing great horses ... Translated by Thomas Blundeville. N.D.

The Art of Riding ... out of Xenophon and Gryson verie expert and excellent horsemen. [Translated by John Astley.] London, 1584.

GUARINI, BATTISTA. Il Pastor Fido Tragicomedia Pastorale di Battista Guarini ... a Spese di Jacopo Castelvetri. Londra, 1591.

Il Pastor Fido or the faithful Shepherd. Translated by Edward Dymock. London, 1602.

GUAZZO, S. The Civil Conversation of M. Stephen Guazzo ... the first three books translated out of French by George Pettie, the fourth out of the original Italian by Barth. Young. London, 1586.

GUICCIARDINI, F. The History of Guicciardin, containing the Wars of Italy ... by Geoffrey Fenton. London, 1579.

GUICCIARDINI, L. The Description of the Low Countries. Trans-lated by Th. Danett. London, 1593.

GUYLFORDE, Sir R. The Pylgrymage of Sir Richard Guylforde to the Holy Land, 1506. Edited by Sir H. Ellis. Cam-den Society, 1851.

HALL, JOSEPH. Quo Vadis? A Just Censure of Travel. London, 1617.

Virgedemiarum. Satires. Edinburgh, 1824.

HARRISON, W. A Description of England in Shakespeare's Youth, 1577–1587. Edited by J. Furnivall. 2 vols. New Shakespeare Society, 1877.

HARVEY, GABRIEL. Works. Edited by A. Grosart. 3 vols. 1884.

Letter-Book. Edited by E. J. L. Scott. Camden Society, 1884.

HOLLYBAND, CLAUDIUS. The Italian School-Maister, Contayning Rules for the perfect pronouncing of th' italian tongue, with familiar Speeches, and certain Phrases taken out of the best Italian authors, and a fine Tuscan historie called Arnalt and Lucenda. London, 1575 and 1597.

HOLLYBAND, CLAUDIUS. Campo di Fior, or else the Flourie Field of Foure Languages of M. Claudius Desainliens alias Holiband. London, 1583.

HUME, M. A. S. Chronicle of Henry VIII. Edited by M. A. S. Hume. London, 1889.

HUMPHREY, LAWRENCE. The Nobles, or of Nobility. London, 1563.

Institution of a Gentleman. 1555.

Italians, Subtlety of. A Discovery of the Great Subtlety and wonderful wisdom of the Italians whereby they bear sway over the most part of Christendom ... By F. G. B. A. London, 1591.

LELAND, JOHN. Næniæ in Mortem Thomæ Viati. London, 1542. De Scriptoribus Britannicis. Oxford, 1709.

Collectanea. 3 vols. Oxford, 1715.

LENTULO, SCIPIO. An Italian Grammar written in Latin by Scipio Lentulo, a Neapolitan, and turned in English by H[enry] G[rantham]. London, 1575.

LESLIE, JOHN. A Treatise touching the Right, Title and Interest as well of the most excellent Princess, Mary Queen of Scotland, as of the most noble King James. [1584.]

LEWKENOR, SAMUEL. A Discourse ... of all those cities wherein do flourish at this day privileged Universities. 1600.

LIPSIUS, JUSTUS. A Direction for Travailers ... enlarged for the behoof of the right honorable Lord the young Earl of Bedford, being now ready to travel. London, 1592.

LOMAZZO, G. P. A Tracte Containing the Artes of Curious Painting, Carving, and Building. Englished by R[ichard] H[aydocke]. 1598.

LUPTON, THOMAS. Civil and Uncivil Life. London, 1579.

MACHIAVELLI, N. The Art of War written in Italian by Nicholas Machiavel, and set forth in English by Peter Withorne. 1573.

The Florentine History written in the Italian Tongue by Nicholo Macchiavelli ... and translated into English by T[homas] B[edingfield]. London, 1595.

MANTUANUS. The eclogues of the poet B. Mantuan. Translated by George Turbervile. London, 1567.

MARLIANUS, J. B. A Summary ... touching the Topography of Rome in Ancient Time. [Appendix to Philemon Holland's translation of Livy.] London, 1600.

MARSTON, JOHN. Works. Edited by A. H. Bullen. 3 vols. London, 1887.

MERBURY, CHARLES. A Briefe Discourse of Royall Monarchie as of the Best Common Weale ... Whereunto is added by the same gent., A Collection of Italian Proverbs, in benefit of such as are studious of that language. London, 1581.

MERES, FRANCIS. Palladis Tamia; Wits' Treasury. 1598.

MINADOI, J. T. The History of the Wars between the Turks and the Persians. Translated by Abraham Hartwell. London, 1595.

MORA, D. Il Cavaliere in Risposto del Gentilhuomo del Sig^r Mutio Justinopolitano, nella precedenza Del Armi et delle Lettere. Wilna, 1589.

MORLEY, THOMAS. Alto di Tomaso Morlei. Il Primo Libro Delle Ballette a Cinque Voci. Londra, 1595.

MULCASTER, RICHARD. Positions. 1581. Edited by R. H. Quick. London 1888.

The First Part of the Elementary. 1582.

MUNDAY, ANTHONY. The English Roman Life. London, circa 1581.

MUZIO, G. Il Gentilhuomo. Venice, 1571.

NANNINI, REMIGIO. Civil Considerations upon Many and Sundry Histories . . . containing rules and precepts for Princes, Commonwealths, . . . Translated in English by W. T. from the French translation by Gabriel Chappuys. London, 1601.

NASH, THOMAS. Works. Edited by A. Grosart. 6 vols. London, 1883–1885.

OCHINO, B. Sermons of the right famous and excellent clerk Master Bernardine Ochine . . . Translated by Richard Argentyne. Ipswich, 1548.

The Tragedy . . . Reprinted from Bishop Ponet's translation out of Ochino's Latin Mss. in 1549. Edited by C. E. Plumptre. London, 1899.

Fourteen Sermons of Bernardine Ochyne concerning the predestination and election of God. Translated by A[nne] C[ooke]. (1550 ?)

Certain Godly and very profitable Sermons of Faith, Hope, and Charity, First set forth by Master Bernardine Ochine . . . Translated by William Phiston. London, 1580.

PALEARIO, AONIO. Of the Benefit that true Christians Receive by the Death of Jesus Christ. Translated by Edward Courtenay, Earl of Devonshire. 1548.

PALINGENIUS, MARCELLUS [MANZOLLI, GIOV. BATT.] The First Six Books of the Most Christian Poet, Marcellus Palingenius, called the Zodiac of Life. Translated by Barnaby Googe. London, 1561.

PALMER, THOMAS. An Essay of the Means how to make our Travels into foreign Countries the more profitable and honorable. London, 1606.

PATRIZI, FRANCESCO. A Moral Method of Civil Policy. Translated by Richard Robinson. London, 1576.

PEACHAM, HENRY. The Compleat Gentleman. 1622.

PHILBERT OF VIENNE. The Philosopher of the Court . . . Englished by George North, Gentleman. London, 1575.

POGGIO [BRACCIOLINI]. Epistolæ. Edited by Tonelli. 3 vols. Florence, 1832–1861.

Epistolæ. Spicilegium Romanum X. Rome, 1844.

POLITIANUS, A. The History of Herodian ... Translated out of Greek into Latin by Angelus Politianus and out of Latin into English by Nicholas Smyth. 1550(?)

PONET, JOHN. A Short Treatise of politic power and of the true obedience which subjects owe to kings. 1556.

PUTTENHAM, RICHARD. Arte of English Poesie. Edited by E. Arber. London, 1895.

ROME. A Letter written from Rome by an Italian Gentleman ... wherein is declared the State of Rome ... Translated by J[ohn] F[lorio]. London, 1585.

ROMEI, ANNIBALE. The Courtier's Academie. Comprehending seven severall dayes discourses: wherein be discussed seven noble and important arguments. Translated into English by J[ohn] K[epers]. London, 1598.

ROWLAND, DAVID. A comfortable aid for Schollers full of variety of sentences, gathered out of an Italian authour by David Rouland. London, 1578.

SANDYS, EDWIN. A Relation of the State of Religion and with what Hopes and Policies it hath been framed, and is maintained in the several states of these western parts of the world. [Known as *Speculum Europæ*.] London, 1605.

SANDYS, GEORGE. A Relation of a Journey begun An. Dom. 1610. London, 1615.

SANSOVINO, F. The Quintessence of Wit, being a current comfort of conceits, maxims, and politic devices, selected and gathered together by Francisco Sansovino. [Translated by Robert Hitchcock.] London, 1590.

SAVIOLO, V. Vincentio Saviolo his Practise. In two Bookes. The first intreating of the use of the Rapier and Dagger. The second, of Honor and honorable quarrels. London, 1595.

SEGAR, WILLIAM. The Booke of Honor and Armes. London, 1590.

Honor Military and Civil. London, 1602.

SHAKESPEARE, W. The Poems of Shakespeare. Edited by George Wyndham. London, 1898.

SIDNEY, Sir PHILIP. Poems. Edited by A. Grosart. 2 vols. 1873.

Apologie for Poetrie. London, 1895.

The Correspondence of Sir Philip Sidney and Hubert Languet. Edited by S. A. Pears. London, 1845.

SILVER, GEORGE. Paradoxes of Defence. 1599.

SKELTON, J. Poetical Works. Edited by A. Dyce. 2 vols. London, 1843.

SMITH, Sir THOMAS. De Republica Anglorum. The Manner of Government or Policy of the Realm of England. London, 1583.

SNEYD, C. A. A Relation of the Island of England about the year 1500. Translated from the Italian by C. A. Sneyd. Camden Society, 1847.

SORANZO, LAZARO. The Ottoman of Lazaro Soranzo. Translated by Abraham Hartwell. London, 1603.

STAPLETON, T. Tres Thomæ. Ed. Duaci (Douai).

STELLA, JULIUS CÆSAR. Julii Cæsaris Stellæ Nob. Rom. Columbeidos Libri Priores Duo. Londini, 1585. [Dedicated by Jacopo Castelvetro to Sir Walter Raleigh.]

SURREY, HENRY HOWARD, Earl of. Poems. London, 1866.

SYLVIUS, ÆNEAS [PICCOLOMINI]. Opera. Ed. Basel. N.D.

TARTAGLIA, N. Three Books of Colloquies concerning the Art of Shooting in great and small pieces of Artillery . . . Written by Nicholas Tartaglia and dedicated to Henry VIII. Translated by Cyprian Lucar. London, 1588.

TASSO, TORQUATO. Godfrey of Bulloigne . . . five Cantos translated by R[ichard] C[arew] London, 1594.

Godfrey of Bulloigne, or the Recovery of Jerusalem. Done into English Heroical Verse by Edward Fairfax, Gent. London, 1600.

THOMAS, W. The Works of William Thomas, Clerk of the Privy Council in the year 1549. Edited by A. d'Aubant. London, 1774.

The Historie of Italie. A boke excedyng profitable to be redde: Because it intreateth of the estate of many and divers commonweales, how thei have ben, and now be governed. 1549.

Principal Rules of the Italian Grammar with a Dictionarie for the better understanding of Boccace, Petrarcha, and Dante. London, 1550.

The Pilgrim. A Dialogue on the Life and Actions of King Henry the Eighth. By William Thomas, Clerk of the Council to Edward the Sixth. Edited by J. A. Froude. London, 1561.

TOFTE, ROBERT. Laura, The Toys of a Traveler, by R[obert] T[ofte]. London, 1597.

TORKINGTON, Sir RICHARD. The Oldest Diary of English Travel. Edited by W. J. Loftie. London.

Tottels Miscellany. 1557. Edited by E. Arber. London, 1895.

TURBERVILE, GEORGE. The Book of Falconry or Hawking . . . collected out of the best authors as well Italians and Frenchmen. By George Turbervile. London, 1575.

Tragical Tales translated by Turbervile In time of his troubles out of sundry Italians . . . London, 1587.

TURLER, JEROME. The Traveler of Jerome Turler. London, 1575.

UBALDINI, PETRUCCIO. La Vita Di Carlo Magno Imperadore. Londra, 1581.

Le Vite Delle Donne Illustri Del Regno d' Inghilterra e de Regno di Scotia. Scritte da Petruccio Ubaldini. Londra, 1591.

VERMIGLI, PETER MARTYR. A brief Treatise concerning the use and abuse of Dancing. Translated by I. K. N.D.

The Common Places of the most famous and renowned Divine Doctor Peter Martyr . . . Translated by Anthony Martin. 1583 [date on title-page, 1574].

VESPUSIANO DA BISTICCI. Vite di Uomini Illustri del Secolo XV. Edited by A. Mai and A. Bartoli. Firenze, 1859.

VIGO, Vigo's Chirurgery. Translated by Barth. Traheron. 1543.

VILLANI, G. Cronica. Florence, 1823.

WATSON, THOMAS. The first set of Italian Madrigals Englished. London, 1590.

Poems. Edited by E. Arber. Westminster, 1895.

WHETSTONE, GEORGE. An Heptameron of Civil Discourses. London, 1582.

WILSON, THOMAS. The Art of Rhetoric. 1553.

The Three Orations of Demosthenes. London, 1570.

WYATT, Sir THOMAS. Works. Edited by J. Yeowell. London, 1894.

YONGE, NICHOLAS. Musica Transalpina ... with the first and second part of *La Verginella* made by Master Byrd upon two stanzas of *Ariosto* and brought to speak English with the rest. London, 1588.

Musica Transalpina ... translated out of sundry Italian authors. London, 1597.

Zepheria. Reprinted from the original edition of 1594. Spenser Society, 1869.

III. WORKS OF REFERENCE

ALDEN, R. M. The Rise of Formal Satire in England. Philadelphia, 1899.

ANDRICH, J. A. De Natione Anglica et Scota Juristarum Universitatis Patavinæ. Patavii, MDCCCXCII.

Rotulus et Matricula D. D. Juristarum et Artistarum Gymnasii Patavini a MDXCII ... Curantibus D^re Blasio Brugi p. o. prof. et J. Aloysis Andrich iur. stud. in Patav. Ath. Patavii, MDCCCXCII.

BASCHET, ARMAND. La Diplomatie Vénitienne. Paris, 1862.

BETZ, L. P. La Littérature Comparée. Strasburg, 1900.

BEYERSDORFF, R. Shakespeare und Bruno. (Shakespeare Jahrbuch, XXVI.)

BOND, E. A. Italian Merchants in England. (Archaeologia, Vol. XXVIII.)

BREWER, J. S. The Reign of Henry VIII. Edited by J. Gairdner. 2 vols. London, 1884.

BURGON, J. W. The Life and Times of Sir Thomas Gresham. 2 vols. 1839.

BURNET, G. The History of the Reformation. Edited by N. Pocock. 7 vols. Oxford, 1865.

Calendar of Entries in the Papal Registers relating to Great Britain and Ireland. Edited by W. H. Bliss. Rolls Series. 2 vols. London, 1893.

Calendar of Letters and Papers, foreign and domestic. Henry VIII, Vols. I–IV, edited by J. S. Brewer; Vols. V–XV, edited by James Gairdner. London, 1880–1896.

Calendar of State Papers, foreign. Edward VI and Mary. 2 vols. Edited by W. Turnbull. London, 1861.

Calendar of State Papers, foreign. Elizabeth. Vols. I–VII, edited by J. Stevenson; Vols. VIII–XI, edited by A. J. Crosby. London, 1863–1880.

Calendar of State Papers, Venetian. Vols. I–VII, edited by Rawdon Brown; Vol. VII, edited by Cavendish Bentinck; Vols. VIII–X, edited by Horatio F. Brown. London, 1864–1900.

CAMPBELL, W. Materials for a History of Henry VII. Rolls Series. 2 vols. London, 1873.

COCKLE, M. J. D. A Bibliography of Military Books up to 1642. London, 1900.

Collectanea. Second Series. Oxford, 1890.

COLLIER, T. P. English Dramatic Poetry. 3 vols. London, 1831.

COURTHOPE, W. J. History of English Poetry. 2 vols. London, 1895–1897.

COXE, HENRY. Catalogus Codicum Mss. qui in Collegiis Aulisque Oxoniensibus hodie Adservantur — Henricus Coxe, 2 vols. Oxford, 1852.

CREIGHTON, M. The Early Renaissance in England. Cambridge, 1895.

DAVIDSOHN, ROBERT. Geschichte von Florenz. Berlin, 1896.

DAVIES, T. S. History of Southampton. Southampton, 1883.

DENNISTOUN, T. Memoirs of the Dukes of Urbino. 3 vols. London, 1851.

Delle Eccelenze . . . della nazione Fiorentina. Florence, 1780.

EHRENBERG, RICHARD. Hamburg und England im Zeitalter der Königin Elizabeth. Jena, 1896.

ELZE, TH. Italienische Skizzen zu Shakespeare. (Shakespeare Jahrbuch, XIII–XV.)

FAIRHOLT, F. W. Costume in England. London, 1846.

FLAMINI, F. Studi di Storia Letteraria Italiana e Straniera. Leghorn, 1893.

FLEAY, F. G. History of the Stage. London, 1890.

FOLEY, HENRY. Records of the English Province of the Society of Jesus. 6 vols. London, 1880.

FRÄNKEL, L. Romanische insbesondere Italienische Wechsel-beziehungen zur Englischen Litteratur. (Kritischer Jahresbericht über die Fortschritte der Romanischen Philologie, 1900.)

FROUDE, J. History of England. 12 vols. New York, 1865–1870.

GAIRDNER, J. Memorials of King Henry VII. Rolls Series. London, 1858.

Letters and Papers of Richard III and Henry VII. Edited by James Gairdner. London, 1861–1863.

GASQUET, F. A. The Old English Bible. London, 1897.

Eve of the Reformation. New York, 1900.

GOTCH, J. ALFRED. Architecture of the Renaissance in England. 2 vols. London, 1891–1894.

GREEN, Mrs. J. R. Town Life in the Fifteenth Century. 2 vols. London, 1895.

HALLAM, HENRY. Literature of Europe. 3 vols. London, 1873.

HASLEWOOD, J. Ancient Critical Essays upon English Poets and Poesy. 2 vols. London, 1811–1815.

HAWKINS, E., and FRANKS, A. Medallic Illustrations of British History. 2 vols. London, 1885.

HEYD, W. Geschichte des Levant Handels. Stuttgart, 1889.

Historical Manuscripts Commission. Calendar of the Manuscripts of the Marquis of Salisbury preserved at Hatfield House. 6 vols. London, 1883.

JEBB, R. C. Erasmus. Cambridge, 1890.

JOHNSON, J. NOBLE. The Life of Thomas Linacre. London, 1835.

JORTIN, J. The Life of Erasmus. 3 vols. London, 1808.

JUSSERAND, J. J. English Novel in the Time of Shakespeare. London, 1890.

KOEPPEL, E. Varia. (Anglia, XI–XIII. Romanische Forschungen V, Englische Studien, 1891, etc.)

LAW, ERNEST. The History of Hampton Court Palace. 3 vols. London, 1885.

LEE, SIDNEY. William Shakspeare. London, 1899.

LEE, VERNON. Euphorion. London, 1899.

LEGRAND, E. Bibliographie Hellénique. 2 vols. Paris, 1885.

MAXWELL–LYTE, Sir H. C. A History of the University of Oxford. London, 1886.

MAITTAIRE, M. Annales Typographici. The Hague, 1719.

MEYER, E. Machiavelli and the Elizabethan Drama. Berlin, 1897.

MULLINGER, J. B. The University of Cambridge. 2 vols. Cambridge, 1873–1884.

Munimenta Academica. Edited by Rev. H. Anstey. Rolls Series. 2 vols. London, 1868.

OLIPHANT, THOMAS. A Short Account of Madrigals. London, 1836.

PATETTA, F. I Caorsini Senesi in Inghilterra nel Secolo XIII. (Bollettino Senese di Storia Patria Anno IV, 1897.)

PIÉRI, M. Le Pétrarquisme au XVIe Siècle. Pétrarque et Ronsard. Marseilles, 1895.

PLANCHÉ, J. R. History of British Costume. London, 1834.

PREZZINER. Storia del Pubblico Studio e Delle Società Scientifiche e Letterarie di Firenze. 2 vols. Florence, 1810.

RASHDALL, H. The Universities of Europe in the Middle Ages. 3 vols. Oxford, 1895.

RYMER, T. Fœdera. 20 vols. Edited by Sir T. D. Hardy. London, 1869–1885.

SCOTT, M. A. Elizabethan Translations from the Italian. (Proceedings of the Modern Language Association. Baltimore, 1895–1899.)

SEEBOHM, F. Oxford Reformers. London. 1887.

SPINGARN, J. E. Literary Criticism in the Renaissance. New York, 1899.

STEPHEN, LESLIE, and LEE, SIDNEY. Dictionary of National Biography. 66 vols. London, 1885–1901.

STRYPE, JOHN. The Life of the Learned Sir John Cheke. Oxford, 1821.

Memorials ... of Thomas Cranmer. Oxford, 1812.

Life of Sir Thomas Smith. Oxford, 1820.

SYMONDS, J. A. Shakespeare's Predecessors in the English Drama. London, 1889.

UNDERHILL, J. G. Spanish Literature in the England of the Tudors. New York, 1899.

VASARI, G. Le Vite. Edited by G. Milanesi. 8 vols. Florence, 1878–1882.

VOIGT, GEORG. Die Wiederbelebung des classischen Alterthums. 2 vols. Berlin, 1893.

VIRGIL, POLYDORE. Polydori Vergilii Urbinatis Anglicæ Historiæ. Ghent, 1557.

WALPOLE, HORACE. Anecdotes of Painting. Edited by Wornum. London, 1888.

WARD, ADOLPHUS W. History of English Dramatic Literature. 2 vols. London, 1875.

WARTON, THOMAS. History of English Poetry. 4 vols. London, 1824.

WYATT, M. DIGBY. On the Foreign Artists employed in England during the 16th Century. London, 1868.

ZDEKAUER, L. Lo Studio di Siena nel Rinascimento. Milan, 1894.

ZIMMERMAN, A. Die Universitäten England's im 16. Jahrhundert. Stimmen aus Maria Laach. Freiburg in Breisgau, 1889.

ZOUCH, TH. Life of Sidney. York, 1808.

INDEX